Our Uncertain World

Challenges and Opportunities in a Dark Time

A Jungian Perspective

Leslie Sawin, Editor

CHIRON PUBLICATIONS • ASHEVILLE, NORTH CAROLINA

www.ChironPublications.com

Interior and cover design by Danijela Mijailovic
Printed primarily in the United States of America

ISBN 978-1-68503-205-0 paperback
ISBN 978-1-68503-206-7 hardcover
ISBN 978-1-68503-207-4 electronic
ISBN 978-1-68503-208-1 limited edition paperback

Library of Congress Cataloging-in-Publication Data

Names: Sawin, Leslie, editor.
Title: Our uncertain world : challenges and opportunities in a dark time / Leslie Sawin, editor.
Description: Asheville, North Carolina : Chiron Publications, 2024. | Includes bibliographical references. | Summary: "We live in times of uncertainty and anxiety. In these times, how can we best navigate our unknowns? Our Uncertain World answers that question through a Jungian prism. Carl Jung's theory has helped many people navigate difficult times. Jungian perspectives facilitate such challenging navigation by not simplifying complexity, but rather by finding the meaningful through-lines that guide the individual toward individuation even in the darkest of times. Using Jung's unique multidimensional approach, this book offers insights and provides answers to questions about life in a state of three-dimensional flux. Our Uncertain World was born from the premise that we are in a period of unparalleled change. The interlocking crises of COVID, national polarization, environmental disaster, and international war can undermine or even destroy the symbols, rituals, and mental structures that give meaning and coherence to our lives. The authors of this book accompany the reader through the current challenges we face and examine new ways of adjusting to the existing condition of protracted uncertainty"-- Provided by publisher.
Identifiers: LCCN 2023053546 (print) | LCCN 2023053547 (ebook) | ISBN 9781685032050 (paperback) | ISBN 9781685032067 (hardcover) | ISBN 9781685032074 (ebook) | ISBN 9781685032081 (limited edition paperback)
Subjects: LCSH: Adjustment (Psychology) | Jungian psychology. | Social change.
Classification: LCC BF335 .O87 2024 (print) | LCC BF335 (ebook) | DDC 155.2/4--dc23/eng/20240117
LC record available at https://lccn.loc.gov/2023053546
LC ebook record available at https://lccn.loc.gov/2023053547

With gratitude to Anne Pickup who held the light
and to Aryeh Maidenbaum for wise counsel and support.

Table of Contents

Foreword   1
John Beebe

Introduction: We Live in Challenging Times   9
Leslie Sawin

Uncertainty: Is It a Gift?   21
Ann Ulanov

Part 1: Living with Personal Uncertainty over the Long Term

Introduction   57

Spirit of the Depths, Spirit of the Times   61
Margaret Klenck

Uncertainty and Healing in the Archetypal End-times   89
Morgan Stebbins

The Faith of the Analyst During Climates of Uncertainty   121
Murray Stein

Part 2: Social Turmoil: A Moment of Social Change for Our Community and Our Nation

Introduction   141

*Inner and Outer Democracy and the threat of Authoritarianism:
Reflections on Psychological Factors at Play in our
Polarized World*   145
Donald Kalsched

Thorns in the Spirit: Trauma and the Uncertain Personal Work of Racial Justice 179
Sean Fitzpatrick

Psychological Responses to Uncertainty in the Individual and Group Psyche 203
Thomas Singer

Part 3: Challenges Facing Our World: Grappling with the Environment, the Pandemic, and War

Introduction 231

The Nature of Uncertainty/The Uncertainty of Nature 235
Jeffrey T. Kiehl

The Three Horsemen of the Apocalypse of Our Time 261
Jan Bauer

Reconsidering Individuation in the 21st Century: When Archetypal Patterns Shift 293
Joe Cambray

Moving Forward 323
Joe Cambray

Author Biographies 333

Foreword

John Beebe

The year I turned twenty-one, I was walking with a friend near the steps of Widener Library, the main library on the Harvard University campus. There was a post box in prominent view. A little girl, maybe eight years old, was approaching it with watchful parents nearby. She had a letter to send, which she inserted slowly and with particular care. As she released the letter into the box, the metal slot-flap closed upon her fingers, still outstretched in the act of letting the letter go. Not only her fingers but her palm slipped out of view. "Oh, I mailed my hand!" she declared to her parents. My friend, an artist whose drawings of animals had uncanny liveliness, remarked on the embodied vitality of her surreal remark. My own reaction was more psychological: I couldn't get over her certainty. As Widener itself seemed to stare down the steps at this mailbox the girl was sure required that her hand must go with her letter, I realized that all the volumes in its formidable collection would not be able to explain away her certainty. What has remained a mystery for me through more than six decades since that epiphany is what became of her uncertainty as to whether the mailbox would actually accept it when starting to release the letter.

On the shelves of Widener Library, we might find a contrast to that little girl in the redoubtable figure of Emil du Bois-

Reymond, a pioneering neuroscientist who stubbornly held on to his uncertainty. Known to students of the 19th century novel as the real life model for the skeptical Bazarov whose emphatic nihilism haunts Ivan Turgenev's *Fathers and Children*, and to historians of science as the positivist who first established the electrical transmission of nerve impulses, Du Bois-Reymond had the temerity to tell his colleagues at the Forty-fifth Congress of German Naturalists and Physicians (Leipzig, 1872) about "The Limits of Science." (Finkelstein, Chapter 12, who gives his own translation from the German throughout; see also Du Bois-Reymond, 1874 for the first English translation). He cautioned these enthusiasts for verified empiricism that despite his own discovery having convinced him, as well as them, that materialism had conquered spiritist vitalism as the only defensible explanation for consciousness, he and his fellow scientists would have to admit that "as regards the enigma of matter and force, and how they are capable of thought, we must resign ourselves once and for all to the more difficult verdict [of] Ignorabimus." [We shall never know.[1]]

One-hundred fifty years later, in an era almost too sure that it will eventually evolve a viable artificial intelligence, it is fashionable to summon du Bois-Reymond both as a support and a ground for challenge. For instance, in a recent online article about the mind-body problem we can read:

> Similar dissatisfactions with contemporary models of the neural correlates of consciousness have been expressed by Chalmers (2010, 11, also regarding Crick's hypothesis) and Block (2009, 1111-2, regarding Tononi's theory). The disagreement expressed by this portion of the philosophical community—as it is remarked in a recent paper by Ned Block (2015)—regards in general the capacity of physical conditions of consciousness to provide a 'ground' of subjective experience: the 'ontological' thesis that only matter exists does not eliminate the

2

'metaphysical' question of which is the 'ground' of phenomenal experiences in different kinds of beings. Block maintains that, even if ontological materialism is true, metaphysical materialism could fail. . . (Block, 2015, 113-4). . . thus leaving open the possibility that 'dualism, in an important sense, is true' (Block, 2015, 133). This . . . suits Chalmers' remark that materialism is 'unstable' and collapses into different metaphysical hypotheses (Chalmers, D.J., 2020).

Against this background, the historical reconsideration of the *Ignorabimus* poses a double challenge: first is it possible that a philosophical or metaphysical explanation of consciousness will expand our knowledge with respect to what the detection of neural correlates can provide? Second is it possible to establish the truth of a determinate explanation—such as a kind of materialism or panpsychism—with respect to the others? The burden of proof—more than one hundred years after du Bois-Reymond—still belongs to a future science of consciousness that denies the *Ignorabimus*" (Pecere, 2020).

Beyond consciousness, the universe we are becoming conscious of cannot be counted upon to behave according to any law or equation that can be put forth to explain its future behavior. According to two of its architects, contemporary complexity theory grants autonomy and creative agency to the universe itself. For example, Kaufmann and Longo announced in 2011:

...there ARE NO LAWS THAT ENTAIL THE BECOMING OF THE BIOSPHERE, and a fortiori, the econosphere, or culture or history, or life in general.

We are at a terminus of Reductionism, the belief that there must be a law or set of laws 'down there' that entails all that becomes in the universe.

Newton taught us that the universe is a vast mechanism, a view that persists in General Relativity and even quantum mechanics with its peculiar measurement process among known possibilities with known probabilities. All remains entailed from below. Heraclitus taught us 2700 years ago that the universe 'bubbles forth'. For the becoming of the biosphere and all of life, we hold that Heraclitus was right. Life bubbles forth. (Kauffman & Longo, 2011).

The autonomy of the psyche was the premise of the analytical psychology founded by C.G. Jung, a psychiatrist specializing in the research and treatment of the parts of the psyche that present themselves about which we are most uncertain. By the end of sixty years of study as to what that autonomy allowed the psyche to become, Jung had realized that its individuation opens up an *unus mundus* in which mind is no longer separate from nature. Jung was born three years after du Bois-Reymond's famous address, and had met Freud in Vienna's "Age of Uncertainty" (Coen, 2007). Jung admired Freud's method of exploration, but was not willing to accept what seemed a rush to closure in the systematizing of psychoanalysis; in his own analytical practice, he distrusted interpretations that attempted to be too exact. Jung preferred to walk around a dream, experiencing it from different perspectives, rather than trying to resolve the dream to one meaning (Jung, 1966, para. 342). He taught his own followers that when engaging with the unconscious it is best to adopt an attitude of not knowing. Jung's understanding that his patients were living boundary-condition lives on the line between certainty and uncertainty made his key conceptions, the *archetypes*, the *Self*, and even *the unconscious*, what he himself called borderline concepts. His own line of thinking in this regard is not, as he anticipated, beyond challenge (Brooks, 2011), but it was central to his understanding of the healing value of the exceptional mental states reported by his patients. Jung realized they had come to him for help because they found themselves forced to live on the edge between what he called "Consciousness and the Unconscious" (Jung, 2022). Their therapies showed him that uncertainty as to what to do with their lives could lead to the emergence of a heightened participation in the unfolding of the world around them, and I think he was voicing what work with patients had taught him when he wrote in old age, "The more uncertain I have felt about myself, the more there has grown up in me a feeling of kinship with all things" (Jung, 1963, p. 393).

The Jungian authors of this book have recognized something that lay just beyond this threshold Jung himself reached in his final years. They have chosen to recognize that today all things are uncertain, kin to the insecurities that people who came to analysis once expected to be cured of. Uncertainly itself has become the subject of contemporary Jungian thought, in which even continuity of the world as a place where we might find love, work, and respite from illness, social unrest, war, economic ruin, and environmental collapse cannot be guaranteed. That these papers take the present insecurity as their premise gives them a standpoint of surprising resilience, because it allows authentic meaning to emerge in its raw form without the scaffolding of certainty. Paradoxically, this gives us more at hand to hold onto. We are reminded, as when climbing a rock, we are safer when we are not sure, and for that reason open to finding what can really make a difference.

–John Beebe

References

Block, N., (2009). Comparing the major theories of consciousness. *The MIT Press eBooks*. https://doi.org/10.7551/mitpress/ 8029.003.0099.

Block, N., (2015). The Canberra Plan Neglects Ground. I*n Cambridge University Press eBooks* (105–133). https://doi. org/10.1017/cbo9781139939539.006

Brooks, R.M., (2011). Unthought out metaphysics in analytical psychology: a critique of Jung's epistemological basis for psychic reality. *Journal of Analytical Psychology, 56:* 492-513.

Du Bois-Reymond, E., (1874). The Limits of our Knowledge of Nature (J. Fitzgerald, Trans.). *Popular Science Monthly* V.5 (online).

Chalmers, D.J., (2002). Consciousness and its place in nature. In *Oxford University Press eBooks* (pp. 103–140). https://doi. org/10.1093/acprof:oso/9780195311105.003.0005

Coen, D.R., (2007). *Vienna in the Age of Uncertainty: Science, Liberalism, and Private Life.* Chicago and London: The University of Chicago Press.

Finkelstein, G., (2013). *Emil du Bois-Reymond: Neuroscience, Self and Society in Nineteenth Century Germany.* Cambridge, MA & London: The MIT Press.

Humphrey, N., (1982). Consciousness: A just-so story. *New Scientist 95,* no 1319: 477.

Jung, C.G., (1916-1928/1966). The Relations between the Ego and the Unconscious. In *CW,* (2nd ed., Vol. 7).

_____. *Memories, Dreams, Reflections* (A. Jaffe, Ed.; R. and C. Winston, Trans.). Fontana Press. (Original work published 1963)

_____. (2022). *Consciousness and the Unconscious: Lectures Delivered at ETH Zurich, Vol 2:* (1934) (E. Falzeder, Ed.). Princeton, NJ: Princeton University Press.

Kauffman, S. and Longo, G., (2011). No Law Entails The Evolution Of The Biosphere. *Lifeboat Foundation: Safeguarding Humanity.* Retrieved January 29, 2023, from https://lifeboat.com/blog/2011/07/no-law-entails-the-evolution-of-the-biosphere

Pecere, P., (2020). Reconsidering the ignorabimus: du Bois-Reymond and the hard problem of consciousness. *Science in Context: 33/1* (online: https://www.cambridge.org/core/journals/science-in-context/article/reconsidering-the-ignorabimus-du-boisreymond-and-the-hard-problem-of-consciousness/8C19E49A253DD5011482AD4252FF563D.

Endnotes

[1] This is the translation of Finkelstein, who says that "According to Nicholas Humphrey (1982) this was one of the four verdicts open to a jury in medieval England when deciding a case, the others being Guilty, Not Guilty, and we do not know."

Introduction

We Live in Challenging Times

Leslie Sawin

*"A modern problem is one which has just arisen
and whose answer still lies in the future."*
—(Jung, 1964, para. 148)

We are living through a time of continuing uncertainty on many levels and for a number of reasons. The past several years have been unusually difficult:

- ❖ The arrival of Covid-19, with its attendant fear, stress, vulnerability, loss, and increasing unpredictability as multiple variants continue to emerge
- ❖ Intensified scrutiny and engagement with racial justice
- ❖ Ongoing bitterness, division, and polarization in our social discourse and political rhetoric, concomitant with increasing gun violence
- ❖ Threats to our planet and the environment
- ❖ The events in Ukraine and the specter of wars—nuclear, biological, or chemical—causing anxieties to heighten in a more global way

Each of us is now called upon to rethink our individual risk and safety, as well as our relationship with our community, the world, and our environment. Some of us are thinking about and tackling new and complex issues. All these challenges require an adaptation to an uncertain future. The uncertainties we each face have personal impact and meaning for us but are also collective and hence, strongly indicate activation of the collective unconscious as a dynamic force in our communities, nations, and the entire world. Can we look to approaches that help transcend the concerns and responses of individuals and develop new means of soulful engagement with these collective forces? Our authors, in their own unique ways, will address such considerations.

Our ongoing reflection and the process of developing strategies for adaptation make clear the need for individual emotional support and insight. New tools, awareness, and responses are needed. These issues also raise questions that, as individuals and as a collective, we must answer. We all need to begin constructing our new way to emerge and live.

Underlying these issues and affecting the available resources for individuals to respond to the increased and long-standing uncertainty is the reality that we are in a time of cultural paradigm shift or, in Jungian terms, a major archetypal shift. Our basic social institutions and structures are being questioned by many. Old cultural and religious patterns are falling by the wayside. This deep cultural and social change process—where old forms of structure and support seem to have lost their power and new patterns that reflect emerging archetypes are appearing—is not something that individuals generally recognize as part of their daily lives. This process has a very subtle yet important impact on the identification of resources and insights to manage our uncertain times.

Why Jung? What Does the Jungian Perspective Bring?

A Jungian perspective on uncertainty, the archetypal change process, and the issues of our times offers opportunities for personal growth, healing, and a process for reimagining the future. For Jung, the loss of some symbols means the opportunity, disturbing as it might be, for new ones to emerge. That is, in a sense, the whole of his political historical theory. Whatever symbols emerge are expressing something from the collective unconscious.

We are in a time of change, and the first step begins with the individual: "As any change must begin somewhere, it is the single individual who will experience it and carry it through. The change must indeed begin with an individual; it might be any one of us. Nobody can afford to look round and to wait for somebody else to do what he is loath to do himself" (Jung, 1955, para. 599).

Recognizing and articulating what is happening, offering perspectives for psychologically understanding current pressures, and offering specific approaches to think about the important social and environmental issues confronting us are crucial now. This book is designed to assist people in developing their new normal on several levels—first, by seeing and working with the new opportunities that a return to regular life offers. What do we want our new lives to be like, and how can we go about creating those lives? The goal of this effort is to help people identify their personal opportunities and to develop strategies for working with them in our changing society and world.

Chapters by ten Jungian analysts explore current sources of uncertainty, both personal and collective, and offer several resources for the reader: exploration of the sources of continuing uncertainty from a new perspective, identifying individual and societal concerns, and offering tools for personal response to these issues and ways to engage in the national encounter with these critical questions.

❖ Living with Personal Uncertainty over the Long Term
❖ Social Turmoil: A Moment of Social Change for Our Communities and Nation

❖ Challenges Facing Our World: Grappling with the Environment, the Pandemic, and War

Each part begins with a brief introduction to the issues being discussed and comprises chapters by individual analysts outlining basic questions affecting our lives in each discussion and offering support and tools as we move forward.

Where Are We Now?

Let us begin with what it feels like to be where we are now. In an interview in 2020, Murray Stein, a contributor to this book, summarized our situation:

> The image that comes to my mind is an *Umbra Mundi*, a world shadow hovering over us and infecting our psychic lives. I see this shadow spreading over the globe like a solar eclipse. The alchemical term for this is *nigredo*. The sun is covered by the shadow of death. It is the familiar stage that signifies the beginning of significant transformation. We are being asked to walk through the valley of the shadow of death. It is biblical. The question is: Will we be able to use this experience for individuation? Or will it just pass like a bad dream of the night that when we awake, we are happy to be free from? (Stein 2020, online interview)

We can all feel this shadow in many ways. We feel it as we watch the news and see the horrific effects of war and the potential escalation to a larger world theater and the threat of using nuclear weapons. We can feel it as the fears about global warming grow and our world sustains more vicious and damaging storms and hurricanes, melting polar ice caps, droughts, fires, and deadly heat waves. It is there as we ponder how best to grapple with the quest for racial justice and how best to personally engage with it. We can see it as our nation struggles to come to terms with ongoing polarization and violence. And let us not forget Covid-19: Are we done with it? Will there be more variants and surges with the coming of another winter? In the summer? What is it safe to do, and how will we feel comfortable and safe in the world? What meaning might the pandemic have for us, including it being a response to climate change?

Chapters in this book will make clear that many aspects of our current situation are not new; we have been here before with the resultant fear and confusion, taking refuge in ideas about conspiracies, alternative realities, and polarization. What are the lessons learned? What are our best options and strategies for navigating these issues?

Introducing *The Red Book*

In the following chapters, you will encounter *The Red Book* a great deal. This book was created by C.G. Jung to honor a period of deep introspection and personal chaos that he experienced in 1913–17, and intermittently until 1932. It was a time of immense personal challenge for Jung that began in 1913 with his break with Sigmund Freud. Jung entered a period of deep mental anguish and began exploring his inner state, dreams, and feelings. He began experimenting with specific techniques to support this inner work. With his background as a psychiatrist who began his career doing experimental research in a clinical setting and social science research later in life, he recorded all his personal experiments of this period in six journals that he named "The Black Books," created in 1913–15 and in 1917. The last volume (number 7) goes through December 1932. As part of this interior work, Jung developed the tools and ideas that would become the foundation for Jungian theory and practice:

> The years …. when I pursued the inner images were
> the most important time of my life. Everything else
> is to be derived from this. It began at that time,
> and the later details hardly matter anymore. My

entire life consisted in elaborating what had burst forth from the unconscious and flooded me like an enigmatic stream and threatened to break me. That was the stuff and material for more than only one life. Everything later was merely the outer classification, the scientific elaboration, and the integration into life. But the numinous beginning, which contained everything else, was then. (Jung 1957)

As the process went on, Jung realized that this effort was central to his conceptual framework, and he decided to memorialize this effort in a very personal way with the development of *The Red Book*.

It is an extraordinary document: 12 by 16 inches, with text and images hand-painted by Jung.

The [Black Books] material went through a number of drafts and was then recopied by Jung in an ornate gothic script into a large red leather folio volume, to which he added historiated initials, ornamental borders and a substantial number of paintings. The work was modelled after the illuminated manuscripts of the Middle Ages.... This publication opens the possibility of a new era in the understanding of Jung's work. It provides a unique window into how he recovered his soul and, in so doing, constituted one of the influential psychologies of the twentieth century. (Shamdasani, Philemon Website)

The text is in German. Jung commissioned the folio-size and red leather-bound volume in 1915 but kept it held in private for the rest of his life. The family approved its publication, which occurred in 2009. References to the artwork in the book will appear in subsequent chapters. Links to each image will be provided in the text.

Jung continued to expand and refine these ideas for the next seventeen years. Later chapters will provide greater context and background on this period. Why do so many of our authors explore and refer to this singular work? Because there are specific parallels with our time and world and because it is a very personal and deep recording of one individual struggle during times much like our own.

The opening remarks at the Eranos presentation 2022, provide a deeper context for why *The Red Book* is part of the current discussion on the uncertainty in our lives. It offers a clear summary:

> Can we find value, individually and collectively, in Jung's *Red Book* for a time like ours, which is so deeply overcast by the *Umbra Mundi* (the World Shadow)? Both the Covid-19 pandemic and the international political crisis and war threat that we are facing right now inevitably shadow all our thoughts.... On an even larger scale, we recognize that we are facing a world historical transition in human culture without the guidance traditionally offered by grand narratives or collective myths. A similar mood of deep anxiety about the future overshadowed the world when C.G. Jung began working on his *Red Book* in 1913.... His approach to the problems presented by the spirit of his times also has prescriptive significance for our times. *The Red Book* has the potential to offer guidance for people living under the disruptive conditions of the first half of the 21st century.

The Red Book is a conversation between an individual and his psychic life on both the individual and the collective level. Therefore, you will find both references to and exploration of *The Red Book* in many of the chapters in this book.

The Structure of This Book

Our book begins with a chapter by Ann Ulanov, *Uncertainty: Is it a Gift?* that offers an in-depth examination of the concept of uncertainty. It starts with an inviting question. Her intensive examination of what it means to experience uncertainty, to grapple with it and to see it as a potential gift, will set the context for the three specific explorations that follow.

Living with Personal Uncertainty over the Long Term

The exploration of living with personal uncertainty over the long term goes a long way toward developing an individual perspective for living more comfortably with Covid-19 and other pressures that we are facing going into the future. We offer here a collection of thoughts from prominent Jungian analysts that develop perspectives, information, and approaches to assist in the framing of an individual's new way of living:

Margaret Klenck: *Spirit of the Depths, Spirit of the Times*

Morgan Stebbins: *Uncertainty and Healing in the Archetypal End-Times*

Murray Stein: *The Faith of the Analyst in Climates of Uncertainty*

Margaret Klenck explores several personal perspectives on responding to the pressures of uncertainty. Contrasting the spirit of the depths (our interior personal world) with the spirit of the times (our relationship to the community), she offers tools and ideas for personal work through art and myth and the language of the blues.

Morgan Stebbins proposes that while there are many useful ways to reduce the stress of a difficult time-period, really lasting results come from taking the image of disaster symbolically. This allows one to radically transform one's view of oneself in the world, and to deeply change psychologically. In other words, the idea that we are living in an apocalyptic time is really the emanation of an archetype that demands our own reflection and change of attitude. In this way, apocalyptic fantasy operates like all other unconscious material in compensating for our conscious position and therefore producing a healing wholeness.

Murray Stein delves into the idea of faith and its potential role in grappling with our current feelings, events, and our world. He talks about the nature of faith both as religious and individual. He then discusses personally having faith and its role in analytic work.

Social Turmoil: A Moment of Social Change for our Communities and Nation

In this part, we will explore the role of imagination as a healing force or as a response to trauma; the collective response to our seminal social issues; and ways to engage with these issues in a personally meaningful manner:

Donald Kalsched: *Democracy and Autocracy in the Individual and the Collective: Reflections on Psychological Factors at Play in Our Polarized World*

Sean Fitzpatrick: *Thorns in the Spirit: Sustained Engagement in Racial Justice*

Thomas Singer: *Psychological Responses to Uncertainty in the Individual and GroupPsyche*

Donald Kalsched discusses the nature of our polarized world and the psychological factors that are part of our national discussion. He examines personal polarization and offers strategies for being part of the process.

Sean Fitzpatrick tackles the issue of engaging with racial justice through a focus on the effect on bystanders present at pivotal events and offers strategies for each of us to engage with this issue.

Thomas Singer gives a historical perspective on uncertainty, offers a tentative model of individual and collective responses to uncertainty, and shows us how the vitality of the mythopoetic imagination can help transcend the effects of uncertainty.

Challenges Facing Our World

In this part, our authors will explore the current climate change situation, our response to the three major environmental issues of our time (pandemic, climate change, and war), and the Jungian concept of individuation in light of new perspectives on emerging systems' science and interconnectedness.

> Jeffrey T. Kiehl: *The Nature of Uncertainty/The Uncertainty of Nature*
> Jan Bauer: *The Three Horsemen of the Apocalypse of Our Time*
> Joe Cambray: *Reconsidering Individuation in the 21st Century*

Jeffrey Kiehl has been a climate scientist for 40 years. As such, he provides a detailed and sobering summary of climate studies and climate change. He also provides perspective and approaches from his work as a Jungian analyst to help in responding to these challenges.

Jan Bauer offers a substantive look at Covid-19, climate change, and the Ukraine war from the perspective of the passions and forces involved at a collective level. She inquires about the collective intensity and mobilization for each area.

Joe Cambray explores a central Jungian concept: individuation. With a deep interest in emerging systems and our understanding of nature, he explores current research on emergent systems and how we understand individuation in the context of nature in light of the new science.

Moving Forward

In this final section, the overarching Jungian principles and perspectives at the heart of this book are summarized and briefly revisited. Where will these ideas go in the future? What new directions might be explored? Joe Cambray offers a glimpse of a potential new viewpoint of Jungian principles. He notes that the field of futurology offers a new possibility to imagine the future.

A Jungian contribution to such an expansion would be by way of a holistic vision of knowledge, including conscious and unconscious forms of knowing.

References

Eranos Conference. Jung's Red Book for our Time: Searching for Soul in the 21st Century, 4/28 – 5/1, 2022.

Henderson, Robert. *A World Shadow: COVID 19.* - (An Interview with Murray Stein, PhD by Rev. Dr. Robert S Henderson). Asheville, NC: Chiron Publications. https:// chironpublications.com/a-world-shadow-covid-19/

Jung, C.G., (1953). *CW, Vol. 7: Two Essays in Analytical Psychology,* Princeton, NJ: Princeton University Press.

_____. (1955). *CW, Vol. 18: Symbols and interpretations of Dreams, The Symbolic Life,* Princeton, NJ: Princeton University Press.

_____. (1968/1988), *Man and His Symbols.* Garden City, NY: Doubleday & Company. (A Windfall Book).

_____. (1970). *CW, Vol. 10: Civilization in Transition,* Princeton, NJ: Princeton University Press. (Original work published 1964)

_____. (1980). *CW, Vol. 9: The Archetypes and the Collective Unconscious,* Princeton, NJ: Princeton University Press. (Original work published 1959)

_____. (1981). *CW, Vol. 17:* The Development of Personality. Princeton, NJ: Princeton University Press. (Original work published 1954).

_____. (1989). *CW, Vol. 11: Psychology and Religion: West and East,* Princeton, NJ: Princeton University Press. (Original work published 1958)

Shamdasani, Sonu, *C.G. Introduction to Jung's Red Book: Liber Novis,* Philemon Foundation Website, www.philemon-foundation.org/published-works/red-book.

Uncertainty: Is It a Gift?

Ann Ulanov

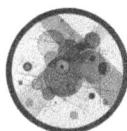

What a disturbing title! Especially now when we face the crossroads of pandemic, racial wounds enlarged due to the killing of George Floyd and countless other people of color at the hands of the police, frightening climate change symptoms of explosive fires, flash floodings, destructive hurricanes and tornadoes, and divisive strife in governments that makes passing any effective and protective legislation in the United States almost impossible. Repeated mass shootings in public places like movie theaters, nightclubs, grocery stores, and children's classrooms are further destabilizing. Additional international shocks arrive with the violence of civil wars starving those who cannot flee the country, unprovoked invasions, terrorist raids on school children, laws that increasingly restrict voters' freedom of speech and electing their own leaders. Uncertainty looms in the present, hanging like polluted air over the possibility of an ordinary future. Calling into question a life where one can count on continuing existence with water, fresh air and vegetables, working a good job, or on ideas like the vibrant sustaining of truth, kindness, and devotion to enlarge justice for all citizens.

Uncertainty expands and catches us furtively when awakened in the night consumed with fear. Can I make enough money? Will my children be worse off than me? What if we lose the house? How can we rebuild after the fires and the winds? Steady broadcasts of disinformation and intentional power grabs poison trust in social manners and mutuality. We feel stripped of usual assurances as if foundational truths we took for granted are now upended. And we have no idea when all this uncertainty will end! Maybe never; maybe this is the new normal.

How can we possibly experience all this uncertainty as gift when practically every aspect of life is shot through with unsureness, perplexity—economically, charitably, the future of societies' peace, education, freedom to be and become, to maintain just external borders of countries and just psychological patterns internally, access to truth, the precedence of beauty, the fact of psychic reality. Now, all this insecurity is a public phenomenon. A radio program broadcasts what to do with uncertainty, suggesting six procedures to live with it. They offer help and point out how prevalent is the fear of not standing on anything solid.

Gifts go nowhere if we are unable to receive them. For that we need the attitude recommended by John Keats that others have also cited, Wilfred Bion among them: "the capacity to be in uncertainties, Mysteries, doubts, without any irritable reaching after fact and reason" (Bion, 1970/1977, p. 70; Hirshfield, 2015, p. 122). Jung urges both of these opposites together: "absolute clarity is a sign of poverty....There has to be doubt" and, "each of us has first to stand by his own truth, which is gradually reduced to a common truth by mutual discussion. All this requires psychological understanding and empathy with the others' points of view" (Jung, 2021, pp. 65, p. 171).

From our small perspective of one great discovery called depth psychology, we ask what does the psyche have to say about this uncertainty? More specifically, what does Jung say as he is the one who fashioned his understanding of psyche from its unconscious language? We read Jung's translations into what I have called symbolic concepts of the raw experience of the unconscious vernacular so different from binary opposites of consciousness represented verbally (Ulanov, 1971, pp. 21, 24). "Therefore man [sic] differentiates, since his essence is differentiation" (Jung, 2009, p. 347). Jung puts it in *The Red Book* (Jung 2009). The tumult of unconscious instinct, affect, intimation, sensation, improvisation may toss an image forming toward an emergent symbol of what this unconscious tongue presents. Jung pulls from these rough fresh instinctual matters dominant images he calls archetypes that are before word or expressible image refined and clear. More often they present a paradox, not a jumble, of hot and cold, good and bad, momentous and banal, ultimate and miniscule in the large reality of the whole.

This level of unconscious in all of us "where instinct predominates" and archetypal images appear like a self-portrait of instinct, which Jung describes as psychoid. Psychoid processes, as irrepresentable, simultaneously show opposing sides of the same coin, such as psychic and physical at once. Psychoid is a perception neighborly to the notion of unrepressed unconscious that other thinkers, such as Sigmund Freud, Matte Blanco, Bion, Riccardo Lombardi, note as that which is there before, antecedent to human construction and definition, teeming with life and full of quiet meaning unexpressed in word or discrete image (Ulanov, 2022, pp. 194-197).

Freud's elegant clarity of writing draws unconscious psyche away into the language of consciousness, giving us abstractions about the psychic apparatus of id, ego, superego in competing and complementary systems—topographical, structural, economic (Rycroft, 1968, p. 128). Jung turns toward the unconscious to fashion its language that is more symbol of what this life is like, yet inclusive of enough concept to talk about the processes personified.

Shadow

Shadow is a good illustration of Jung's perspective, picturing what falls behind us that both haunts us and gives us three dimensions, a solidity to our psyche-body. Nothing can change if we do not see our shadow. We experience it, engage it. That is the action that precedes understanding it. Freud gives us clear words about how shadow manifests (resistance, aggressiveness, death instinct, defensive system). Jung gives us images arising from living experience; only then is understanding grounding, rather than abstracting.

We attend how shadow shows itself to us through lived experience—fear of menace, humiliation, seizing its power to enhance our ego. That is the accent from this psychoid layer of psychic life that precedes rationality. We may find, I suggest, our responses to the prevalent uncertainty that seems now to interpenetrate every aspect of life precisely in the uncertainty that inhabits our basic psychoid process. Jung writes, for example,

> The shadow is...a narrow door, whose painful constriction no one is spared who goes down to the deep well. But one must learn to know oneself in order to know who one is. For what comes after the door is, surprisingly enough, a boundless expanse full of unprecedented uncertainty, with apparently no inside and no outside, no above and no below, no here and no there, no mine and no thine, no good and no bad.... all life floats in suspension...the soul of everything living, begins; where I am indivisibly this and that; where I experience the other in myself and the other-than-myself experiences me" (Jung 1954/1959, para 45).

Jung characterizes the relation of conscious and unconscious itself as unsure, unsettled, not fixed: "Between the conscious and the unconscious there is a kind of 'uncertainty relationship,' because the observer is inseparable from the observed and always disturbs it by the act of observation....exact observation of the unconscious prejudices observation of the conscious and vice versa" (Jung, 1959, 9:11, para. 355).

Reading Jung's psychological conversations with people, it is noted "he responds individually to their concerns but always points to the archetypal reality he recognizes behind the respective problem" (Jung, 2021, p. 3). For example, in pursuing a problem of abandonment, it can happen a new personification emerges in the person's dream, fantasy or simply appears and surprises, as an image. Here is an example:

A woman engaged in a long analysis describes a new event. A Chinese girl appears in a dream and the analysand engages her imaginatively. She has not thought her up. *What is she doing*, my patient asks and watches as the Chinese girl surrenders to the dark of neglect, making no attempt to flee or fight it, nor reproach or resolve it. The Chinese girl just accepts her plight of lying in the dark, abandoned, split off from the lively girl who dealt with her family's neglect by jumping into any life she could find. The Chinese girl personified a part of the woman's psyche unknown to her before. This foreigner depicted a part that had remained alien in response to the trauma of neglect. This pictures surrender to the suffering of it in contrast to the compensatory vigorous engagement in life through all the activities open to a school girl and later to an adult. Her long surrender to abandonment pictures the personal element of suffering and, eventually, another surprise: an archetypally accented perception of a new area of being existing for everyone, that is, an element of objective external reality. The woman discovers through the Chinese girl that the dark was not only loss and suffering. It led to perceiving a different aspect of life itself, a dark blackness of reality of outer space, not bad but just there, non-human centered cosmic dark of which she was a tiny part (Ulanov, 2022, pp. 86-89). In retrospect, I see that outer uncertainty dominating her society of her adult years dumped her into her deepest and earliest personal fears of literally no one there for her with welcoming interest in her specific life.

The upending of social foundations we citizens had relied on resulting in collective uncertainty stirs up our most personal intimate fears. What individuals make of this frightening uncertainty contributes specific personal realizations as answers to universal sorrows. Our personal work builds up links between our finite personal lives and the largeness of belonging to our human tribe and its place in the whole. This is no small feat. I have often felt such psychological work in even one person's particular life is a form of social action for the benefit of everyone. Through that person, the capacity to hope, enjoy pleasure, engage humor feeds the spiritual atmosphere in which we all dwell.

The irrational unconscious gains a voice through this particular person's life, a voice they hear and from the encounter fashion a form of living relation to it. These essential unconscious processes to do with instincts and pictured as archetypes are invisible and unthinkable. Jung hypothesizes the psychoid realm and helps it have a voice in daily personal and collective life (Ulanov, pp. 93, 147).

Projection

How to tackle uncertainty? Where to begin? The painter Paul Klee shows a way. British art critic David Sylvester notes Klee's paintings "keep the exact point of access remaining open" (1920, p.25). Like the psychoid unconscious, no single point of focus in this "all over" type of painting is the entry point, but "any point within the image may serve as the beginning of a journey" (Klee, 2017 pp. 25). These 'all over paintings' distribute a field of equality, each part its ownness as well as sharing the space with the rest of the painting, just as with the psychoid realm, wherever you are touched by it, enters in all its presence. The ego has no role, except, perhaps, as beholder. Thus, we make a trip back to the primal, to "the land of deeper insight." Klee said, "I want to be as though a newborn...to be almost primitive" (Klee, 1898-1918, p. 8; Klee, 1920).

Such all-over accessibility to all available entry points to experience, touches on our fundamental event of projection, which is natural. It happens to us. Projection hurls out of ourselves attitudes, emotions, intentions, even thoughts, putting them onto other persons, even on places. I heard in analysis of the same beach from two individuals who did not know each other about the balm they experienced at that same beach; it felt numinous to them. Projection can fall on the beauty of the curve of that table leg both strong and delicate, or on a fetish object that feels endowed with power. It happens in religious objects, or spiritual places or even actions of others that embody precious values like kindness, justice, let alone the sensate evidence of deepest values of freedom and law, like a Constitution or Declaration of Independence. Yet it can also cause strife and trouble. We can learn to be aware of its happening through attention to its signs of agitation, compulsion, identification. Often, we project onto others negative attitudes even of intense malignity, intent to diminish, to harm in body and spirit. We see in the other sly evil thoughts, or aim to ruin.

All schools of depth psychology recognize this shared experience among us. Jung says through projection we make a world for ourselves—endowing others and places and things with meaning, interest, attraction and joining groups we endow with values we hold dear. Lack of projection begets depression, withdrawal of a serious kind from the world outside us that we fail to make our own by contributing to its value to us. Unconscious energy falls away from making connections with outside events, persons, nature. We then suffer from being cut off; as one adult man said to me, "I am like a marble rolling around in the universe." Or a woman described the blank terror she suffered: "I am in outer space, outside the spaceship and the umbilical cord attaching me to it is fraying." Jung comments the mentally ill… "withdraw into primal experience; they are being drawn back," invent special power-words, "into the magic words of the primitives" (2021, p. 197).

Jung asserts anything unconscious automatically gets projected. Projection happens when our state of identity with an emotion or idea is breaking up. Then it vaults outward landing elsewhere on someone else, as different group, a far-off paradise. The pivotal point to grasp in projection is the first step toward our getting conscious of what this psychic item is. I project you are angry. I get a bit more aware of what anger is in seeing it as yours, in you. Three relationships inaugurate: dim awareness of you who has some kind of "hook" that attracts my projected anger; dim awareness of the anger itself as an emotion in me, maybe a danger or thing of power in me; and dim awareness that anger seems to exist itself hovering between us, carrying archetypal energy. Maybe a new experience entirely? We have a choice whether or not to take up these relationships. Jung emphasizes this change in us initiated by projection: we notice the other person and mark them as carrying this forbidden or attracting anger; we see we are angry; we see anger itself blowing up between us and within us. It cannot be reduced to personal interaction between us. It flares in and catches us both. If noticed and dealt with, projection can promote consciousness.

If not noticed, projection misses the otherness of the other and uses them to carry our psychic content that we reject as our own. We blame. It is you who are angry, not me. Curiosity, expanding into interest is needed. Are you angry? Why did I choose you to carry my anger? What is my history with it? What is this anger anyway? Projection has been studied from many angles and insightful things are written about it (Freud 1906, page 184; 1917, pp. 70-71; pp.61-65, 92-93; Jung 1979, pp. 541-543; Von Franz, 1980, passim; Klein 1975, 463; 1980; pp 361-362; Ogden 1982, passim, Ulanov A. and Ulanov B. 1975, pp. 39-41, 220-238; Ulanov A. B., 2001, pp. 92-107; Ulanov A.B., 2022, chapter 6).

Recalling Projections

What is not much written about and yet worth addressing, is recalling projections and asking where does that energy go? How is it employed instead? To take up these questions now is especially important given the pervasive strife and animosity characterizing our present political life. Comparatively, the United States has fewer imposed restrictions, fewer threats to jail anyone who speaks against the leader or government system. We live in the midst of flagrant projecting onto the other person, political party, group, religion, sexual orientation, persons of color and various other identity groups. The sense of gap between haves and have-nots in economic, educational, ethnic divisions make us doubt we can identify truth. We become uncertain that truth exists. There is a great need to recall our projections, both personal and between groups and nations. What then happens when we withdraw our projections? Where does the energy go?

Recalling our projections means we cease to be identified with them. We can see the projected content going over to the other, see a bit of the other or the object as it exists in itself, not cobbled together as a bundle of our projections. Now there are three items—me, you, the content in itself. Space aerates between them. Jung says straight out, withdraw all projections in life: "They make life poor and steal libido.... This is when real life can start! Otherwise one lives in an autoerotic fashion, loving one's projection in the other" (Jung, 2021, p. 71).

Jung stands with real life as having its own "mana." He wants to be human, not a myth, not a god; he writes, "with the projection gone, one can see the true value. Nothing is ever only this way or that, but has multiple facets that are alive and reveal new ones all the time." When oneself or something becomes "mythic," it gets fixed as this or that: "full of the highest projection" (Jung, 2021, p. 71). This fixed definition is dead-making, an incarnation gone wrong. The amplitude of the psychoid psychic basis, so to speak (for who knows what exactly to call it) is alive with plenitude, like the *multiplicatio* Jung and the alchemists find in the lapis, the *aqua permanens*, the conjunction of Self and ego. For all Jung's taking as the most important imaginal experience of his entire life the archetypal fantasies recounted in his Red and Black Books, he ends up, if I understand him rightly, praising human life—finite, limited and full of mistakes, as well as talents, and breakthroughs to full hearted living. A life lived in this world and in connection with the infinite.

Like the philosopher Ricoeur, Jung sees that the sacred wants to step over into the ordinary, incarnating in time and space while harkening still to the all and the vast, the totality of reality and its bright centers heralded in religious icons. Of course, we want to reify those gems, to be able to hold them in our mitten, keep them like Pascal's document skin-close next to our heart. But then we reduce it to ego terms, under our ego power and must de-reify, disidentify with the live burning gems, the sigh too deep for words, the heartbeat from the center of the galaxy. Let it go, let it be, boundless, undefined, and yes, uncertain! We cannot keep it in a fixed form; it exceeds; it hides; it keeps its own most real.

The alternative to this lively surprising uncertain relationship with our libido if we do not withdraw our projections, becomes dangerous because our libido, our psychic energy, "flows backwards into oneself.... The blood empties itself toward the inside and worthlessly seeps away, instead of pouring out into a creative act, full of joy and strength!" (Jung, 2021, p. 31). This shows up in how we show up to an encounter—seeing an analyst for the first time, hearing the drumbeat in a jazz quartet—have we "put a considerable stream of libido into our meeting?" If not, "nothing happens…and you get nothing out of it" (Jung, 2021, p. 34).

Remember, projections make libido available; they are the first beginning step toward more consciousness of all this energy and to whom it belongs. If we fail to take notice of being in the grip of projection, its infusing, say, a shadow conflict with another, but persist in insisting the other is as bad as we think they are, then the other damages us. We fill them up with the unlived life in ourselves, and the other person may simultaneously do the same to themself. In one instance of this, Jung counsels do not avoid that person, do not run away; do not evade your negative mother complex that you find in interchanges with this other person. Jung urges, "You are each other's unlived life! .... You have to fill undeveloped land with real life!" Do not "fall into projections…. Imagine you are walking a path, and on either side are 'pieces' (parts of your life) scattered about. You have to collect them all and take them with you!" (Jung, 2021, pp. 75-76).

If we fail to recall our projections when we see how they block off the otherness of the other because all we perceive is our projected form of the other, we become dangerous to others too, because "the libido-drain into the unconscious 'spreads' and then endangers" others around us Jung, 2021, p. 31). We become a 'monster' infecting others, as we fear the monster of the pandemic infecting us. Libido flowing backwards into oneself and not into life is a bit of poison within that may combine with a poison external to us. The two separate poisons mix and become one and we can spread it from us to contaminate another. Then the task is detecting where the lesion is in oneself. Where has the libido gone—what blocks its flow into life? A dream or an active imagination may locate where the block is, as might a neighbor's comment, saying for example, you must speak up! Or an inner figure may say, you must do something!

When we recall projections and try to accommodate their energies within ourselves, the ingress of libidinal energy for desires, new acts within ourselves or in the world, and insightful surprising thoughts, expand our finite daily being. This directs us specifically, I suggest, to unlived life: that life we are not living yet could be, thoughts we could be thinking, love we could be absorbing and beaconing out like light cast into the world. We remember Jung being confronted with hordes of the dead lamenting in *The Red Book* who could not die and rest in death because they could not get answers to questions they never dared ask when alive. Their plight was specifically unlived life which Jung, through the voice of Philemon, told them about. When we withdraw projections and all that energy currents its way into us right now, it presses into the borders of what we have not dared—to feel, to try, to think, to have presentiments of, and recognize as fact belonging to actual living.

We see this in our cultures in unusual bursts of freedoms and people taking heretofore unimaginable choices. Single people decide to embark on becoming a parent. Science makes it possible and their choice makes it actual. Unheard of before. Same sex lovers insist on marriage ceremonies to lasso the sacred into their public declaration of loving this particular other person. Unheard of in previous centuries. Transsexual transitions or even simply public acknowledgement of their nature never before allowed into cultural discourse, now suddenly is allowed and makes inroads to take up all kinds of opportunities—in military service, leadership government, business, moving next door. Recalling our projections introduces new life, overcoming melancholy for what we fear we missed in life, saying no, try for it now. This jumbles up ideas of what is possible and impossible and makes for cultural uncertainty and opportunity.

Even more remarkable than this active living the unlived life is engaging its opposite: inwardly to let things happen, to stand still, to consent to your own life, say yes to yourself totally. Pay attention to the merest hint of an unguessed feeling, an incipient strange thought. Trace it out. What might it be? Let it be, do not refuse. The goal is completeness; stand still, "Say yes to yourself, then life will come to you!" "Seek life humbly! Beware, it wants to find soil in you!" (Jung, 2021, pp. 76-77).

Integrative Projections

With more familiarity with one's projections happening, recalling them and employing the returning libido to investing in living fully, another kind of issue to do with good may appear. This event figures in projections of an ultimate value one holds, to the God-image one has created, to meditations on the good as a force in life and how to relate to it. Here we have projections onto the good itself which show in our small versions of it and in how we try to relate to it.

People may have an ideal figure of goodness they admire. They may feel enlisted into beliefs in the good as part of what makes life possible at all, of what sustains us even in time of misery and abject disempowerment. These images of the good get projected toward the ultimate, toward God, toward ideal figures who embody it in action and attitude—heroes of courage, survivors of torture and imprisonment, moments of such remarkable generosity toward others even to the point of self-sacrifice—remember the butcher, father of six children, exclaiming *no* as he is next in line for the gas chamber in one of the horrid camps. Max Kolb, further down in this death line, did. Remember the perception of Julian of Norwich of God as the author of all good who suffers all evil.

These filaments toward the good, like delicate tendrils advance from us toward the good, because we cannot envision the whole of it. We even may feel dread in the face of its bigness that could squash us, or call us out, seeing every demon we harbor. This green shoot or maybe it is not yet even green but white, just emerging from the dark earth and into the light that turns green with vital life; it is like a delicate thread between us and the good itself. This projection is a linking to the object good (or is it subject?). Our tiny version of the good makes it possible to imagine a relation to the good as something big, external to us (Ulanov, 2001, pp. 102-106). It is not our possession nor do we fall possessed by it. We spy it, intimate it and through this projective link can bear the burden of its huge majesty and tolerate the veneration it evokes in us. Such projections as these seem to gather uncertainty and certainty, both. Somehow our projection links us to this good. We take it in; it favors integration. Yet what does that mean? How do we live that? It really happens, hence certain, yet the variety of ways it is lived astonishes, hence uncertainty what unfolds for me—a gift that extends in time.

The Issue of Locality During Uncertainty

Uncertainty dislocates us. Where is it exactly? In our minds? Or in our faltering feet? Or around us, outside us? Or everywhere? Or are we rooted right here where we find ourselves to be? Or maybe we do not know, especially if we take seriously Jung's observation, "Compared to the vastness of the unconscious, our consciousness fits into the size of a thimble" (ibid, p. 104). Our consciousness has made great strides in developing, even to knowing we must include our split-off sides in ourselves and in our societies. But unlike the Romans who knew there was a spirit, a *genius loci*, a god to be honored in a new location they discovered and settled, with our current emphasis on globalization and internet connectiveness, we are uncertain where we are rooted. Central to that unsureness are the remarkable technological and digital advances of computers, tablets, phones, and all their sundry subsidiary apps that speak of virtual reality. This is contact with many others, known and unknown, even though we live in vastly different spaces and different time zones around the world (and even off the world with spaceships and astronauts) and do not share actual common ground, except in the air of the internet.

What do we make of this essential element, one of the four great ones of earth, air, fire and water? Air in astrology is associated with communicativeness, mental activeness, thinking, rationality, and being civilized, "being the one element in the zodiacal wheel which does not contain any animal symbolism" (Greene, 1984, p. 63). That implies living at a distance from entanglements with instincts and emotions. Air is associated with being human; the symbol of air, Aquarius, is a human being handling the foundational source, water pouring from one container to another.

Coupled with the pandemic lockdown where customary work and meetings in person ended to avoid infection through air (!), we got a taste of the air of a tacit virtual reality that appears real in the image of the homework or of the other person on Zoom, implying even a possible intimacy, but in fact is an illusion. We look at the camera and the other person does too; we do not see each other but a camera version—surely better than no picture but a trick of technology that omits a basic vital sense of touch and smell, scent made up of self and other breathing the same air in the same time and space.

In computer-land or digital-land we are not grounded on the actual earth but as if in the invisible air, a true emblem of the Aquarian air sign where the living water is in the hands of a human being. That figuration pictures humanistic values, good for society, the pouring of the alchemists' *aqua permanens* from one container into another, orienting a horizontal axis that bespeaks more equality than hierarchy of previous eons. We think we gather together around a shared idea, but are we? The terms have changed—different spaces, different time zones. Appearing present, we listen to the presentation but sometimes long after the Zoom presentation was made. Zoom relativizes our sense of space and time.

My experience on Zoom is mainly through hearing material from others, or delivering material myself to others. I find giving material easier because it links me to the people listening. It is as if I am talking to them and listening to their discussion and inquiries. It is harder than being in person to sense and gauge the emotional field we create, but it is possible once one consents to the tacit virtual quality in their presence. When I am part of the audience I find it hard to be quick enough to do the technological maneuvers to ask a question or join a discussion. When listening, I find it tiring, as if fixed into a posture that stiffens my limbs. Sometimes I feel I am lined up in the third grade class picture and must not wiggle. The fixed in place quality drains energy from me.

A more serious shadow side of virtual reality in the air shows up in match-make-dating which I learn from younger friends. A kind of ruthless deletion of another is well known and named ghosting. A passionate actual date in person, or sometimes an exciting virtual meeting up, is followed by no message, no acknowledgment, no thank you, or we must talk, only the delete. Effort to contact the other who disappears is never responded to even to say I find I am not able to continue meeting. One never knows what happened—did the other die? Have an accident? Hate me? Scorn me? Want to harm me? Uncertainty is made manifest by subtraction rather than action and addition. One is discounted, rendered deletable. This puts into the shared atmosphere, the now discounted spirit of the times in which we all dwell, a sort of sorrow, self-doubt, rage. On the other hand, however, I am impressed by how lectures on Zoom gather from across cultures a world-wide community of different ages, abilities and disabilities into one group to hear what is said. This widens and deepens, at least potentially, the richness of communication. This is in contrast to previous audiences limited to who has time, money, health, and leisure to travel to hear what will be said. The emotional field is different, but still there and worth giving attention to nurture it.

My point in even mentioning locality as a factor to consider in facing uncertainty is because of its prevalence everywhere not only through the air of new expanding technology, but also down on the ground for millions of people fleeing their homes to find a home, a location they can build to call their own. Many want to return to their homeland and may never be able to do so. Others hope to plant their roots elsewhere and what does that feel like? The change of locality exists in the midst of uncertainty, both in personal and in collective terms. We could devote an entire study to locality, tracing the lines from Gaston Bachelard's meditations on space of corners, nests, and dresser drawers to air as liberating flight upward or a falling down into sin or Hades (Bachelard, 1964, 2002) all the way to intangible networks of friends, congregations worshiping the same God, and piercing space/time barriers into a new kind of grounding in the air beyond the boundaries we used to call fixed.

Reckoning with this new collective of the air from digital technology and virtual reality expands the notion of collective unconscious with the click of an electronic mouse. Where is my self in this and where is Jung's symbolic concept of Self as the subject of totality? Uncertainty and paradox prevail. On the one hand we must take seriously our finite limits, what we do not understand and cannot master and avoid all triumphalism based on denial, like the former president of the United States who simply could not accept he lost the election to become president for a second term. He gave the impression that losing equated becoming a loser— he was a loser whose father would dismiss because only winners counted. More than being a poor sport by denying the loss that was evidentially correct and affirmed by more than a few repeated counting of votes and multiple lawsuits to claim his victory, all of which failed, my impression was he crossed a line into being gripped by fantasy replacing reality. Never, ever, was he a loser but always and ever a winner. Any individual, government official, or agency who disagreed must be repudiated, gotten rid of, or ruined.

Some experts about virtual reality and digital technology see it as subverting our usual sense of self and other and intersubjectivity (Krebs, 2013, pp. 31-38). I see the merit of that paradigm but prefer a different one that emphasizes expansion and addition over subtraction and loss. I see the new feeling-thought of uncertainty threatening us from all sides as forming into consciousness a new perception of interpenetration of all levels of psyche that Jung's notion of psychoid tries to name but says is not possible to represent in image or word. All that is, is present simultaneously and distinctly, not one aspect of reality annulling another, nor subsuming it in a hierarchy, nor containing it. Instead, the sheer multitude of reality pressing can make one uncertain to a severe degree of wanting to deny and hide, or open to possibility of which choice to follow. However finite and tiny we are in the bigness of the whole, we exist and can choose which aspect to develop.

Naming the New

I perceive gifts that our current state of uncertainty and changing world offer. We are in the process of forming new structures and realities. One of the ways that forming happens is in a new version of naming something, or someone we love, for example, that recognizes and speaks to the essence of the other, their otherness, not our version of it. Essence here is not fixed and defining. By essence I mean epiphany—a showing, an opening of beingness that is a unique streaming-forth. The new is nonlinear and renounces progress, sometimes even growth. It is closer to Klee's all-over painting where all the parts are represented and one can enter the composition anywhere at any time. It includes the unlived life as well as a shout for joy at all the livingness registered, celebrated. Surprise, spontaneous bursting forth or simple quiet showing of life here and now, spurs an incredulity matched by wonder.

Uncertainty shifts the focus from ego management and understanding by deep thinking, to what Jung calls the Self, the subject of totality of us, completeness of bad and good of us, of the world, of others. Potential and actual realized life, grief, loss and the acute charge of the new to come through and see differently persist. Jung's soul chiding him for still getting stuck in explaining and understanding, says outright "You will no longer think from cell nuclei of your brain...[but with] thought-feeling, it crawls around like a worm" (Jung 2020 Black Book 5, p. 242).

When given a name, in baptism for example, or a pet name by one who loves you, or in public as an awardee to your acclaim, one comes into one's individuality. Particularly in ritual, like baptism, Jung says, the child becomes an individual and capable of *Viseo Dei* (Jung 2021, p. 20). In contrast to the primitive who lives, Jung claims, as part of the collective, the rite of baptism lifts one out of anonymity to a position of individuality in relation to nature and others (Jung,1964, para. 136). This kind of sacred name is felt as a secret recognition of your own mostness. Sabi Tauber dreamt Jung whispered in her ear her secret name which only he and Sabi know "So that I may recognize God and he recognizes me" (Jung, 2021, p. 29). Tiny, finite, flawed, a jumble of potentials and failures, talents and mistakes, our little selves matter, even to the Ultimate Source, however we conceive it to be or not. It is through our human lives the infinite can step over into ordinary life. "The self is being crystalized in the name" (Jung, 1964, p. 31).

In making the numinous welcome in the ordinary, we must accept our limits to what we are able to do, "to stay within the frame of what is possible" (1964, p. 74). Jung advises Sabi Tauber to work on her own understanding of synchronicity as her creative project, not to get lost in scientific articles about it for which she lacks the background. She has an understanding of it "from the depth of the earth" that the scientists do not have (1967, pp. 74-75). Stay with that for "the absence of a goal is the premise for such work (as in active imagination); it arises from the unconscious and has an effect in the collective" (Jung, 1964, p. 75). The process of individuation goes on its own way, whether we tend it or not: "One has to go with the current, 'grow in the forest....' We must do what we hold to be right and what is possible. In that way we answer the question that our destiny puts to us" (Jung, 1964, p. 72).

This is a secret the finite shares with the Source—the necessity of being the individual you are makes possible the incarnation of the numinous, the God if you like. "God cannot incarnate... on unhealthy grounds—not in folly and stupidity....the plant of eternity...wants to grow in this world, here and now" (Jung, 1964, p. 86). What is needed is daily to be who you are, to get into right relationship with your own horse, to learn to ride it, not kill it by racing all the time, nor to sink into a quicksand of passivity by sloth. The archetype is invisible, it comes as a gripping, a lightning flash, a quiet word that deposits certainty but of the next step only. Take, for example, your projection of the good that attaches onto some part of the large good of life. Take in what it offers you, integrate that projection. It brings a bit of the good itself toward you, "so one knows who one is and what one has to do.... inwardly say 'yes' to life.... Say yes to yourself, then life will come to you"

(Jung, 1964, p, 76; Ulanov, 2007, pp. 201-206). Move somewhere else: to the end of projection, or recalling projections.

New Creative Gestures

What then happens in this surrounding, both inward and external to us, to uncertainty? Uncertainty can stir up creative gestures. They communicate their possibility to us. Here are three examples. The first is noticing synchronicity which operates by different laws from our usual discourse. A second is the shift of the place from which communication comes between tense opposites, like those dogging racism and the mystery of good and evil. A third is a shift in the psychic placement of our ego in personal and in collective consciousness from being the center of attention and as the main actor in life to the Self as center of the whole psyche including the unconscious. Sometimes something gets announced that can no longer be contained within our personal psyche. It bursts out to make an external form to which we work to create and must learn to relate.

Synchronicity

Jung designates synchronicity "the meaningful coin-cidence... of a psychic and physical state or event that has no causal relationship to one another .... Simultaneous occurrence of two meaningfully but not causally connected events which have the same or a similar meaning" (Jung, 1963, p 400). Synchronicity is not new in that people know, speak and write about it. But the acuity of our awareness of its happening is sharpened. We do not cause it. At our best, we recognize it, do not spurn its occasion. Its happening bespeaks a different way of organizing perception of meaning. Uncertainty can confuse and frighten; synchronicity can astonish and elicit wonder. Wonder becomes a new marker of awareness in contrast to the dread accompanying uncertainty that anything can happen at any time. Now the push of synchronicity into creative act and attitude demonstrates the wonder that anything may happen at any time. As a simple opposite to uncertainty that confuses and frightens, synchronistic events astonish and elicit wonder. And they convey that meaning exists.

New life comes from outside our familiar parameters of cause and effect, linear progression, logical sequence. Jung writes, "Synchronicity… doesn't work causally, but meaningfully, and only when emotion is involved….Mere coincidence is more than we assume—it's not just 'chance,' it's all arranged! Synchronicity is a reality" (Jung, 2021, pp. 72-73). Our response to uncertainty is a creative gesture; it enlivens soul.

Synchronicity is a new organizing of experience into making meaning, in contrast to the model of ever extending the line of producing with the exclusive goal of more growth for more money. Meaning making seems slower and less efficient if looked at from the perspective of produce more, gain more profit. This meaning way is to live more now, together mutually. This creative response to uncertainty brings moments, nexus points of meaning we take in, build on and live from.

Shift of the Place of Communication

The second gift of uncertainty is a new mode of communication antecedent to word and image that differs from tried and true ways of crossing distances in verbal representations and pictures. It applies to speaking to the tension of opposites. How can communication happen in the riotous, stubborn conflict of antagonistic divorce? Political polarization? Racism? The gap between opposites appears abysmal.

We cross by joining in depth places of recognizing analogous suffering among us. Without words, without images, silence may make us reach down with our toes to a space before such usual ways of communicating. We touch where we ourselves experienced a violent erasing force exerted by another against us, a group excluding us, one people erasing another people. We do not have the same experience but one akin to our neighbor's suffering.

We each have our version, analogous to but not identical with what the other suffers. Annihilation is the thread of connection between us. In listening for each other, receiving whatever emerges in the silence, we respond to the other from, not about, our experience. We respond from what arises in us of similar but not identical terror, humiliation, rage, shock, helplessness, or loss of hope that feels resonant with the other's experience. That creates a network of potential recognition. Uncertainty keeps us from rushing.

From there communication may begin. We are not so much trading stories as we are sharing a space from which stories originate. We recognize great pain in each other, this fact of human existence; we are members of the tribe of humanness. We begin to find another language. More surprising still, this sharing requires a different mode of speaking. What could it possibly be? What came to me was how trees are reported to communicate through fungal roots, canopy sharing, fueling tree health to a young sapling in danger of collapse. Grammar and syntax occur in tiny membranes, fertile humus. We communicate through growing not explaining. We lend growth to one another, not verbal discourse. From there communication may thrive (Wohlleben, 2015; Simard, 2021; Brewster, 2019).

An example comes from James Baldwin saying, Blacks don't have a 'race problem;' this is a whites' problem (https://www.jstor.org/stable/3252049#:~:text=%22'It's%20not%20the%20Negro%20problenm,you're%20white.%22'&text=doing%20it%2C%20where%20we've,re%20going%20in%20whiteness%20studies). In my view, White people should not expect Black people to educate them about how to behave and speak about racism. Black people are busy already surmounting racist acts cruel to the point of death in the most horrible circumstances, as if meant to broadcast a White supremacist attitude that White people are stronger, bigger, better. No. The wounding war is not over. Killing attitudes persist and break out into collective consciousness in terrible episodes. This is a White problem spurred on by their terror, fear. Black people are occupied solidifying hard won success in elections and appointments to high office, daring to create an abundant culture of all kinds and levels. Black people are busy surviving and thriving.

The Shift of the Placement of the Ego

The black/white opposites offer as well a significant example of getting pulled into the opposites of good and evil. When who is good and who is evil are interchangeable. Both sides can be seen at different time to be either. When in fact, we are all both. Uncertainty that pulls us loose from our moorings in definitions of good and evil, may make space for simpler access to our living with these opposites. Jung discovers that good and evil go together as long as we are growing. When we stop growing, they fall apart in deadly rivalry.

The Self is the subject of the whole psyche, including the unconscious. We experience the Self personally, as one analysand put it, "I feel myself under regard" conveying a sense of superior authority to which he felt beholden. Contemporary and ancient cultures draw on religious, mystical, spiritual notations of Self such as samadhi, isness, God images, which supervene binary ego positions. Archetypal manifestations of Self circle around figures of the center, the point, the world-axis, Source without source.

We can ask, what does the Self viewpoint tell us about good and evil? The Self view includes all the parts of us, the whole of us. We may imagine through a Self-perspective we see that ordinary people of all kinds and types experience good and evil already living together in themselves, their neighbors, even their enemies. We can describe someone we know well, the good of them—their priceless first-rateness, the merit, geniality, worth of them—and also perceive in them where they are unprincipled, petty, nasty, ignoble, even malicious too. They are already living those opposites of good and evil together in one person. They are not split apart, nor wildly alternating from one opposite to the other. Are their opposites integrated? Usually no, but maybe in small bits they coincide and

43

even interpenetrate into a complexity of character. They make efforts at growing.

This image of us trying, failing, mistaking and achieving all mixed in, combats scapegoating and projecting, aiming to get rid of unwanted parts of ourselves by blaming the other. We live with opposites, trying to corral them like horses to move together, even like Plato's horses that draw the chariots that circle the spheres (Phaedrus, pp. 250-51). We see blunt evil when we try to take one opposite and avoid the other, for example, when a political party leader muscles all party members to vow to defeat any legislation the new president of the opposite party proposes. The leader's personal opinion takes precedence over the vow of his office to serve his constituents and the whole governing process elected by the citizens. We can see glints of utter good in simple acts of kindness that without fanfare one person shows to another. This ordinary effort to live with two sides of our nature is a surprising gift of uncertainty. What feels monumentally important in splitting good and evil in an effort to keep one and banish the other yields to more ordinary living their going together if we are growing.

The next example is dramatic and, to me, extraordinary. It features the burden of the good. Something that has existed inside us—a possibility surrounding our dominating complex—bursts outside us and we must learn now to relate to it there, instead of falling back into inward identification with the complex. A shift takes place from the ego view to the Self view and an announcement happens from Self to ego that something can no longer be contained within our personal psyche. It is a possible good though may not initially appear to be such. It arises from what Jung, using language of the unconscious, describes, "A new sun broke away from the flaming primordial mother. A dragon crept up and spat out the sun. It could no longer endure the light in it" (Jung, 2021 BB vol 6, p. 271; Ulanov, 2022a, 2022b).

This light is brighter than the known lights; they pale in comparison. In the example I suggest here, this new light so bright offers a shift from entanglement in complex to instead take the creative gesture offered. In this uncertainty of transition to do a new and heretofore unthinkable thing, the dogging complex moves from within to outside us. The new possibility surrounding the complex is fire that "reaches the light and the light went pale" (Jung, 2021, 6, p. 271). This fiery light becomes external to us; we encounter it and must learn to relate to it. It is the turning away from the complex because of this light so bright, its luster makes the dragon spit it out of ourselves which is a new possibility symbolized by this new light. This is good as burden, encountered and related to as an external form we must shape and learn how to relate to. The good is symbolized by the light so bright. The energy to surge out of ourself toward this good is symbolized by fire and comes, I suggest, from the energy availed of recalling our projections.

The change of mode from assimilating something within us to finding and creating a new form outside us, means we do not integrate this content but encounter it as an other, not a personal part of us, but something in its own right. Something new is on the scene. This response to the newly shaping form is the creative gesture uncertainty offers as a gift. Instead of being embroiled once again in the old complex, a new possibility appears on the horizon, hard to define, that disrupts our ways of handling complexes. This is present even dare I say in Jung's case in the signature of the God image of the spirit of the times where good and evil are sharply defined and made certain as unredeemed opposites. Some other force moves this radical change. We experience this new form forming with uncertainty, doubt and wonder. It is not something we control but attend, serve. The energy to do this comes from the energy recalled to us when we withdraw our projections.

I think of the slogans of different people's dominating complex: the tormenting critic that makes a person so anxious they cannot function but succumb to despair that they are nothing; or a fortified determination to be free of sadistic attack and neglect but clinging to freedom has cost spontaneous feeling which now must be allowed to be felt; or swirling in guilt for not putting one's foot on the earth incarnating a life, no longer hovering in the air above life; or a sense of nonbeing vying with being that has cut off easy interaction with the world, one copes but alone. What makes us get free of such a dogging complex?

Uncertainty upends foundations we counted on. We knew good from evil, safety from danger. We cannot use those old references to orient ourselves, but hearken to some new note we hear or scent, spy, touch, even taste that is so amazing that it must be untrue. Our old dogging complex is also upended, dug up at the roots so its heretofore dominating power withers. It can be gone. We used hard work to manage the complex but this bursting out goes further. Some creative gesture appears; we search and find the forming good and it takes up all the room and there is no oxygen for the old complex, no fuel to sustain it now.

The creative gesture that may among uncertainty's gifts is the shift of placement of ego from center stage to serving a bigger source. This can feel like a defeat of the ego. But we usually experience this shift with surprise, I believe, when we look at it from the point of view of the Self. The shift inaugurates a new relation to the complex that had overcome our ego. The ego is no longer in charge but gets stripped of the complex in service to the creative gesture. The good here is the possibility now formed to be real. Upending the old complex, giving it up, undoing it, not listening to its whisper and threats, not hearing them. All energy goes elsewhere.

I used to think that at best we could with hard work analyze the complex, then put it in its place and stay alert to its rising up again to throw us into a pit of depression or shake us with agitation of massive anxiety (Ulanov, 2017, pp. 83-84). We constructed ways to care for ourselves and not repeat the old drama of trauma. We protect our presiding over our life. The new thing in this shift, I propose, is we may heal the complex; it is upended and gone; it dissolves. What makes this happen?

It is by the fire of the blazing light of love, a new feeling colder than the grave bursting out of the insight that your complex, my complex, hurts something or someone we love. We see that clearly, with horror. If it is one of our children, we see we could brand them with pain because we are caught up in the script of the complex. Or it may be a cause of justice we love and we see that this complexed behavior undermines the very justice we serve. We renounce the complex; a sliver of freedom turns us to the creative gesture of giving up our enthrall to the complex—lest we damage the very cause we serve, hurt one we love. Or it may be an ideal—a way of living, a vision of kindness, a value of education for all, or the power of beauty to comfort.

A sliver of new space appears, a turn of the head away from repeating the complex's ingrained pattern and the wound that feeds that pattern. We turn our head to the creative gesture, the bursting out of the old pattern into a new emerging form we then must find, create, attend. A different ethic impacts us and bursts out from within us: we love this other and will not inflict pain on them, will not abuse their life with our complex—be it a child, a beloved, a cause of justice, a spiritual option. We feel an encounter with the ultimate, however we describe that. Uncertainty accompanies the unfolding of this force of love for the other. It feels like a leap of aliveness. We see our inflicting pain on the other and say no, no more, uncertain what form this loving the other will take. With a sliver of freedom, we refuse to enact the complex on the other. No more of that. Uncertainty accompanies this freedom.

This nexus point of interpenetration of ordinary event by extraordinary creative burst of new tone, action, feeling inspired by a Self point of view brings insight, tissues knitting together in the body, a kiss given and received. Often synchronicity accompanies this meeting, a flowing current of aliveness felt in relation to meaningfulness of eternal presence. Some people call this God, Jung included. Others eschew that nomenclature preferring Self and ego in cooperative dance. Others say chance, fate, mystery of wholeness showing itself. It does feel like wholeness happening, space made for something new that rearranges everything, rounding out a completeness. It brings a kind of happiness. Gratitude abounds.

The shortest way to grasp this new gift of being done with the complex is to give examples. An analysand suffered a car crash that totaled the car, injured one hand that required surgery. The other driver was at fault but nonetheless sued in court for a big cash amount for medical claims that were false. My patient hired a lawyer and an investigator who collected evidence of the falsity of the claim of back injury in photos of the man playing golf and moving around easily. The claimant lost in court. My patient chose not to retaliate by countersuing for punitive damages although she initially considered it. Instead she was moved out of devotion to her Buddhist teachings to seek peace and not act out of rancor, not to put violence into the world.

A second example was the shock of an analysand to discover her dominating complex of catastrophic anxiety hurt her adult child who came to give needed help with a flooding problem. His help was crucial; he was glad to give it even though it required he give up two days of his demanding work and life schedule. But he was enraged at being met when he arrived with a massive wall of her anxiety that made her criticize, resist, and try to control everything he proposed to do. He let her have it, saying, *you ask for help; I give up two days of my life and work to help you. I am glad to do it and you beat me off and beat me up with your anxiety. That is your problem; deal with it. Don't make me do it; I don't know how. But you hurt me and enrage me as if my gift to you is like so much shit.* What struck into her with clarity like a knife to the heart was the pain of hurting a son she loved: her problem hurt him. She said it felt as if her complex branded, burned into his flesh. The bright light that burst out of her was loving him. She went with that, into its current. Could we say the dragon in her spat this current of light out of her? With massive effort she checked her anxiety and went with the force of love. She felt like the mother who moved a car to free her baby from its wheels. How was this possible? She had no idea, only that it was necessary. The anxiety no longer ruled her. She attended to that shock and how to form an ongoing relation to this force of love. She turned her head away from the old catastrophic anxiety into this new form forming. The energy for this big change comes, I suggest, from recalling our projections and putting their newly liberated force to use in this way of accepting the burden of the good.

Such a defeat of the complex for the sake of loving the other and the wholeness of the whole puts into the world perception of the bigger event without dismissing the smaller one. I think of Alexei Navalny whose fearsome presence stands up to Vladimir Putin, president of Russia. Putin had Navalny poisoned; he survived and returned to Russia to stand up again and Putin arranged a tax charge against him and a nine-year sentence in maximum-security penal colony. His wife and son are also to be recognized in standing against dictatorship in their support of husband and father and thus also contribute to the rest of us. Navalny stands out in his unique view that "Postwar Russia must be the central issue" as the way to end Putin's war inflicted on Ukraine and by proxy on the West.

Navalny asks what is the post-war future we imagine for Russia? He urges not to get stuck in opposites that inflame each side to even more aggressive tactics. Look to that future where Russia might endorse the participation of its whole society and take its place as a good neighbor in the world, not perfect and with no perfect guarantee, but with enough freedom for other citizens also to have a life, not just one man at the topmost point of the pyramid. Navalny argues for a government of participatory republic, against the dictator model of a presidential republic. Psychologically, allowing citizens' votes to count would be comparable to diluting a complex by building up other psychic functions, analogous to other ways of protesting that don't land you poisoned or in a maximum-security penal colony. Even from prison this man signals his creative gesture toward a parliamentary, not a presidential republic that Russia inflicts on itself.

Navalny argues against Russia's continuation of war as the solution to all domestic political problems and the proliferation of its "resentment and imperial ideas....in a state of permanent military mobilization" (Navalny September 30 at 8:00 am; www. washingtonpost.com/opinions/2022/09/30/alexei-navalny-parliamentary-republic-russia-ukraine/.

A parliamentary republic promotes more success in the world as evidenced by the countries who adopted that style in the collapse of the soviet socialist republic. Navalny offers his creative gesture, I suggest, to see a third way out of the lethal clash of opposites of Ukraine fighting for its land and Putin saying this land is Russia's.

References

Bachelard, G. (2002). *Air and Dreams: An Essay on the Imagination of Movement* (E. Farrell & C. F. Farrell, Trans.; 3rd ed.). Dallas, TX: The Dallas Institute Publications. (Original work published 1943)

_____. (1964). *The Poetics of Space.* (E. Gilson, Trans.). New York: Orion Press.

Bion, W.R. (1977). *Attention and Interpretation.* London: Tavistock Publications. (Original work published 1970)

Brewster, F. 2019. *The Racial Complex: A Jungian Perspective on Culture and Race.* New York & London: Routledge.

Freud, S. (1917). *The Standard Edition of the Complete Psychological Works of Sigmund Freud: Introductory lectures on psycho-analysis (part II) (1916-1917).* London: Hogarth Press. (Original work published 1906)

Greene, L. (1978). *Relating, An Astrological Guide to Living with Others on a Small Planet.* Weiser Books. (Original work published 1970)

Hirshfield, J. (2015). *Ten Windows: How Great Poems Transform the World.* New York: Knopf.

Jung, C.G. (1959). *CW, Vol. 9.1: The Archetypes and the Collective Unconscious.* Princeton, NJ: Princeton University Press. (Original work published 1954)

_____. (1959). *CW, Vol. 9.11: Aion.* Princeton, NJ: Princeton University Press.

_____. (1960). "On the Nature of the Psyche" *CW, Vol. 8: The Structure and dynamics of the psyche*. Princeton, N.J.: Princeton University Press.

_____. (1963). *Memories, Dreams, Reflections* (A. Jaffe, Ed.; R. and C. Winston, Trans.). Fontana Press.

_____. (1964). *CW, Vol. 10: Civilization in Transition "Archaic Man."* Princeton, NJ: Princeton University Press. (Original work published 1931)

_____. (1979). *CW, Vol. 20: Index*. Princeton, N.J.: Princeton University Press.

_____. (2009). T*he Red Book: Liber Novus*. S. Shamdasani (Ed.); J. Kybuz, J. Peck, S. Shamdasani. Trans.). New York & London: W.W. Norton.

_____. (2020). *The Black Books* (S. Shamdasani, Ed.; M. Liebscher, J. Peck, & S. Shamdasani, Trans.). New York & London: W. W. Norton & Company.

_____. (2021). *The Journal of Sabi Tauber* (1951-1961). (I. & A. Gerber, eds. and trans.) Einsiedeln, Switzerland: Daimon Verlag.

Klee, P. (2017). Ten Americans: After Paul Klee. Munich, London, New York, Bern: Zentrum Paul Klee; Washington D. C.: The Phillips Collection; Munich: Prestel Verlag. Egglehofer, Fabienne, "Inciter to Invention: Paul Klee and a New Path for Abstract Art" (ibid, pp. 17-32).

_____. (2013). *"Creative Confession & Other Writings"* Gale, M. (ed.). London: Tate Publications.

_____. (1964). *The Diaries of Paul Klee 1898-1918*. Klee, F. (ed.). Berkely and Los Angeles: University of California Press.

Klein, M. (1975). *Love, Guilt and Reparation and Other Works 1921-1945*. New York: Delacorte/Seymour Lawrence Press.

_____. (1975). *Envy & Gratitude & Other Works 1946-1963.* New York: Delacorte/Seymour Lawrence Press.

Krebs, V. (2013). "The Power of Ghosts" *Jung Journal of Culture and Psyche 7:4,* 31-38.

Mayo, J. (1992). *Teach Yourself Astrology.* London: NTC Publishing Group Clays Ltd. (Original work published 1964)

Ogden, T.H. (1982). *Projective Identification and Psychotherapeutic Technique.* Lanham, MD: Rowman and Littlefield Publishers.

Plato, P. (387). *Phaedra: The dialogues of Plato, Vol. 1.* (B. Jowett, Trans.). New York: Random House.

Rycroft, C. (1968). *A Critical Dictionary of Psychoanalysis.* New York: Basic Books.

Simard, S. (2021). *Finding the Mother Tree.* New York: Alfred A. Knopf.

Ulanov, A, & Ulanov, B. (1975). *Religion and the Unconscious.* Louisville, KY: John Knox/Westminster Press.

Ulanov, A.B. (1971). *The Feminine in Jungian Psychology and In Christian Theology.* Evanston, IL: Northwestern University Press.

_____. (2001). *Finding Space: Winnicott, God and Psychic Reality.* Louisville, KY: John Knox/Westminster Press.

_____. (2017). *The Psychoid, Soul and Psyche: Piercing Space/Time Barriers.* Einsiedeln, Switzerland: Daimon Verlag.

_____. (2022a). *Back to Basics.* Einsiedeln Switzerland: Daimon Verlag.

_____. (2022b). "The Shadow's shadows" Buenos Aires: Proceedings from IAAP International Congress August-September 2022, to be published soon.

von Franz, M. -L. (1980). *Projection and Re-Collection in Jungian Psychology, Reflections of the Soul.* (W. Kennedy, Trans.) LaSalle, IL & London: Open Court.

Wohlleben, P. (2015). *The Hidden Life of Trees.* (J. Billinghurst, et al., Trans.) Vancouver & Berkeley: Greystone Books.

Living with Personal Uncertainty over the Long Term

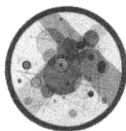

"As any change must begin somewhere, it is the single individual who will experience it and carry it through. The change must indeed begin with an individual; it might be any one of us. Nobody can afford to look round and to wait for somebody else to do what he is loath to do himself."
—(Jung, 1961, para. 599)

"To ask the right question is already half the solution of a problem."
—(Jung, 1959/1969, para. 49)

Introduction

We are all living in a time of prolonged and continuing uncertainty for a number of reasons. Our period of intense uncertainty and fear began with the sudden arrival of the pandemic. It changed everyone's lives in one way in the short term and other ways for the long term. Donald Kalsched chronicled the short-term effect in a July 2021 paper: "The isolation and loneliness in COVID-quarantine, the fear of death, the loss of a dependable future, the economic anxieties—all these [are] very real collective traumas" (Kalsched, 2021, p. 4). These traumas were felt by everyone, but they affected individuals and the community differently.

With the advent of vaccines and the increasing number of people receiving them, hope was on the horizon. States were opening up again, whether wisely or without regard to managing Covid-19 surges. Spring emerged, optimism began to return, and the country continued opening up as the year went on. As time goes on, everyone hopes that the pandemic is now mostly behind us. At the same time, there is hesitation and concern:

❖ How do I know when I am ready to return to "normal?"
❖ What should my first steps be?
❖ What would a new normal be? Feel like? Include?
❖ What do I want to keep from my pandemic years, and what should I discard?
❖ Am I really safe? How do I assess the recurring risks?

The last few years have constrained us on many levels. This section offers ways of developing an individual perspective for living more comfortably with all the pressures that we are facing going into the future. We offer here a collection of thoughts from prominent Jungian analysts that include perspectives, information, and ways to assist in the framing of an individual's new way of living.

References

Jung, C.G. (1969). *Archetypes of the collective unconscious* (R. F. C. Hull, Trans.). In H. Read et al. (Eds.), *CW, Vol. 9 pt. 1. Archetypes and the collective unconscious* (2nd ed., pp. 3-41). Princeton, N.J.: Princeton University Press. (Original work published 1954)

Kalsched, D. (2021). "Intersections of Personal vs. Collective Trauma during the COVID-19 Pandemic: The Hijacking of the Human Imagination," *Journal of Analytical Psychology* 66, (3).

Spirit of the Depths, Spirit of the Times:
Dread and Hope in A Turbulent World

Margaret Klenck

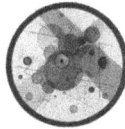

> *"...the spirit of the depths spoke to me: 'You are an image*
> *of the unending world, all the last mysteries*
> *of becoming and passing away live in you.'"*
> —Jung, *The Red Book*, page 121

We are all being swept up into a time of great strife and dread. We are challenged by upheaval, isolation, anger, exhaustion, grief—and change. So much is in flux: climate change and weather catastrophes, war in Ukraine, the excitement and pain of social justice movements, the glaring realities of economic inequality, waves of refugees fleeing untenable situations, the rise of fascistic autocrats and waning of democracies around the world, the upswell of violence against women and minorities, and a global exhaustion and grief as we process wave after wave of Covid-19 illness and death. We are all affected by the *Spirit of the Times*, Jung's term for the zeitgeist. We're affected inevitably, perpetually, consciously and unconsciously.

How shall we cope? How can we help? How shall we understand? What must we encounter in ourselves, in our depths, to be able to tolerate these uncertain times and not splinter into pieces? What is dying and what is being born, in the world, in each of us? How shall we live into our futures with hope?

These are big questions. They are questions that people have been asking forever, as history never ceases to present confounding, exciting and often terrifying times to live in. Jung's theory and clinical method grew out of just such times and many of the same questions. His answers not only have consequences for our work in Jungian analysis, but also for our capacity to understand and find hope, both for ourselves and for the world. The Jungian view of psyche offers us many tools to help us through our fears—to find meaning in the midst of turmoil.

At another intense and troubled time, just as WWI started, Carl Jung recorded his encounter with inner images which eventually became *The Red Book*, a major work that both chronicled his personal experience of his unconscious and laid the foundation for the field of analytical psychology. In the *Red Book*, Jung identifies two spirits which are often in opposition: the spirit of the times and the spirit of the depths. The spirit of the times refers to the zeitgeist, the political, social, day to day reality we live in. This spirit affects us profoundly as it carries us along on the waves of history. The spirit of the depths is not concerned with current situations. It is the energy from the deep unconscious, from both the collective unconscious—everything that humans have experienced since the dawn of time—and each person's personal unconscious. The spirit of the depths also affects us profoundly, although we are often unaware of how we are being moved by it. The often difficult and disorienting interaction between the two can provide a path for healing and hope.

One of the lessons of Jung's experiences as explored in the *Red Book* is the psychological truth that we must engage our depths, especially when the times are fraught. The essential way we engage with our depths is through our own inner images.

The study of images is central to and at the heart of Jungian psychology. It will be the focus of our work here. By images, Jungians mean more than visual images; we mean all the ways that human communication happens—languages of words, of body, of sound, of thought. In our search for some of the answers to our current uncertainty, we are going to journey down three paths, focusing on three aspects of image, from the Jungian point of view. Jung famously said "psyche is image" (Jung, 1967, para.75). He also said "The psyche consists essentially of images.... A picturing of vital activities" (Jung, 1958, para.889, 769). Image and imagination are linked, and as we shall see, they are woven throughout the Jungian method in such a way as to promote healing and also help in dealing with the struggles of the times.

James Hillman puts it this way,

"In the beginning is the image; first imagination then perception; first fantasy then reality.... Man is primarily an imagemaker and our psychic substance consists of images; our being is imaginal being, an existence in imagination. We are indeed such stuff as dreams are made of." (1975, p. 23)

The three aspects of image we will consider, our three paths, are:

I. Personification: Working directly with images as in Active Imagination and Dream work

II. Encountering the Arts: The emergence of images into symbols that move us, and can bring healing

III. Amplification: the craft of discerning the most apt archetypal story emergent from the Depths, to express the Spirit of the Times, so that we can adapt in strong and authentic ways

I. Personifying Image: Jung's encounter with his unconscious and the invention of Active Imagination.

In 1913, Jung found himself in chaos. At 37, he was well regarded in his profession and had become strongly associated with Sigmund Freud, who called him his "son and heir." But Jung had broken with Freud after their many heartbreaking struggles. While he embraced Freud's theories and became the preeminent spokesman for the psychoanalytic movement, Jung never fully agreed with some of Freud's ideas. That disagreement, and Jung's refusal to toe the party line, pulled the two giants in the field apart. Jung ended his last letter to Freud with a quote from Hamlet: "The rest is silence." It was a devastating breakup for both men, and an intellectual turning point for Jung.

In his autobiography, *Memories, Dreams, Reflections*, Jung writes, "After the parting of the ways with Freud, a period of inner uncertainty began for me. It would be no exaggeration to call it a state of disorientation. I felt totally suspended in mid-air..." (Jung, 1961, p. 170).

Several things happened for Jung during this period. One was that he "felt the necessity to develop a new attitude towards my patients. I resolved for the present not to bring any theoretical premises to bear upon them, but to wait and see what they would tell of their own accord....The result was that the patients would spontaneously report their dreams and fantasies to me ....I simply helped the patients to understand the dream-images by themselves without application of rules and theories" (Jung, 1961, p. 170).

This was a tremendous move on Jung's part: from being the doctor as authority who would tell the patients what was going on with them to being the doctor as partner who would treat the spontaneous images as "the facts from which we must proceed" (Jung, 1961, p. 171). This decision could be said to be the beginning of the Jungian analytic method as we have come to understand it.

I suggest this is a good example of something new being born spontaneously from a period of disorientation and chaos. It was a new idea, a new method, a new imagination of what might heal. Without Jung's willingness to engage in what was for him a terrifying struggle, he would never have come to this remarkable new method.

Another thing that happened during this time for Jung was that he had big, frightening dreams, dreams that confused him, dreams that wouldn't let him go. Dreams of the dead, dreams that gave him, as he said, "constant inner pressure;" he feared that "there was some psychic disturbance in me" (Jung, 1961, p. 173).

So, he made the psychoanalytic move: he reviewed his life, trying to find his footing. A childhood memory came up, of playing with toy blocks and building structures, houses, towns, etc. Despite feeling sort of ridiculous—Herr Dr. Professor Jung gathering stones from the lake and building a small town of buildings—that is what he felt compelled to do. This "building game" as he called it "was only the beginning. It released a stream of fantasies which I later carefully wrote down" (Jung, 1961, p. 175). This became *The Red Book*.

It was during this time as well that Jung had visions of Europe being covered in ice, and then of Europe being awash in blood with dead bodies floating by. He was terribly shaken by these visions and again feared for his sanity. And then, WWI broke out. He understood that his dreams and visions were not only his own personal story, although they were that, but they were also in conversation with the world, with the Spirit of the Times and the movements of history, the collective psyche. Jung wrote, "Now my task was clear: I had to try to understand what had happened and to what extent my own experience coincided with that of mankind in general. Therefore, my first obligation was to probe the depths of my own psyche" (Jung, 1961, p. 176).

This was not easy for Jung. As he was struggling between the Spirit of the Times and the Spirit of the Depths as he describes it, he found himself at first siding with rationality, with all his books containing all the world's knowledge, his educated and brilliant mind, and his significant place in the society. But the Spirit of the Depths pressed and Jung found that he could only speak in images, not ideas. "With nothing else can I express the words from the depths" (Jung, 1961, p. 123). Only images. He would eventually come to that classic formula, "Everything of which we are conscious is an image, and that image is psyche . . ." (Jung, 1967, para. 75).

Hear what else he says:

" to the extent that I managed to translate the emotions into images—that is to say to find the images which were concealed in the emotions—I was inwardly calmed and reassured. Had I left those images hidden in the emotions, I might have been torn to pieces by them. There is a chance that I might have succeeded in splitting them off; but in that case I would inexorably have fallen into a neurosis and so been ultimately destroyed by them anyhow." (Jung, 1961, page 177)

Jung concludes: "the essential thing is to differentiate oneself from these unconscious contents by personifying them, [turning them into characters] and at the same time to bring them into relationship with consciousness" (1961, page 187).

We can hear how essential it is to have connection to our inner lives, our inner personifiable images, especially now, with so much stress swirling around us. Jung gives us a method and a guide: *The Red Book*. Let's look at the structure and process of that experiment in encountering the depths by personifying and conversing with inner images.

Active Imagination: Working with Personal Images

To work with his inner images, Jung developed the process of active imagination. First, Jung would put himself, as he said, in a mood, and drop down into the feeling of it, allowing his will and his intellect to recede. Then he would open himself up to the images, let himself be drawn in, let the images personify themselves, take human or mythological shape. Then, he would engage those figures; he'd talk to them and listen to them. It was often terrifying, or confounding, but he let them speak to him, surprise him, challenge him. Then he would surface back into full consciousness and write his encounters down, just as they happened, no embellishment. Lastly, he would wonder about the experiences, trying to put them into some context for himself; that is when his intellect would get re-engaged. Then the process could begin again.

If you have read the *Red Book*, you are familiar with this rhythm: surrender will and intellect, sink down, encounter, experience, surface and record, then wonder.

This is the process for encountering *all* inner images, whether they are actively sought as in active imagination exercises, or arise in dreams, prayer, or even in metaphor in conversation. All images can be processed in this way. By lifting up the technique of Active Imagination, I am not suggesting dissociation as a coping strategy—not at all. Active Imagination, dream work, prayer life, sticking to the image, are not dissociative processes. Rather they are <u>associative</u>, eventually associating the images of the unconscious emergent from psyche with our lived lives. Dialoguing with personified inner images is not an escape. It is a weaving together of the outer and inner so that we are strengthened, by our encounter with ourselves. Jung (1961, p. 123) described this as "the spirit of the depths in me was at the same time the ruler of the depths of world affairs," connected, deeply entwined.

Here is an example: When I was writing the essay that became this chapter, I got rather stuck in a kind of writer's block. I found myself thinking, *It's as if a troll is not letting me cross the bridge*. I didn't consciously select that image of a troll, it was a spontaneous image from the depths, and one I could engage with in just this way. It's just as real and as important as a big Active Imagination or a nighttime dream.

Part of what calms us, whether we are suffering a writer's block or facing a pandemic, war, discrimination, natural catastrophe, etc., is the knowledge that we are part of what Jung called an unending world; whatever happens, time continues. Our psyches are connected through our personal unconsciousness to the collective unconscious and the great web of humanity. Our experiences contribute to the vast wealth of human history and the human condition. We carry the essential nature of all humanity, of creation itself. In our own births, lives and deaths we manifest the endless cycles of rebirth and transformation. Further, by engaging with the events of the zeitgeist with consciousness, informed by this knowledge of the depths, we can find purpose and meaningful actions in our day-to-day lives. In this way, the spirit of the times and the spirit of the depths are not only in a struggle with each other, but they are also in relationship to each other. They are an interrelated whole. As Jung put it, "...the spirit of the depths spoke to me: 'You are an image of the unending world, all the last mysteries of becoming and passing away live in you'" (2009, p. 121).

This first path has led us to a process for dialogue with our inner images, a method of listening and differentiating from raw unconscious material, while at the same time being influenced and affected by it. This path has brought us to the possibility of orienting ourselves through our encounters with our intrapsychic realities, as if we had a psychic compass that will always point to our own true north—we just have to learn how to read it.

II. Encountering the spirits of both the depths and the times through the Arts

The second path: The Arts. With art we engage with the Spirit of the Times and the Spirit of the Depths viscerally. That visceral encounter moves us, stretches us, changes us and can heal us. When we hear music, when we see a painting, watch a dance, experience an opera, a play or a film, when we read poetry or a novel, we are encountering the fruits of other people's encounters with their unconscious and their inner images. We absorb their insights and conclusions directly, without thought. We are fed new food, food we have not cooked ourselves. Being open to art in all its forms requires a similar willingness to surrender that Active Imagination does, a willingness to simply react, not to judge or control, a willingness to see what happens to you.

Of course, this is also true when we make art ourselves, when we sing, compose, paint, sculpt, dance, film, photograph, write. This attitude of openness and willingness to be affected by images is paramount. Whether you doodle or paint in oils, compose a symphony or make up a little tune as you walk down the street, you are being prompted by your unconscious, your inner images, the spirit of the depths—to express something new. So often, it is art that carries us through hard times. Art presses us into our emotions, making it impossible to pretend that nothing is affecting us. Art reconnects us to humanity.

Another way to say this is that the potential for transformative symbols to arise is ever-present in works of art, both when we create them ourselves and when we experience the creations of others. Symbols are living expressions "for something that cannot be characterized in any other or better way" (Jung, 1971, p. 816). Jung makes a clear distinction between symbols and signs, with signs being expressions of a known thing—such as street and traffic signs, official insignia, icons on our computers, etc. But symbols express something inexpressible in any other way. "Every psychic product, if it is the best possible expression at the moment for a fact as yet unknown or only relatively known, may be regarded as a symbol" (Jung, 1971, p. 817). It is this unknown aspect that gives the symbol the transforming potential. A sign is useful for navigating the known world, but it is dead. A symbol is always "pregnant with meaning" (Jung, 1971, para. 816).

When images become symbols, they transform psychic energy. Symbols connect us to past, present and future. Jung says that "it is the essence of the symbol to contain both the rational and the irrational" (Jung, 1964, p. 24). As such, they connect the Spirit of the Times and the Spirit of the Depths in fascinating ways, guiding us to understanding. "The psychological mechanism that transforms energy is the symbol" (Jung, 1960, para. 88). Symbols are the lifeblood of meaning.

In a 1929 letter, Jung says, "I am indeed convinced that creative imagination is the only primordial phenomenon accessible to us, the real Ground of the psyche, the only immediate reality" (Jung, 1973, p. 60).

And the Jungian analyst Sherry Salman explains it this way, "Symbols are living, emerging images, reflecting active psychological process and pregnant with meaning. They are capable of acting like transformers of psychic energy...a symbolic image evokes the totality of the archetype it reflects... creating links to affective experience which heals splits" (Salman, 2008, p.70).

However, we need to be on the emotional, psychic alert for symbols. They don't just do their transformative work by themselves.

In his introduction to *The Red Book*, Sonu Shamdasani describes Jung's understanding of the dynamic of symbolic meaning this way: "...the creation of symbols was the most important function of the unconscious. While the compensatory function of the unconscious was always present, the symbol-creating function was present only when we were willing to recognize it" (Shamdasani, *Red Book*, p. 57).

For example, when I was caught in the writer's block mentioned earlier, if I had not noticed that I said to myself it was as if a troll was keeping me from crossing the bridge, that image, and the whole symbolic potential embedded in it with stories of trolls, and what is required when stopped by a troll—all of that wealth of information would have just passed me by. I wouldn't have gotten the message from psyche and I would not have been fed symbolic food there. We must be on the look-out.

As it turns out, I did look up trolls and discovered that they are Nordic creatures, rather ugly and mean-spirited who often waylay people as they walk through the countryside and eat them.

They will ransack barns and storehouses and are generally greedy. They cannot abide church bells. Yes, I felt that I was being stopped by a dangerous ugliness (my own writer's block, my troll complex if you will). But I also learned that only two things can defeat trolls: 1) a lightning bolt from Thor, or 2) some kind of trick. You can't fight trolls directly. This helped, when I sat with that information. I saw that I shouldn't keep fighting my writer's block directly, it would just eat me up. I either needed to rely on inspiration (a lightning bolt out of the heavens), or I had to approach this block sideways, with some humor and a slyness. I had to trick this little complex. Amplifying troll, just learning this bit of the image, moved libido (psychic energy) and moved me out of the writer's block. Psyche sent the image of troll specifically; it was a precise message and exactly the image I needed. I would have missed it all if I had not taken the image seriously and engaged it, encountering my own inner troll.

Here is the famous quote from Jung in *Memories, Dreams, Reflections*, Jung's autobiography in which he admonishes us to take our inner images seriously:

> "...I took great care to try to understand every single image, every item of my psychic inventory, and to classify them scientifically—so far as this was possible—and, above all, to realize them in actual life. That is what we usually neglect to do. We allow the images to rise up, and maybe we wonder about them, but that is all. We do not take the trouble to understand them, let alone draw ethical conclusions from them. This stopping-short conjures up the negative effects of the unconscious....The images of the unconscious place a great responsibility upon a man. Failure to understand them, or a shirking of ethical responsibility, deprives him of his wholeness and imposes a painful fragmentariness on his life." (1961, pp. 192-193)

As with Active Imagination, there are systematic ways to engage the arts so that they can help you through difficult times, bringing you clarity, inspiration, courage and hope. Making art, expressing yourself in any medium unlocks the doors between consciousness and unconsciousness which, in turn, allows the spontaneous emergence of surprising and transformative feelings, thoughts, symbols. Creative endeavors come in all forms. Having an active relationship to your own self-expression challenges the stuckness of ego consciousness and subverts the hold of the zeitgeist. The key is to let yourself be moved—by your own creations and those of others.

One suggestion is to choose a piece of music and sit with it, not having it in the background while you are doing other things. Follow it, go where the musician(s) are taking you. It can be a folk song, a symphony or pop song. It can be jazz or sea shanties. But really listen. And then notice where your mind goes, where your imagination takes you. In this way you will be bridging between your conscious and unconscious and making room for something spontaneous to emerge. As Sherry Salman said, "affective energy …heals splits" (Salman, 2008, p.70).

Even if where the experience takes you is to painful feelings, the process will be useful. Suppressed grief, anger, longing, confusion can keep us frozen, unable to fully engage with life. That kind of suppression dissociates us from others and from ourselves and eventually leaves us open to despair.

Another process for encountering one's depths is to look at pieces of art, in the same ways as with the piece of music—fully. Here are some photographs to use as exercises in this work. Let yourself take in the images, look at the composition, look at the expressions of the faces. Go back and forth between your reactions and feelings and the image. Let yourself be surprised by what you feel; let yourself be affected. Let yourself connect to the humanity of those in the photographs. Take your time; follow your memories and your associations. Continually try to see with fresh eyes. (I suggest you look at them, spend time with them first, and then read the identifying descriptions; let yourself respond viscerally first).

Migrant Mother: Dorothea Lang

This 1936 iconic photograph by Dorothea Lang is part of a series she took during the Great Depression, which chronicled the lives of those caught up in the economic/ecological disaster of the dust bowl and the ensuing poverty. Lang took several shots of this mother with her children, but asked the children to look away for this one, to rest on their mother. What emerged was this photograph which has become synonymous with maternal despair and hope all in one image.

Dance Film Still, *Can You Bring It*:
Bill T. Jones and D-Man in the Waters

This documentary asks the question, what is the role of Art in the time of crisis? "Thirty years ago, Bill T. Jones embedded motifs of risk and sacrifice, love, loss and resurrection in the choreography for D-Man in the Waters. Through an extraordinary series of interviews, archival material, and uniquely powerful cinematography of movement, this 90-minute, lyrical documentary uses the story of this dance to illustrate the triumph of the human spirit in art and within the community" (www.d-mandocumentary.com).

Guernica: Pablo Picasso

This extraordinary painting was Picasso's response to the horror of the bombing in 1937 of the small Basque town of Guernica by German Nazi war planes. The town was targeted because it was located on the only road between the front and the Republican stronghold of Bilboa. It is said that the town's men were all away fighting, so that only the women, children and animals were there to be massacred. This painting has come to represent the true horror of all war.

Eve Arnold: fisherman and family, Island girl.
Bahia Honda, Cuba, 1954.

This photo of a joyful moment with a Father, Mother and Child is iconic for its representation of an archetypal family relationship. The experience of a child held by her parents may bring up many emotions and memories.

You can do this process with any image, painting, sculpture, etc. This technique helps build the psychic stamina to experience the Spirit of the Times in dialogue with the Spirit of the Depths, to suffer, tolerate, and to find hope and courage.

A third exercise is, of course, to make your own images—painting, drawing, sculpting, collaging and so on. Even if you are not "an artist," what emerges will be authentic and have the potential to move you, to become symbolic.

When speaking of the healing power of creativity, the oft quoted words of the great Blues singer Alberta Hunter come to mind: "Blues means what milk does to a baby. Blues is what the spirit is to the minister. We sing the blues because our hearts have been hurt, our souls have been disturbed." Or, as another great Blues singer, Odetta, has said, "The blues is celebration, because when you take sorrow and turn it into music, you transform it."

When the tumultuous times feel like they are overwhelming you, sit with a painting, a song, a film, sculpt something, get out your crayons, dance, sing. Truly engaging with the images as they emerge will keep you from being stuck and overwhelmed. You could be moved from expressions of mere signs to symbols "pregnant with meaning." Deeply engaging with the arts will bring you the joyful knowledge that, "You are an image of the unending world, all the last mysteries of becoming and passing away live in you."

III. Spirit of the Times/Spirit of the Depths: Amplification and the Illumination of Meaning

The third path: Amplification, which is the craft of recognizing the dominant aspect of an image, its core, its essence. Amplification is a method of deepening, broadening, expanding an image and its pattern. It is a way of understanding what is being communicated in the fullest way by an image (as with my troll). It is the opposite process of free association. In free association, you let your mind wander from association to association, memory to memory. This leads to the Complex and is a useful tool and a key technique in Freudian analysis. But Jung said that there was a deeper and more useful tool, amplification, which discovers the collective core of any image, and as such, is a deeper communication from psyche to the dreamer. Amplification is a fundamental technique of all Jungian work. Jung says "I amplify an existing image until it becomes visible" (Jung, 2008, p. 26).

On this path, we will ruminate about which archetype/ archetypal story might be emerging in our times. What is the most apt story or cluster of stories for our moment? And, how does that story help us to connect the outer and the inner, to tolerate the tensions of the spirits of the times and of the depths? Importantly, we will remember that all outward stories must always be seen as intrapsychic stories as well. As the Alchemists said, *As above, so below*, and Jungians add, *as outer, so inner*. Any story that resonates will do so in part because it will reflect the deep inner situation as well.

The word archetype itself comes from Plato who envisioned perfect forms or types that were eternal. Archetypes are the very foundation of the Depths, the oldest, most universal aspect of psyche. Jung calls archetypes the images of the instincts and he saw that the interplay between these forms and personal experiences created both neurosis and healing.

In psychological terms, we project our inner images, our inner ideals, thoughts, feelings onto the world. Just as the ancients projected the stories of their gods and goddesses onto the patterns of the stars, we are seeing our stories manifesting in the world around us. Projection is both a normal human activity and a cause of much suffering, especially when what we project is our shadow. Shadow, in Jungian terms, are the parts of each of us that are cast off, disallowed, disowned, thrown into the basement— because the family/culture/religion says those parts of us are bad, and because we agree. Once aspects of our personalities are exiled from consciousness, the only way they get expressed is through projecting them onto others. The process is at the root of so much racism, misogyny, political hatred. One of the main projects of analysis is to help the analysand identify his/her shadow and withdraw the projections.

The Shadow lives in the area of psyche Jung called the personal unconscious. Jung also identified a psychic layer which he called the collective unconscious. This layer consists of the most ancient images. And these images, these realties, do not change their nature. Archetypes, these ancient hovering possibilities, have manifested in myriad ways throughout history; cultures and the spirits of other times have brought forth new iterations of archetypal energies. Chief, king, prime minister, all partake of the same archetype, for example. Jung says,

> Archetypes are like riverbeds which dry up when the water deserts them but which it can find again at any time. An archetype is like an old watercourse along which the water of life has flowed for centuries, digging a deep channel for itself. The longer it flowed in this channel, the more likely it is that sooner or later the water will return to its old bed.
> (Jung, 1964, para. 395)

Part of our task in times of chaos and upheaval is to seek out and recognize the archetypal story that is being expressed anew. In other words, which of the oldest riverbeds is now filling up, beginning again, filling with the waters of the collective, the Spirit of the Times? It is essential to discern which archetypal story/myth, god, dynamic is arising so that we can realign ourselves, inwardly and outwardly, to a new story in a conscious way and not get simply swept away by the rushing waters as they refill the old riverbed.

Archetypes do have tremendous energy, but only when they are constellated by circumstance. Archetypes hover, they are empty until they are needed. There is the classic story of someone walking down the street and hearing cries for help from a window of a burning building. The person finds herself rushing into the building to save those in danger, even though it is dangerous for herself. That is not only because she is a good person, it is because she got gripped, filled with the heroic archetypal energy that is called for at that moment. Similarly, what is it that keeps new parents loving their infants who wake them up every two hours and won't go back to sleep? Donald Winnicott calls this Maternal pre-occupation. I call it being gripped by the mother archetype: filled with the water of that deep Mother riverbed.

Archetypal energy also can grip a culture. Mobs are examples of an archetype taking over and people losing their individual agency. Political movements, for good or ill, shift the individual's autonomy as each person gets caught up in the newly re-filling archetypal riverbed. You can feel this shift; it is visceral. Think of a sporting event where you get swept up in the spirit of the moment, or a music event, or a political rally. Soldiers are trained to be more attuned to the archetype of soldier/hero than to have individual reactions to fighting and encountering enemies. These are just a few examples. The Spirit of the Times is often fed by this archetypal energy flooding the political, social moment—just as it was for Jung before the first World War.

It is essential to remember that our response to this emergent energy is fed by our own projections. We each add to the water that is reanimating the ancient riverbeds with our own projections, our own prejudices and ideas, our own loves and hates. "Jung has shown us that the psychic behavior of the individual is bound up with the psychic behavior of the nation and vice versa. What the nation does is the sum total of what every individual does" (Aumuller, 1950, p. 7).

What is the mythic energy emerging today? What archetypal story or dynamic is being summoned from the depths in our present time? Or said another way, what inner archetypal experiences are being projected onto the world right now?

Here are 3 possibilities:

1. *Sleeping Beauty*: The story could be being animated today. The whole tale gets set in motion when the 13th fairy is excluded from the table, because there were only 12 gold plates. The 13th fairy, in her fury, with the full force of the envy of the marginalized, excluded, disrespected and impoverished curses the princess, who is the embodiment of the future. And all that potential sleeps for 100 years. The young hero hears the story through the mists of time, about a princess in a far off land, and seeks to find her. His diligence and love overcome the power of the curse. But it takes a long time.

My particular sensibilities gravitate to seeing this story as amplifying the economic inequalities, the racist and sexist underpinnings and religious intolerances rampant in our world. But, even if you do not share my politics, I'm sure you can identify the many 13th fairies alive in the world today, who are furious and envious and destructive. This amplification points to the weight of the time it will take and the remarkable tenacity it will take for the future of the innocent, potential of a new kingdom to be awakened.

As an intrapsychic story, this is a tale of how our own envy curses our futures, pulling everything into unconsciousness so that all our potential is thwarted. Only some energy from outside the envy-cursed kingdom of our psyches can break the spell. We all know how cursed we feel when overcome by envy, how powerless we are to get out of it, how only love can release us. So, Sleeping Beauty is a possible amplification describing one aspect of the Spirit of our Times.

2. *The Emperor Has No Clothes* is another apt story for these days. Let us remember two things about this tale. One is that everybody is scared of being seen as stupid, that's why they all pretend to see the clothes. The second is how that tale ends. For an amplification to be useful, we cannot just look at one part of the story. We must look at the whole story, the whole dynamic, beginning to end, to find its psychic meaning.

"But the Emperor has nothing at all on!" said a little child. "Listen to the voice of the child!" exclaimed his father. What the child had said was whispered from one to another. "But he has nothing at all on!" at last cried out all the people. The Emperor was upset, for he knew that the people were right. However, he thought the procession must go on now! The lords of the bedchamber took greater pains than ever, to appear holding up a train, although, in reality, there was no train to hold, and the Emperor walked on in his underwear. (Anderson, 1837)

That's how the story ends. The truth only calcifies the emperor's position and everyone goes on knowing it's a lie.

Hannah Arendt writes about this conundrum extensively in her book *The Origins of Totalitarianism* (1951). The more the Nazi elite knew that the whole process was crazy, inhumane and evil, the more they had to cling to their positions of power and actually took a kind of pride in suppressing the truth. There was a valor in holding onto the lies of this story they had helped create. We have heard this kind of adherence to a story that has been proved to be false from folks closer to home. Again, whatever your politics, in this amplification we can witness a kind of identification with a lie, and a hope that by continuing the lies one can gain and maintain power by keeping close to the power of the lie and the liar. We see this happening all over the world.

Intrapsychically, we all have inner Emperors—ruling ideals, complexes. And how stubbornly a complex can grip us, how irrationally we can hold onto our narcissistic insecurities and needs, how desperately we can be scared of being seen and seeing ourselves as stupid, as imposters, unworthy, etc. The complex torments us to hide our inadequacies at all costs, bullying and manipulating those around us. How corrupting such an inner ruler is to our whole psychic economy!

While these are good amplifications, they are also ever-present stories; they speak to the continual condition of human civilization: envy is ubiquitous, corrupting power is endemic. Is there a new archetype arising, one that has been sleeping for a while? Is there an old dried up archetypal riverbed filling up again with the water of the zeitgeist?

3. Archetype of Apocalypse: What might be emergent is the archetype of the Apocalypse. The Archetypal pattern of apocalypse is: revelation, judgement, punishment and/or destruction and a birth of the New. The energy of this archetype is righteous, judgmental, full of guilt and shame, merciless, chaotic, violent, overwhelming, and global. All for a cleansing of the world and the possibility of a new way.

There are Apocalyptic stories in most religious traditions, stories of the gods wiping out humanity for being disobedient. But we are not going to be looking at these stories from a religious point of view. Nor are we going to focus on a moral point of view that is implicit in the religious stories. Rather, we will examine Apocalypse as a universal archetype.

The story of St. John's Revelation found in the Christian New Testament is but one example of this archetypal story. John hears a voice telling him to write down everything he sees, and he has a huge vision filled with terrifying and inscrutable images. Terrible things are predicted—every kind of destruction, four horsemen spreading war, plague, famine and death. There are myriad monsters and angels of destruction. Hail and fire mixed with blood rains down on the earth which is trembling with earthquakes and floods and fires. Wave after wave of catastrophe, pestilence, plagues and sufferings—death all around. The New Babylon, i.e. the current world, is destroyed through cycle after cycle of battles between monsters and angels fueled by the righteousness of God until finally, the New Jerusalem is built, and those who have been carefully hidden, the saints, can emerge and God and the Lamb can live with the people in the Heavenly city.

The arc of this story describes a relentless press for the destruction of the old, corrupt, disobedient, sinful, world and the building of the totally new world into which it is safe for the hidden goodness to live.

The Jungian analyst Edward Edinger wrote a thought-provoking book, *Archetype of the Apocalypse, Divine Vengeance, Terrorism, and the End of the World.* In 1999 he foresaw many of the realities we are experiencing now. Let me quote from his introduction:

> What we are about to discuss is a primordial psychic pattern of the collective unconscious that is at the same time a dynamic agency with intentionality. When it constellates, it generates itself and manifests itself in the individual psyche and the collective psyche of the group it happens to touch. [So, both—individual and collective—this is important] Put differently, archetypes live themselves out in whatever psychic stuff they can appropriate; they are like devouring moths—finding little egos they can consume, and then living out of those egos. (Edinger, 1999, p. 5)

He concludes this section: "This is what the content of the Apocalypse archetype presents: the shattering of the world as it has been, followed by its reconstitution."

Reading Edinger's book clarifies some of where we are now. We are particularly frightened right now, in these times, because we know history, we know of whole civilizations that have crumbled, disappeared, been destroyed. Equally frightening is our innate knowledge that we can be internally destroyed, disoriented, or psychically dismembered—by a new idea, a revelation of some kind, by love or hate, by trauma, by grief, by fear.

We also know that when a revelation breaks in, we don't survive in an old way. "The experience of the Self is always a defeat for the Ego" (Jung, 1963, para.778). That famous quote from

Jung highlights the fragility of ego consciousness; it is always at the mercy of the Self, of the spirit of the depths, of a relativization. Those relativizations often feel like defeats, like loss on a grand scale, or like the destruction of our personal, emotional foundations. Think of times when your life has been upended by a new truth breaking in: the discovery that you must leave a relationship, or the realization that you are in the wrong work, that your sexual orientation is not what you and your family had thought. Perhaps you have a religious conversion, or you suddenly become ill and all your plans for the future crumble. Perhaps you have been shaken to your core as the zeitgeist demands that you confront our own racism and privilege, even your understanding of our country's actual history. Likewise, the onset of a deep depression or a sudden anxiety disorder can shatter one's sense of security, essential wellbeing and Self.

All these examples carry a certain experience of judgement, of being in the wrong somehow with yourself, with the culture, even with God. And any time a revelation exposes us to judgement, we are in the Apocalyptic archetypal field.

Edinger points to analysis and says: "Every depth analysis is a miniature 'apocalypse': as if there were a 'destruction of one's world' from which conscious 'civilization'" (Edinger, 1998, p. 178) has to start all over again. Is the myth of the Apocalypse the myth we are living in now?

According to Edward Edinger, apocalypse means "uncovering what has been hidden." When pressed by this archetype, we are forced to wonder what has been hidden in our culture, in ourselves, that deserves revealing, judging, punishing? (In this I hear Greta Thunberg as our new St. John the Divine.) This kind of self-scrutiny is called for when encountering this particular archetypal field. Edinger suggests that the only way to avoid the catastrophe is for enough people to deeply understand what is going on (1998, p. 172).

All archetypal stories are expression of the human condition. All are living in us and we project them onto the world. We fill up the ancient riverbeds with the water of our own psyches. From that perspective, these archetypes arise into the zeitgeist when enough people are projecting them onto the world—not recognizing them as intrapsychic realities.

If we can discover how these stories are living in each of us, we will be less inclined to project them onto others. We will be less likely to project our shadows, envy, righteousness, complexes and evil onto the world. This is the ethical obligation that Jung spoke of that I quoted earlier: "The images of the unconscious place a great responsibility upon a man. Failure to understand them, or a shirking of ethical responsibility, deprives him of his wholeness and imposes a painful fragmentariness on his life."

Jung insists that we have an ethical responsibility as humans. He is not speaking politically, although this idea is the foundation of a political ethos, and he is not speaking legally, although this idea is foundational to a just world. Rather Jung is emphasizing that our first task is to take ourselves seriously, to listen to our whole selves—our inner images, complexes and specific psychologies. Two things then occur: we can learn to recognize our Shadows and our projections so that we don't impose them on others, and we can strive toward a kind of wholeness we can then bring forth into the world. He calls this work individuation; he is clear in all his writings that individuation does not stop when the person feels good and centered in him or herself. He is clear that our ethical obligation is to do this inner work so that we can be fully engaged in the world—both for our own sakes and the world's. Jung's depth journeys, his apocalyptic time after his break with Freud and discovery of Active Imagination, serve as models for the courage, perseverance and true unknowing required to individuate.

The story of the Apocalypse promises us that a new Jerusalem is possible, if we can suffer the revelations, guilt and destruction and come to more consciousness about ourselves and the world. This archetypal story predicts that then we can find a new peace, between Self and Ego, between ourselves and Others.

To conclude: Our hope lies in two directions. One is engagement with the Spirit of the Times, the world as it is and history as it is unfolding, using ourselves, our consciousness and our courage to help in ways that make sense to each of us. Doing something in the face of so much despair, even singing the blues, moves libido and psychic energy. Individuation, as Jung insists, requires us to engage with the world, to bring our full understandings to the world, to participate.

The other direction is inward. In this direction, we also can look to Jung as our guide. Jung's encounter with his unconscious, his descent into his own depths, his profound experiences of the power of the images in his own psyche and that of others, led to an extraordinary method of engaging the images of the psyche. When we notice the images, take them seriously, personify them, speak with them, listen to them, amplify them, they can become symbols—symbols of transformation.

If we can hold both—outer and inner, the world as it is and our personal inner worlds, then we can have a meaningful, restorative, and revelatory conversation between the Spirit of the Depths and the Spirit of the Times. And then, we can find comfort and encouragement from Jung's message from the spirit of the depths: "You are an image of the unending world, all the last mysteries of becoming and passing away live in you."

References

Aumüller, A. *Jungian Psychology in Wartime Germany*, printed by the Analytical Psychology Club of New York, of her lecture given on February 17, 1950.

Anderson, H.C., (1837). *Fairy Tales Told for Children*, Copenhagen: C.A. Reitzel Publisher.

Arendt, H., (1951). *The Origins of Totalitarianism*, New York: Schocken Books.

Edinger, E., (1999b). *The Archetype of the Apocalypse, Divine Vengeance, Terror and the End of the World*, Chicago & LaSalle: Open Court Publishing Company.

Hillman, J., (1975). *Revisioning Psychology*, New York: Harper Collins.

Jung, C.G., (1961). *Memories, Dreams, Reflections.* New York: Pantheon Books.

_____. (1967). *CW, Vol. 13, Alchemical Studies.* Princeton, NJ: Princeton University Press.

_____. (1969), *CW, Vol. 11, Psychology and Religion: West and East.* Princeton, NJ: Princeton University Press. (Original work published 1958)

_____. (1969). Synchronicity: An acausal connecting principle (R. F. C. Hull, Trans.). In H. Read et al. (Eds.) *CW, Vol. 8. Structure and dynamics of the psyche* (2nd ed., pp. 417-519). Princeton, NJ: Princeton University Press. (Original work published 1952)

_____. (1970). *CW, Vol. 14, Mysterium Coniunctionis.* Princeton, NJ: Princeton University Press.

_____. (1970). *CW, Vol. 10, Bollinger Series XX.* Princeton, NJ: Princeton University Press. (Original work published 1963)

_____. (1971). *CW, Vol. 6, Psychological types.* Princeton, NJ: Princeton University Press.

_____. (1973). *Collected Letters: Vol. 1. Letter to Kurt Plachte, January 10, 1929.* A. Gerhard & A. Jaffe, (Trans.). R.F.C. Hull, Bollingen Series, SCV. Princeton, NJ: Princeton University Press.

_____. (2008). *Children's Dreams, Philemon Series,* Princeton, NJ: Princeton University Press.

_____. (2009). *The Red Book: Liber Novus.* S. Shamdasani (Ed.); J. Kybuz, J. Peck, S. Shamdasani. (Trans.). New York & London: W.W. Norton.

Salman, S. (2008). *True Imagination.* Thompson, CT & New York: Spring Publications.

Shamdasani, S. (2009). *Introduction to the Red Book,* Philemon Foundation, New York: W.W. Norton & Co.

Uncertainty and Healing in the Archetypal End-times

Morgan Stebbins

"Repent! The End is Nigh!"

    This is the refrain from many prophets over many centuries, from across the spectrum of religious traditions in response to cataclysms of different kinds. Another word for this sort of cosmic catastrophe is apocalypse. Below is a definition that we can use to orient us as we explore our current time period and possible responses to it:

The word apocalypse can be defined as:

1. The end of the world as we know it; breakdown
2. Revelation of the divine; new understanding
3. The dawn of a new age; living and seeing differently

We can see from the above that in all cases the call by the prophet is to change our attitude toward the divinity; that is, to repent of the old ways, as well as to live differently with each other in the context of day-to-day life. What does it mean to repent and change this attitude today in a secular world facing a plethora of difficulties?

    For many people, recent events have made it clear that the world is a scary place. The combined threats of war, pandemic, loss of meaning, dictatorship, violence, global warming, and social disruption all cause great anxiety with their threat of tremendous and unwanted change. These challenges will demand great courage and wisdom if our civilization is to develop in a positive way. However, looked at psychologically, these events show us that an *archetypal end-time is at hand.* This means that the personal and internal perceptual system is ripe for far-reaching change.

What does it mean to look at something psychologically? First, it's important to differentiate between the scary situation itself and the *anxiety and resulting fantasies* caused by thinking about it. The former needs action—the wiser and more mature the better. However, the latter, if understood symbolically, can become an impetus to, and even guide for, psychological growth and change. Even if action is then needed, understanding the fears and underlying assumptions about the situation can make that action all the more salient. Our usual human perception of the world around us—such as when we refer to war and pestilence to which we have not been subjected—is to rationalize and concretize. That is, it happens out there, and typically to someone else. This attitude leaves the question and opportunity of soul-work out of the equation.

The thesis here is that healing from the highly affective states of end-time anxiety comes from seeing those very events that stimulate our end-of-the-world fantasies as symbolic indicators of our own minds—and that furthermore they chart a course toward wholeness. In fact, it is manifestly the lack of wholeness in a person or society that produces these excess fantasies, and their final purpose is to help us reintegrate lost aspects of ourselves.

This leads back to our original quotation. We will explore some other ancient prophecies of doom, but psychologically they all come down to an intrapsychic demand to repent of our lack of symbolic awareness that is in itself causing fantasies of some kind of apocalyptic world end. We can call the end-times archetypal because they are seen and expressed in exactly the same form throughout history. This shows us clearly that they are not about our times per se and not about the ostensive world, but rather they are factors arising from our shared brain structures and mental faculties in response to certain triggers. In fact, *the end* in this case refers to the necessity of terminating our current conscious standpoint in favor of a more nuanced, psychological, and soul-building orientation. This may seem like an extreme or world-denying standpoint. However, it is neither. Rather it is the only way to understand the excess and often paralyzing stimulation caused by actual world events —in order to both know ourselves and therefore also to be more effective actors in the world.

Our chapter will work with the personal anxiety response to the world situation. That is, we will explore our personal resources and show how to work with images, which leads to growth from the experience and to better understand and act in the world around us.

Experience of the world as apocalyptic

We are bombarded every day with news, changing times, and exposure to troubling events and images. Mostly, we wring our hands and pull out our hair. Sometimes we are called to some kind of action, but often our worry is an indicator of internal conflict— that is, our inner tension reaches a point of being resonant with outer events, and that resonance triggers apocalyptic fantasy, language and fear. That is, frequently our reactions are about our internal state and the need for personal change.

Here's the paradox: change is scary and disagreeable if it's unpredictable, if the outcome is different from what we (as the ego) had hoped, or if it doesn't feel good. We shy away from chaos, the frustrations of our conscious wishes, and negative feeling states. The conundrum is that these are all the same indicators as an encounter with what Jung has called the Self.

The word Self, in this context, means more than our knowledge of our conscious minds or our personal history. Jungians understand that a person is much more than their conscious parts— in fact the decisive parts are not conscious—and so the Self means the whole thing, the known and unknown parts of each of us. Cognitive science agrees wholeheartedly—most of our decisions are made before we are aware of them and mostly, we are run by our unconscious cognitive biases. So, a reference to the Self means a connection with a wholeness that is beyond awareness but which also impacts us in measurable ways. Wholeness in this context can be seen as a process, one that is aware of our fragmented parts and committed to reconnecting with them little by little. In this regard wholeness also means a connection with the idea of the divine, as that which is bigger than we are, and the arising of new meaning as we relate to the previously shunned parts. This connection is what *constitutes healing in the analytic realm.*

What is more, any encounter with the Self takes on transpersonal proportions. That is, since the total Self is more comprehensive than the ego, it almost always feels overwhelming. This state is what Jung calls an encounter with the *numinous*, and it is embedded in language of all encounters with the divine across time and tradition. It is hard to overstate what a difficult situation this is for the personal ego. Unless there is a means of mediating this experience, it becomes necessarily projected into the world, and ends up, for example, being one of the many inauthentic political view struggles we see across the world. The ancient religions have been the mediators of this experience for millennia but for many people they are not speaking in relevant symbols any longer. It is now everyone's personal responsibility and personal path to understand these experiences, and to build up a personal symbolic relationship with, as Jung puts it, "all things which cross my willful path...and change the course of my life for better or worse" (Jung, 1973, p. 525).

Furthermore, change always involves letting go of what's here now. In alchemy this is described as the dying of the old king, or ruling principle of the psyche. In these stories the king, representing the executive function, becomes decrepit. One can tell because the land (and so, the personality) becomes dry, barren, and unfruitful. Decisions are ungainly, effort does not further the cause. So, the king becomes ill and eventually dies. The king, our current ego stance, never enjoys this part. Eventually a new king or queen emerges, the land regains its fertility and the kingdom thrives. In the best scenarios there is mourning for the old ruling principle, for it served us well in its time, and there is celebration of the new orientation and rejuvenation of the whole.

When the old way of being has become stale and sickly, the psyche does not work well. This experiential state of confusion and chaos then becomes projected onto the world, which in turn is perceived as unsettled and dangerous, and this causes excess anxiety and stress. Jung, in his great psychological history of the western world, *Aion,* describes this state as "philosophical disorientation" (1959, p X) which amounts to existential dread, excess worry about the state of the world and one's place in it, as well as deep personal discombobulation. The solution for that is to "illuminate the secret chambers of the soul," which means to understand how we project our inner world onto the world at large, how to understand that process, and finally how to make ourselves whole by retracting and claiming those lost parts. For this we resort to a psychological amplification of the symbols that are projected into the world.

A Psychological Call to Insight

How do we distinguish the great problems of our age or the things in life that need action and physical change from a psychological call to insight? Sometimes the difference can be subtle. To make the distinction as to which are psychological challenges, several hurdles must be passed. First, the person must not be in a panic or trauma state. Whenever we are in a panic state there is no capacity for reflection. Instead, calming measures are called for including a move toward a safe environment and the passing of time. Second, the threat must not be unfolding in the present moment and require bodily action. This is differentiated from fears that are located in the present in a general sense, such as war in another country or global warming, but which do not demand immediate action as would be the case if there were a bear in the house.

So, a key differentiation is whether an action is needed in response to a fear or anxiety or not. Evolutionary psychology tells us that fear is an adaptive response to danger, and that humans are wired for extra fear and anxiety since a false positive (every shaking bush is a tiger) is not a mortal error whereas a false negative (I'll ignore that bush…and it's a tiger!) is a mortal error. We can see which group would pass on their genes!

In summary, if we think that there is some urgency that needs action, then by all means we should act. If we are not in a situation where action is relevant or when we've done the actions that we can do, and yet we find our reactions, fears, and fantasies are still rampant, then we can be sure they are due to psychological stressors. It should be clear at this point that panicky thinking about terrible worldly situations is deeply psychological.

The Nature of Psychological Change

This understanding of an apocalyptic fantasy as reflective of an inner state is what gives us our opportunity for change. In depth psychology it's often said that that change is good, perhaps one could say that it's even the goal of professional work. This can be confusing since, according to the psychological language used, many different things may be meant by the word change. Many times, what is meant is some kind of conformity to a norm or the proper execution of ego intentions. However, Jung infers that the deep change called transformation comes about through a confrontation with the unknown parts of ourselves. The most important aspects of that are the core principles of the Self.

This confrontation initiating this deep kind of change may not feel good, in fact it may seem downright disastrous. There are many reasons for our lack of ability to change but in a nutshell we can say that *any substantial change of attitude is in itself a turning point of life* and means abandoning some thoughts and feelings that have been important, perhaps for a long time. This can cause a fear of investigating the images of our fantasy. As Jung says,

But the unconscious is also feared by those whose conscious attitude is at odds with their true nature. Naturally their dreams will then assume an unpleasant and threatening form, for if nature is violated she takes her revenge. In itself the unconscious is neutral, and its normal function is to compensate the conscious position. (Jung, 1963 para. 184)

This difficulty is behind one of our most persistent habits: seeing our imaginal fears as identical to world events. Seeing our own psychic process as a form of virtuality can initially be a difficult task. Furthermore, understanding that we produce our perceptions as much as receive them, again corresponding to modern neuroscience, is a great undertaking. One approach to that undertaking is a process of psychological amplification.

Psychological Amplification of Perceived Threats

Jungians use the word amplification as a way to specify a particular hermeneutic lens. There are many of these lenses, or ways to see things. We can look at events from an economic viewpoint, political viewpoint, moral viewpoint, and so on. For Jung, the way toward healing and illumination of the lost chambers of the soul begins with a psychological amplification. To begin with, amplifications are in order of our perceived threats. The depredations of war, pestilence, evil rulers, and planetary death are ancient and ubiquitous – they are even biblical! In fact, every turning of a calendar age has engendered its own end-time narrative and many disasters have been seen as indications of an imminent cosmic end. And importantly, many of these effects are apparently first predicted in scripture. It should be noted that none of these end-times has occurred in a literal sense and yet the impact on individuals was still profound.

The Ubiquity of Apocalyptic Times

For instance, in many religious traditions the predicted end time includes a judgement, as in Christianity, or a resetting of the cycle of the cosmos, as in Buddhism and Hinduism. In most of these cases the predicted end demands a change of lifestyle in the here and now. These situations reveal the immanence of the divine or collective in the daily life of the ego. That is, whether or not some outer end arrives, the end of an attitude in fact occurs and the birth of a new attitude arises.

Let us look at a few examples among many others and see what they infer to the extent that they are manifestations of an inner state rather than as literal events. One of the Hindu texts, the *Vishnu Purana* tells us that the universe consists of great cycles of time. Just one cycle, or *Chatur Yuga* lasts for 4.32 million years, and there are hundreds of thousands of cycles. The last phase of one of these yugas is called the Kali Yuga and it is the one in which we currently reside. As we might expect, this period has been foretold to be characterized by impiety, violence, and decay. In fact, the Vishnu Purana defines the evils of this period as follows:

> Social status depends not upon your accomplish-
> ments, but in the ownership of property; wealth is
> now the source of virtue; passion and luxury are the
> sole bonds between spouses; falsity and lying are
> the conditions of success in life; sexuality is the sole
> source of human enjoyment; religion, a superficial
> and empty ritual, is confused with spirituality.
> (Dawson, 1923, p. 76)

Not only that, but perhaps even more prophetic for today's headlines, the scripture continues to say that rulers "in the fourth age will be godless, wanting in tranquility, quick to anger, and dishonest. They will inflict death on women, and children, and will rise and fall to power quickly. Undisciplined barbarians will receive the support of rulers" (Dawson, 1923, p. 76).

Sadly, no solution is offered apart from a quite regressive one, temporally speaking. We can work to achieve the ultimate union of Atman with Brahman, or soul with Godhead, which may take one hundreds or thousands of additional lifetimes. Nevertheless, the call is to change one's life so that this process will not take any longer than necessary.

Farther west, we encounter an Assyrian clay tablet dating to around 2800 B.C.E. that bears the inscription: "Our Earth is degenerate in these later days; there are signs that the world is speedily coming to an end; bribery and corruption are common; children no longer obey their parents; every man wants to write a book and the end of the world is evidently approaching" (Strauss, 2009).

Again, no solution is offered but we can see that problems endemic to apocalyptic thinking are spread widely across time and space. From about the same locale but a few thousand years later we have the prophets of the Hebrew Bible. Many speak of the coming of the Lord due to problematic behavior by humans, and Joel is no exception:

Book of Joel:

15 Alas for the day!

For the day of the Lord is near,

And it will come as destruction from the Almighty

This predicts an apocalypse and yet continues with the emergence of a new type of person:

28 It will come about after this

That I will pour out My Spirit on all mankind;

And your sons and daughters will prophesy,

Your old men will dream dreams,

Your young men will see visions.

29 Even on the male and female servants

I will pour out My Spirit in those days.

We can see from this that again, destruction of the old, at the hands of the divine, and a new way of being are both ushered in by the end-times.

Finally, we can refer to the Christian New Testament and The Book of Revelation. This is also, tellingly, referred to as the Apocalypse of John. The seven signs of the apocalypse as elaborated in this work include the arrival of the Antichrist (or antagonist), war, famine, plague, judgment, chaos, and silence or rebirth. In fact, the four horsemen of the apocalypse and seven seals are frequently and seamlessly applied by Biblical believers to current events, and it is easy to see why. Today we indeed have problematic rulers, war, famine, plague, and chaos.

This mapping of this kind of apocalyptic writing onto current events made many people quite nervous in the ancient world, just as now. In response, the people changed their lives accordingly. In the early Christian example, believers proceeded to sell their property and live communally, as well as sharing the priesthood among all (men and women), while waiting in expectation for the return of Christ which was supposed to happen any day now.

Their response is a part answer for us, if we can understand it symbolically. In psychological terms these prescriptions would mean changing our attachment to physical goods, living in a way that is more connected to others, sharing the spiritual and worldly authority, and being open to the influx of cast off personal or social elements. All of this shows that living in the end-times is a change of orientation in attitude and life.

In fact, in all of these religious traditions, the prediction is that the human situation will be brought to a kind of fulfillment, for better or worse. This illustrates that inner change can be a threat to the current conscious standpoint and that the needed change will be apocalyptic for that standpoint—though it will be an opportunity for growth of the whole personality. After all, we remember that all substantial psychological change is *directed by the unconscious* and it's also usually experienced as a crisis by the ego.

Amplification of Apocalyptic Traditions

In investigating both these traditions and personal fantasy narrative there are two relevant lines of amplification. On one hand, the content of the apocalyptic event is crucial to understanding an unconscious fear. That is, the specific events of an imagined disaster are symbolically important to describe a person's inner landscape. On the other hand, the ideas or fantasies about what kind of preparation is needed to meet those end-times are also relevant as psychological cues about what kind of change is being suggested.

This chapter presents the idea that the *fantasy of disastrous negative change* is a psychological indication of opportunity. These fantasies can be mined for symbolic information and then grounded in life. They show a way out of a neurotic state and into radical growth if their content can be understood and lived out. Even more so, the extreme types of this thinking, which we could call *fantasies of apocalypse,* have a particularly salutary effect if they can be understood and integrated.

A Proposal for Healing

To further our understanding of our title, *healing in the archetypal end-times*, let's look at the potential problems listed above as a group. Later we can unpack them individually. As we have said, if these events can be thought of as archetypal lenses due to their ubiquity in sacred texts and across time as responses to outer events, then we can conclude that they are embedded in the human condition; they are structures of the psyche that get activated in certain situations. This is important because if the scourges of humanity have always been with us then we can see two things.

One is that our time is not special, at least not on the literal level. The idea of the specialness of our time is specifically part of apocalyptic fantasy. However, if we understand that these fantasies are part of the human condition in general, arising when there is an opportunity, then we can take a more reflective view of the situation. The idea of literal temporal uniqueness makes the projective externalization of events even more difficult to overcome. Second, if these problems are spoken of in religious texts, and typically in situations of existential change from one relationship with the self, cosmos or divinity to another, then we may conclude that there is actually something spiritual about how our relationship with the cosmos unfolds.

What is more, the worldly solutions to modern problems (whatever the age of the world, modern refers to the status of what is current for the reader), are unknown to the extent that we have to live into them in the future. No external answers are given that are relevant for all time, due to the specificity of individuals and events. However, since the collective responses or apocalyptic images remain the same as ever, we may conclude that there are stable approaches to the inner scene—and if we learn from those, we become wiser, calmer, and better oriented. Jung reminds us that "a modern problem is one which has just arisen and whose answer still lies in the future" (Jung, 1959 par. 148). In that sense our time is actually special in a different way, in the same way that all moments in time are special. That is, we do not know the future and the task is to understand our own unconscious reactions so that we can be best prepared for what unfolds.

So, we are dealing with the *fantasy* of apocalypse, indicating that someone is haunted by the image of various disastrous events whether they refer to an end-time or not. However, we are categorically not saying that by calling the experience a fantasy it can be sloughed off or made light of. In fact,

> A collapse of the conscious attitude is no small matter. It always feels like the end of the world, as though everything had tumbled back into original chaos. One feels delivered up, disoriented, like a rudderless ship that is abandoned to the moods of the elements. So at least it seems. In reality, however, one has fallen back upon the collective unconscious,

which now takes over the leadership. (Jung, 1959 para. 254)

This understanding allows us to take fears and fantasies as a spiritual challenge, as a psychological opportunity, *as a call to individuation*. Individuation is Jung's term for psychological maturity that leads to wholeness or at-one-ment. That is, it is becoming ourselves as more independent than before from the mass thinking of our social fabric. As is true for any call, the possibility of results demands that we be listening for and heed the call and that takes courage. Indeed:

> Instead of being at the mercy of wild beasts, earthquakes, landslides, and inundations, modern man is battered by the elemental forces of his own psyche. This is the World Power that vastly exceeds all other powers on earth. The Age of Enlightenment, which stripped nature and human institutions of gods, overlooked the God of Terror who dwells in the human soul. (Jung, 1964, para 471)

Responses to Psychological Distress

Once we understand the threat as something more than literal, we can take an attitude appropriate for soul building. When we are confronted with psychological distress of great magnitude, there are a few typical responses. Jung outlines four kinds of responses to psychic intrusion:

The first is an unwelcome disintegration in the face of chaos. This includes falling apart, shutting down, and severe splitting. Next, we might pursue what he calls a *regressive restoration of the persona*. This is a kind of retreat back to a social role that was mastered, thus avoiding the threatening content by reverting to an earlier stage of adaptation. Next, we can embrace or identify with the archetypal content, usually through concretizing. This looks like digging bunkers for preparation or getting ready for the jump to Haley's comet.

Finally, and of course most creative, is symbolic understanding of the image or problem, meaning that one sees it as an internal event or at least one with internal significance and so can take the view that it is actually a part of themselves that could be understood. Of course, this is the preferred model that we will expound upon. We can see that three of these approaches have to do with responses that hold on to the present situation in some way and that do not lead to understanding of the symbol or change of attitude.

In fact, if we return to the fantasy that our current time period is special, we see that this stance only exacerbates the neurotic status quo and the rejection of the spirit of the depths. Jung reminds us that much of our suffering arises from a conflict between worldly and inner or spiritual needs, what he called the Spirit of the Times and the Spirit of the Depths (cf M. Klenck in this volume for a deeper discussion). If instead we can spare a moment to consider that our worldly problems are ancient and likely eternal, then we can potentially see them as most probably archetypal lenses through which we see the world. Also, as said above, this in no way invalidates them as physical occurrences with real life consequences as well.

Moreover, the fantasy of the specialness of our time period exacerbates the middle two responses from the above list, the regressive and identifying standpoints. From the regressive we see a blame of the outer situation and a heightening of neurotic anxiety. This leads to inaction and shutting down, along with utopian thinking and hand wringing. It also engages in the splitting of good and bad, and the projection of the problem to over there.

The other way of identifying with the collective threat leads to a personal acceptance of the fantasy as literalized concretization. This often leads to its systematization into good and evil, the concept of holding the singular great truth and the impetus for dramatic and purifying action, such as seen by MAGA agitators, religious terrorists, and historically in ethnic cleansing. Again, we see the splitting and projection, as well as radical solutions engendered by that projection in a futile attempt to cleanse the offending impurities that, in fact, stem from one's own psyche. It should be clear that neither direction does anything to enhance symbolic understanding and instead they get stuck in the literal, rejecting the call of the spiritual and the possibility of self-transformation.

The last approach mentioned above is to understand both the image of disaster and the fantasy of a response to that disaster as compensatory nudges from the unconscious. This transition of attitude is what practical spiritual practice is about, which is why Jung uses the term *transcendent function* to describe it: "The tendencies of the conscious and the unconscious are the two factors that together make up the transcendent function. It is called 'transcendent' because it makes the transition from one attitude to another organically possible" (Jung, 1960, para. 145).

The Nature of the Apocalyptic fantasy

Now we can discuss the nature of the apocalyptic fantasy—what it entails and what it leads to. In treating it symbolically, we first differentiate the apocalyptic fantasy itself and also the fantasy of how life would change because of it. Great examples of the latter abound among the religions, and we know from reading the early Christian literature that they lived lives wholly transformed in terms of sharing goods, emotionally supporting each other and with an egalitarian power structure due to the understanding of the immanence of the coming or return of Christ.

The apocalypse generally conveys the radical approach of the numinous which Jung describes in a letter to M Leonard cited above as "That which changes me, for better or ill." It is a *thinning the veil between the divine and human*, the temporal and eternal, the whole and the part, meaning and meaninglessness. Psychologically we can say that the ego gets very close to the Self in these moments, and that is always a matter of some stress for the ego. However, this very proximity is what makes these moments ones of opportunity. After all we want a solution, and we know the solution is to connect with the whole, the eternal, the divine and the meaningful. The concepts of wholeness and divinity are related to the religious experience of God, and this brings up some difficulties from Jung's point of view:

> To this day "God" is the name by which I designate all things which cross my willful path violently and recklessly, all things which upset my subjective views, plans and intentions, and change the course of my life for better or for worse.

> Also: [God] "is an apt name given to all overpowering emotions in my own psychic system, [which] subdue my conscious will and usurp control over myself" (Jung, 1973, p.525).

Experiences with the numinous, something eternal or transpersonal, do not refer to religion or organized practice but to an internal process for bringing the two sides together.

The Ego and the Self

We can see that the problem can be described as one of wholeness, or lack thereof. That is, the parts of ourselves we split off are then projected onto the world. This projection makes us partial beings and ascribes causation of our problems to the world. Our internal conflicts instead become an inflammable view of the world at large. "Certainly, one of the commonest causes of suffering is a moral conflict, which ultimately stems from the apparent impossibility of affirming the whole of one's nature" (Jung, 1960, para. 204).

More simply Jung reminds us, "Projections change the world into the replica of one's own unknown face" (Jung, 1959 para. 17). The creative and curative move is to recognize them as such, understand them, and live accordingly.

The Nature of Projection

Whatever we don't know about the world, and much more insidiously, whatever we don't understand about ourselves, is projected as what we do or what we fear: "Our ordinary psychological life is still swarming with projections, you find them spread out in newspapers, books, rumors and in ordinary social gossip. All gaps in actual knowledge are filled with projections" (Jung,1958, para. 140).

In fact, there is nothing pathological about projections. Projections are the way we first perceive elements of the unconscious. This can happen in a sudden dislike of someone whose difficult attitude we unknowingly share, and so on. However, Jung's understanding of projection goes far beyond the standard psychological norms. On one hand it is a perception of an inner state as an outer event or drama. At that level it is a kind of mistake that can be corrected, and at this most psychological schools agree. For Jung, projections give us information about who we are, and are, in fact, lost parts of ourselves that are critical to value. That way, once we can see the apocalyptic narrative fear as projected, we can start the project of understanding them symbolically, and finally we can get around to translating this strange language of the psyche into something we can assimilate.

Beginning the journey

But the problem is that: "Nothing endangers this connection more in a man than a successful life; it makes him forget his dependence on the unconscious" (Jung, CW 5, para. 457).

So, what are we to do, to illuminate the lost chambers of the soul? Since the parts of ourselves that we disavow end up as projections in the world, the task is to withdraw our projections and understand our fantasies. The second part of that task is to see those fantasies and projections as real but psychological, and finally our job is then to act in the world through our transformed attitude. After all:

The psychological rule says that when an inner situation is not made conscious, it happens outside as fate. That is to say, when the individual remains undivided and does not become conscious of his inner opposite, the world must perforce act out the conflict and be torn into opposing halves. (Jung, 1959, para. 126)

However, neurosis itself is always already a partial solution. More so, it is a future personality trying to emerge and running into the old attitude. In order for us to help this process along a few things are needed. There must be sufficient motivation to let the old ways die (the old king as noted above) and sufficient courage or desperation to see what the new orientation may bring. What this new orientation will be cannot be fully predicted and part of the sacrifice made is that the result will be a surprise to the ego.

Another way to put this is that a new symbol has to be at least potentially present in order to be healing – and it is! The paradox is that the apocalyptic fantasy is itself the new symbol, if only it can be understood as such. The simplest way to say this is that the fear, the symptom, the uncertainty itself must be seen to have some information. This information is actually the guiding path itself if it can be seen symbolically.

How do we do this? We do this, again to refer to Jung's *Aion*, by understanding the images of our time, especially the *relationship between the personal and collective images*, that is, by amplifying in a psychological way. As noted above, there are many kinds of amplifications, from economic to political to theological, but the psychological one is that which cures this particular problem. "Neurosis is intimately bound up with the problem of our time and really represents an unsuccessful attempt on the part of the individual to solve the general problem in his own person" (Jung, 1953, para. 18).

This practice is the solution because "disturbances of conscious apprehension [are] caused by the admixture of archetypal images. The exaggerated action due to the interference of instinct are caused by intuitive modes of apprehension actuated by archetypes and all to likely lead to over-intense and often distorted impressions" (Jung, 1960, para. 279). That is, our inner conflicts become triggered by outer events. Since this triggering is an ancient part of the human psyche, we can call it an archetypal response. Thus, the solution is to translate the archetypal additions into conscious language and render them powerless by exposing them to consciousness.

To put it more simply: when collective events activate a resonant inner complex, neurotic suffering ensues. Again, as Jung says, "Individuation is an at-one-ment with oneself and at the same time with humanity, since oneself is part of humanity" (Jung, 1954 para. 227).

The Role of Imagination

Neurotic suffering involves alienation, which can happen in many ways. All of them depend on human beings having an imagination which is not constrained by physical adaptation. This gets back to the virtuality of the psyche. The great human achievement is the imagination which has the almost magical power of constructing scenarios which do not exist. According to most current models of the workings of the prefrontal cortex, the purpose of this modeling is to test their viability. Of course we can see a downside, which is that imaginative scenarios involving danger and escape can be triggered by modern stimuli. Some of the most prominent triggers are any kind of social interaction in which reality and meaning-models are exchanged. These include social gatherings and social media, all sorts of gossip inclination, all types of news, and any collective orientation or activity from politics to sports. It's a wide range and obviously none of the triggers are nefarious in themselves.

So, uncertainty is a kind of gateway. As Heraclitus reminds us, "war is the father of all things" (Jung, 1960, para. 99). He is talking here about the regulative function of opposites, or what he (and Jung after him) called *enantiodromia*, which is a great change caused by the opposites in conflict. Too much or too big a dose of *enantiodromia* can be crippling and it leads to neurotic suffering, or what Jung also calls *philosophic disorientation.* This is very serious because it usually involves a threat to core meaning structures. These core meaning structures carry an independence and an authority that is very similar to descriptions of divinity. This is why Jung uses the term God-image to designate the psychological center of values, akin to what Paul Tillich has called the ultimate concern.

But what can we do about this *philosophic disorientation*? Jung indicates (and practice confirms) that there is a remedy! Again, referring to *Aion*: we can cure it "by shedding light on the psychic background and the secret chambers of the soul" (Jung, 1959, p. X).

> Tears, sorrow, and disappointment are bitter, but wisdom is the comforter in all psychic suffering. Indeed, bitterness and wisdom form a pair of alternatives: where there is bitterness wisdom is lacking, and where wisdom is there can be no bitterness. (Jung, 1963, para. 330)

A Clinical Example

Although this work can certainly be done outside of an analytic situation, I will now give a clinical example that shows a number of these fantasies at work, and the moment in which they were understood as something other than the literal constraints that they seemed to be:

Rachel is 42 years old. She has been quite successful in all outer parts of life, that is she has good friends, is proud of her career, and she is in a stable relationship. In most ways you'd have to say she's very well adapted, and, in fact, people almost always like her due to her hard-working attitude, intelligence, and sunny demeanor. We had worked for a long time on some issues of her feeling not-good enough and also of feeling like a fraud, both of which had softened a bit but not substantially changed.

Recently, a number of things had begun to trigger her. As always, the clinical question is, *why now?* Is it that events in the world are measurably worse, in which case the problem is literally the external occurrences (that is, the Spirit of the Times as discussed by Margaret Klenck), or have similar sets of events happened before but perhaps now for unknown and unconscious reasons the psyche is having a new reaction?

Rachel came in, on this particular day, in an unusually foul and combative mood. This was a striking difference from her usual upbeat attitude, as she didn't usually like to complain. Although I felt slightly apprehensive about a possible negative transference headed my way, I also understood that this might be an opportunity.

Her heightened affective state was visible in her body language, facial expressions, and tone. She seemed angry, sad, and frustrated. Of course, I asked about it in as neutral a way as possible, and the response was for her to look at me with a level of fury and to say in a way that implied it was my fault: "How do you think I am? I feel like shit, and everything is falling apart."

The absolute language and the strong affect showed me that a complex had been activated, and as mentioned above, complexes in the analytic situation are pure gold if you can mine them for their value. It is also important to remember that as a clinician, the outbreak is, in some ways, your fault since this kind of deep process is the one goal of the work.

In any case I tried to look as neutrally curious as possible and decided not to prod, but rather to see what unfolded. Usually there is no need to interfere once an image is arising, since one tenet of analytic behavior is to get out of the way of the patient's process and to stick to their images. So, she continued to describe how there was a sense of "nothing moving, of not getting anywhere, of being stuck," and described in despairing terms that it was always going to be this way.

Indeed, after a pause came the expression of some of the going to shit. As she began, these images all had a collective cast: the problems with Covid-19, the question of where do you wear a mask these days or not, and people are still getting sick, what is the government doing. This evolved into comments about the recent escalation of warfare and how unsettling it was, how unfair and why are people like that anyway. That led to a despairing comment on Roe v. Wade, assaults on women and related injustices, then came a sudden turn into guilt about privilege and how she shouldn't really complain.

Listening to this I realized the thing that was in imminent danger of being shut down was actually the complaining, so I did a rough and ready translation of the things that were mentioned. We have to remember that lengthy and detailed amplifications are important for training and can be extremely helpful when studying psychic disturbances, but in the moment we have to make do with a quicker process guided by our training, intuition, and the evidence of the images. So, I wondered to myself about the various angles that each of those world-problems could take. Are we talking about Covid-19 as psychic infection, or about the difficulties with social interaction as internal isolation from the Kidhr or internal verdant one? Perhaps the concern about warfare was also indicative of an inner conflict that is projected somewhere. The questions of injustices perhaps were hinting at an internal moral stance concerning a lack of response to autonomous images, or the guilt (as Jung understands it) as a debt-to-the-self, that is, something to be enhanced and lived but along symbolic lines?

It seemed—and these things are never that obvious— that in the debt-to-self department some challenge to privilege-compromised complaining was the most promising. However, I didn't know where that complaining would be most fruitful and so I asked what of those items seemed most pressing. In response she surprisingly expressed that what really seemed pressing but perhaps were "too petty to mention" were some more personal concerns. Although I didn't expect this, it in fact bore out my caution since none of the particular images stood out to me.

Many people in therapy are aware of their privilege and it can be hard to justify talking about situations that are much worse for others. We often don't feel entitled to talk about our suffering but the truth is that we all encounter our suffering personally in whatever form it arises and the key thing is to pursue those images.

Of course, I said I wanted to know about these concerns. Not surprisingly she spoke in a more engaged way about such extremely non-petty struggles as distress and anger about a recent visit with her mother which brought up an almost overwhelming amount of searing, even crippling, self-hatred. These two were related, as we knew through years of working with her mother complex, and then she also talked about how her usual self-care processes had been coming up short.

Amplification

We should remember that for Jung, the psyche itself has a timeline and that a neurosis changes our view of the world by creating an alternate reality, one that is often related to superstition. This allows the world to correspond to internal logic but not to outer reality. He reminds us that, "The outbreak of neurosis signalizes the moment when this [making unreal by the ego] can no longer be done by the primitive magical means of apotropaic gestures and euphemisms" (Jung, 1960, para. 207).

Or one could describe this moment as the *end-times for a particular attitude* and as when something happens in the mind is as if to say, *you can't make nice anymore*. This is one reason we can (carefully) cheer for the arrival of a new neurosis, even though it brings a certain suffering. A neurosis is the beginning of a change of internal structure. In fact, Jung claims that,

"A neurosis is truly removed only when it has removed the false attitude of the ego. We do not cure it—it cures us. A [person] is ill, but the illness is nature's attempt to heal [them]" (Jung, C, 1964 para. 361).

The Nature of the Therapeutic Relationship

A note about case presentations should be made here. They are, of course, constructions of an artificially edited narrative that is based on literal experiences cut together in a certain way to illuminate some small piece of understanding. I say that because any encapsulation of personal process cannot remotely do justice to the many hours of slow careful work listening to narrative and building rapport. It should be noted that this moment came after a long period of quiet, listening, sympathetic understanding, and a slow building of a relationship in which the little moves of symbolization brought both relief and change.

I am going to relate a kind of turning-point moment in a long process. It's important to remember that it takes quite a long time to, in the words of Yoram Kaufmann, "find this unique imaginal language of each analysand" (Kaufmann, 2009, p. 6). Not only that, the proper timing is critical, and this can be thought of as an invitation from the psyche. That is, an image will arise that asks for a response. This can be as simple as the analysand asking your opinion or as subtle as a long pause or an aspect of a dream image or fantasy.

This process is of course harder to accomplish than to describe, but if we describe it even as a theoretical possibility, then we can look for it in analytic dialogue. Nevertheless, the quality of being stuck is an indication that libido (or psychic energy) is pushing back into the unconscious where it will stimulate a new image. It is the job of the analyst to be on the lookout for the new image, since usually one arises after a cathartic release. And the phrase "always going to be this way" is one way of saying we feel like we are fated to never change. When we hear that we can remember that:

The psychological rule says that when an inner situation is not made conscious, it happens outside as fate. That is to say, when the individual remains undivided and does not become conscious of the inner opposite, the world must perforce act out the conflict and be torn into opposing halves. (Jung, 1959/1969, para, 126)

This implies that we need to find the inner conflict, which is delicate for a few reasons. First, most of us live life out there in the world and it would be insulting to try to refer to the internal pattern before we are invited. However, in this case, I was being invited by the image of the apocalyptic scene. And it may go without saying that we would rather feel together than become divided internally, and it is never that pleasant to take back our projections even if the result is salutary.

Our first job as analysts or as stewards of our own process is to collect the triggers and collective images themselves in order to see them together and in as specific form as possible; that is, we listen to the narrative in an active way, we explore it and feel its emotional and bodily reality, and then we look at as an independent and advisory entity, like a dream.

When I heard her talk about her feeling of stuckness, I reflected only to myself on the recent very good work we had done, but I did not mention it. I was able to not react since I did not take the comment personally, rather I saw it as a part of her unfolding process as described above. I waited for the image to unfold, as it seemed it would.

Although the self-hatred seemed more emotionally pressing, I asked about the self-care as a more gradual way to get to it. She related that vacation no longer offered rejuvenation, her typically soothing activities failed to soothe, her mild drug use no longer offered the respite of a change of consciousness, and working out no longer satisfied her bodily critique not to mention the bad feelings.

I thought to myself that this was probably important because again, the stopping of the making unreal was happening, but I couldn't think of a way to say, *oh this is good news*. Instead I sympathized but mentioned that although distressing, all of these things happening at once might be showing us that something big was brewing. In this context I asked about the recent visit with her mother.

Now it should be noted that in the history of her family dynamics she had the very bad misfortune of winning the Oedipal battle, meaning she became the apple of her father's eye and so the focus of her mother's envy. When the family broke up due to an affair, the father was no longer available and the only parent left was the somewhat vicious mother. This very understandably led to a pattern of self-hiding and self-denial in order to avoid the mother's wrath and yet survive in the current environment.

Her visits to her mother were never enjoyable but were done dutifully and cheerfully for the most part, which, in itself, was quite adaptive but also self-denying. During the recent weekend visit to her mother, a particular event arose. At the end of the weekend she asked Rachel to stay another day. This was the last thing Rachel would have wanted in any case but she demurred, saying she had to make a long drive home to her own family and that she had to work the next day. Her mother became irate and called her selfish, and then raised the stakes by tearfully claiming that "all she wanted was a little time with her daughter before she died."

It's pretty clear from this short vignette how Rachel felt she had to hide anything very authentic in terms of emotional response—and the nascent arrival of her new attitude, represented by staying firm about going back to her own home, was exactly what was setting off the self-hate. In our therapeutic dialogue we had already related the self-hate to a place of paradoxical safety, since from within that painful place one could not be accused of aggrandizement, which was always the major sin in her family of origin.

Like many complexes, this one served a purpose in child-hood but later in life it has become no longer useful, or even overtly destructive. In her firestorm of self-destructive hate, we can also begin to see what might actually end, in the end-times, as her attitude of conciliation begins to crumble.

The discussion around her mother reminded her of a dream: *This woke me up - crying out...*

I was riding in the back seat of a car (unclear who was driving but there was a driver and a passenger riding in the front seat). I was kind of low down and I was looking at beautiful scenery along the water, the breeze was coming in the window (a gorgeous mountain out front in the distance) then the car suddenly went off the road and was submerged in water and I had the panicky feeling of not only being locked in a small car unable to get out but then totally underwater – I was thrashing around beginning to drown and saw my window was open – and I hesitated – should I try to save them?

We explored the dream a little. The panicky trapped feeling of the dream was already resonant in the room so this seemed like a good segue. We worked through the images together. The quality of not driving shows that a complex is in charge. That much was eminently clear! Her status as riding in the back, and being low down, felt like being a kid (and reminded her of some of her happiest childhood memories when she was not the positive focus of the father nor the negative focus of the mother but just cruising through life with both parents).

In the front seats were adult figures, not exactly her parents but just where the parents would be. This can indicate that we are dealing with parental *imagos*, meaning the parts of our parental experiences that we internalize. These are the real culprits in later life since they haunt us without regard for distance in time or space from the actual parents.

The sudden crash was reminiscent of both her historical experience of how things went bad in the family all of a sudden but perhaps more importantly, tracked the current feeling of things going off the rails, of crashing, being submerged and trapped. And one more thing arises in this dream: the choice.

At this point, and because of the element of choice, we could map out this dream onto her current apocalyptic experiential landscape, one that included feelings of disaster, suffering and a pretty imminent end-time. We had over a number of years developed a common language that included some amplification and she was used to my style. So, what I said next was not a big deviation from the kind of things I had said before that had been helpful. I say that because everyone has a different style, and everyone will get to this kind of turning point in their own way.

I said that it seemed like her situation had come to a head, and that there was a kind of desperation she felt and it was a kind of culmination. She nodded in agreement and said 'yes that's really how it feels.' I then suggested that feeling like it's the end is a kind of apocalypse, and that the experience of apocalypse is a *thinning of the veil between you and the divine*. We had talked about spiritual matters quite a bit so that wasn't a leap on my part.

In response her eyes slightly widened and although it was a mouthful, she took it in in the way I meant, which was that something important in her psyche was on the verge of happening, and not in a bad way. She said, "it seems like something is trying to break out of me, but it's so scary." I responded that, "it makes sense that your usual ways of soothing the rough waters and calming yourself do not work anymore, and in fact that is a good thing." She looked at me quizzically and I said that vacation in the sense of getting away from the work one needs to do, soothing the problems instead of wrestling with them, changing one's mind through substances instead of in a permanent way were all indications that a new way of thinking about things was emerging.

I went on to say that of course it would be a kind of scary end time for the ego if it were to be supplanted by a new attitude. So, *the world is in fact ending for that attitude*, and that is very painful because that is what we know as ourselves. In the dream language, she was being given the choice to leave behind her childhood (and ongoing) role of caring for others in order to be safe, and of abandoning the parental *imagos*. For many women, individuating from the mother *imago* brings up an experience of abandonment, and it was doing so now.

We agreed this was the choice: to go down with the ship again or swim to safety and let the others die. This is never an easy choice, since that former person is, in fact, oneself and it is all one has known. Furthermore, those *imagos* or internalized parental images have guided how we live, they have become our values and priorities. Giving any of that up in favor of a somewhat unknown future is the analytic sacrifice.

Tears welled up, she started to cry softly. She said, "it does seem like something new is coming. Now that I think about it, I've been acting differently – but it's all so scary, I don't know what's next." And we never do.

So, the old attitude was indeed in jeopardy as anything new and manifested in the world would upset the delicate balance of social role and internalized mother *imago*. These connections were made mostly by her since we had mapped out much of this beforehand over the years. The big change was that a moment of apocalyptic revelation could be seen as success rather than failure to the extent that it was seen as referring to the internal and emotional landscape, rather than being allowed to dry up in the arid air of concrete references and external problem solving.

This mention of apocalyptic experience as revelation proved to be a new bit of shared vocabulary, and the experience of *absolutely all bad* was from then on seen as a different kind of signifier, one that from then on meant: *something new is close* and *what is arising next?* What was arising was a new chapter in

117

her quest for self-expression, as the manifestation of that change of attitude. This change showed both a courage to encounter envy by personally expressing herself and a feeling of heady powerfulness as the gaze of shame was inverted, becoming the projection of soul and appreciation of its pull into life.

In conclusion, we remember that individuals carry a set of automatic imaginal responses within them. These responses to collective events are also in themselves archetypal, in that they use a routinized format to process stressful events. However, when these responses are not relevant to action in the world, they can be seen as reflecting an inner state. This inner state can be either specifically symbolized by a particular problem in the world or, as in our example, it can be a generalized apocalyptic complex. It can be very fruitful and even healing to work with this material as indicative of an inner situation if it can be understood symbolically. This process brings to light potential unconscious conflicts in order that they can be contended with consciously and so assimilated. This symbolic view never need occlude the reality of worldly troubles. Rather, it shows the efficacy of having a spiritual approach to situations which come up at regular intervals in the sacred writings of all major religious traditions across the whole span of their history, and which are very much alive today across the globe.

References

The New Oxford Annotated Bible, Revised Standard Version, (1977), Book of Joel - Joel: Chapt. 15 & 28. New York: Oxford University Press.

Dawson, M., (1923). *Nineteenth Century Evolution and After: A Study of Personal Forces Affecting the Social Process, in the Light of the Life-Sciences and Religion.* New York: Macmillan.

Jung, C.G., (1950). *CW, Vol.18: Symbols and interpretations of Dreams, The Symbolic Life.* Princeton, NJ: Princeton University Press.

_____. (1966). *CW, Volume 7: Two Essays in Analytical Psychology.* Princeton, NJ: Princeton University Press. (Original work published 1953)

_____. (1966). Principles of practical psychotherapy (R. F. C. Hull, Trans.). In H. Read et al. (Eds.), *CW, Vol. 16. Practice of psychotherapy* (2nd ed., 3-20). Princeton, NJ: Princeton University Press. (Original work published 1935)

_____. (1989). *CW, Vol. 11: Psychology and Religion: West and East.* Princeton, NJ: Princeton University Press. (Original work published 1958)

_____. (1980). *CW, Vol. 9: The Archetypes and the Collective Unconscious.* Princeton, NJ: Princeton University Press. (Original work published 1959)

_____. (1970). *CW, Vol. 10: Civilization in Transition.* Princeton, NJ: Princeton University Press. (Original work published 1964)

_____. (1969). On psychic energy (R. F. C. Hull, Trans.). In H. Read et al. (Eds.), *CW Vol. 8, Structure and dynamics of the psyche* (2nd ed., 3-66). Princeton, NJ: Princeton University Press. (Original work published 1928)

_____. (1970). *CW, Vol. 14, Mysterium Coniunctionis.* Princeton, NJ: Princeton University Press. (Original work published 1963)

_____. (1970). *CW, Vol. 10: Civilization in Transition.* Princeton, NJ: Princeton University Press. (Original work published 1964)

_____. (1973). *Collected Letters: Vol. 2. "Letter to M. Leonard, December 5, 1959."* A. Gerhard (Ed.), A. Jaffe, (Trans.). R.F.C. Hull, Bollingen Series, SCV. Princeton, NJ: Princeton University Press.

Kaufmann, Y., (2009). *The Way of the Image, The Orientational Approach to Psyche,* New York: Zahav Books.

Strauss, M., (2009). "Ten Notable Apocalypses That (Obviously) Didn't Happen" November 12, *Smithsonian Magazine* Website, Smithsonian.com.

The Faith of the Analyst During Climates of Uncertainty

By Murray Stein

Faith is a mystery. Some people have it and some don't. Its presence or absence may depend on childhood and the attachments of a loving mother who lays down the psychological foundation of trust in life. Paradoxically, I have also noticed that people who had serious health or emotional problems or traumas in their early years, often have an uncanny connection to mystical spiritualty, another source of trust and ultimately faith. Sometimes between life and death, uncertain whether to stay in this world, it's as though the supernatural hovers about them, and participation in another invisible world is an ever present possibility. Sometimes this frightens them, but if it does not, it can turn into faith in their destiny as individuals. If they become Jungian psychoanalysts, they often show a gift for sustaining the pressures of taking a deep dive into the unconscious with their patients. Their faith, which is based on personal experience of the transcendent, sustains them through thick and thin.

In times of uncertainty in life, faith has an enormous benefit. Perhaps even sheer survival itself can depend upon it. One thinks of Victor Frankl in Auschwitz, who sustained himself not only with a sense of meaning but also faith that he would survive to live his meaning. A similar story is shared by Rabbi Leo Baeck, who survived several years in Theresienstadt while in his 70s. Faith contributed powerfully to their amazing resiliance in the face of uncertainty about survival. They lived, literally, from day to day without certainty that they would be alive tomorrow. At times in the analytic process, it comes down similarly to a matter of psychic survival and endurence as the waves of emotion rise high and the earth shakes beneath our feet. What can we cling to for hope? It becomes a matter of faith.

In this reflection, I will address several questions, all of which fall under the larger issue of the analyst's faith when working with the inevitable crises and moments of despair that arise in the course of analysis. The questions to be considered here are:

1) What is faith?
2) "Have I faith or a faith or not?" (the question Jung asked himself in a letter to Fr. Victor White, O.P.[1])
3) Does the presence or absence of faith on the part of the analyst make a significant difference for the course and outcome of analytic work?

Following the response to these questions, I will consider some typical moments of crisis that arise in analysis and are sketched briefly in Jung's essay, "The Psychology of the Transference," where he writes: "The collapse and disorientation of consciousness may last a considerable time, and it is one of the most difficult transitions the analyst has to deal with, demanding the greatest patience, courage, and faith on the part of both doctor and patient."[2]

Question 1: What is faith?

I will begin by asking a basic question: what do we mean when we use the word "faith?" Within traditional religious contexts, faith has a clear metaphysical and supernatural reference. It means "faith in God" (or "Goddess") as named and revealed in

---

[1] A. Lammers, *The Jung-White Letters*, p. 119.
[2] C.G. Jung, "The Psychology of the Transference," para. 476.

the Sacred texts and rituals of the specific religion in which it is used. The English word's etymology, however, is actually devoid of explicit reference to anything religious or supernatural. In the SOED, we find that the English word "faith" derives from the Latin *fides, fide-, fidere* and that the Latin *fides* translates the Greek *pistis*. The basic meanings of these Latin and Greek root words are: confidence, reliance, trust. This can be trust in anyone or anything—in one's own creative abilities and powers, for instance, as Louise Bourgeois, the famous sculptress, used the word when she was asked, "How were you able to continue working for so long without public recognition" (she was not "discovered" until she was in her 70s and had been busy as a sculptress for decades), and she said, "I just had faith in my work!"[3] One can have faith in one's business or intimate partner (to be reliable and "faithful"), or in one's political party or leadership. Here faith is purely of this world and without any spiritual or religious connotation. It means confidence and trust in someone or something visible, knowable, tangible. It is more or less equivalent to, "I trust you," or "Your handshake is as good as a legal contract." Faith is trust, pure and simple, in anyone or anything. It is faith in this sense that we speak of when we say that it is grounded in early childhood attachment to an emotionally reliable mother or caretaker.

For many people, however, the word "faith" has a strongly religious connotation. Having faith speaks of reliance and trust in God, and hence it affirms a sense of contact with and knowledge about a supernatural Being. In the Bible, the great exemplars of faith—such as Abraham who trusted God and left his home country to embark on a journey into the unknown, and Moses who trusted God to provide nourishment during the years of wandering in the wilderness—place their trust in Diety, not in their fellow human beings or their own powers or in anything material and visible. This

---

[3] "Louise Bourgeois: The Spider, the Mistress and the Tangerine," a film by Marion Cajori and Amei Wallach, Zeitgeist Video, 2008.

is not faith that the sun will rise tomorrow. Faith, in this sense of the word, exceeds the capacity of reason and the requirement for evidence. It is not based on mundane experience. It leaps to another type of cognition (as in Kierkegaard's famous "leap of faith") where existential risk is involved. It rests on intuitive knowledge or on what we might call Gnosis, following the ancient tradition of visionary knowing.

In the New Testament, there is a classic definition of faith in this religious sense: "Now faith is the assurance of things hoped for, the conviction of things not seen. For by it the men of old received divine approval. By faith we understand that the world was created by the word of God, so that what is seen was made out of things which do not appear."[4] Faith here means a kind of knowledge of the unseen, of a supernatural and ultimate Power operating behind the scenes and responsible for there being something rather than nothing, and for destiny both individual and collective. Additionally, in the New Testament faith in Christ is made the condition of the soul's salvation, an idea that was powerfully propounded by Martin Luther in the Protestant Reformation. Faith becomes the requirement for salvation and insures one's blessed condition, if not always to one's physical satisfaction in this life, then surely to one's spiritual satisfaction in the next. Here, faith is not trust in just anything, it is trust specifically in Christ. And the mystery of faith is resolved by John Calvin in his notion of predestination: the people who have faith are blessed and have been given their capacity for faith by divine Providence. Faith is rooted in a transcendent source. Those who do not have faith have not been blessed with this capacity by God. This is Calvin's answer to the question of why some people have faith and others do not.

This religious understanding of faith is what has been passed down through generations of people embedded in the biblical traditions, and so it is not surprising to find that it is this

---

[4] Hebrews 11: 1-3.

understanding of the term, rather than the more neutral one as indicated by the word's etymology, that has been adopted also by the more or less secular culture of the West. It is commonly understood that the content of faith is made up of: a) the conviction that invisible and supernatural forces are at work behind the scenes in nature and history; b) knowledge, based on "revelation," about how these forces affect and impact visible reality in time and space; and c) trust in them regarding the ultimate triumph of good over evil and salvation for the souls of the believers. The term, "faith," belongs most authetically to the vocabulary of the religious, and its existence separates the faithful from the unbelievers.

No wonder, then, that modern people generally have shunned the term. Logical positivism, for instance, considered all faith statements to be nothing but superstition, basically discardable nonsense. Faith belongs to the Middle Ages, to the Age of Faith, which has now been superceded by the Age of Reason. In the period of high modernity (19th - 20th centuries), to have faith was generally considered pre-modern, meaning that the "believer" remained mired in the mythological stage of human consciousness and had not yet evolved culturally into the modern age, which adamantly rejected the notion of the supernatural and committed itself to the methods of empirical science and logical rationality. Faith in the religious sense of the word is not admitted into scientific discourse. In fact, it is anathema, to use another religious term. Banished!

As a modern man committed to scientific method and research, Jung struggled with the concept of "faith." In a letter to Father Victor White dated May 21, 1948, he questions himself and writes: "Your paper ["Notes on Gnosticism"] has made me think: *Have I faith or a faith or not*? I have always been unable to produce faith and I have tried so hard, that I finally do not know any more, what faith is or means. I owe it to your paper, that I have now apparently an answer: faith or the equivalent of faith with me is what I would call *Respect*. I have respect of the Christian Truth… There is however nothing specific in it, since I feel the same kind of respect for the basic teachings of Buddhism and the fundamental taoistic ideas."[5]

Typical of cultural moderns and trained scientists, Jung has great difficulty with the term "faith." To his mind, it generally meant "belief"—assent to a particular set of doctrines and creeds, be it Protestant Reformed, Roman Catholic, Moslem, Jewish, Hindu, or whatever. It does not necessarily imply a first-hand, primary religious experience or a hard-won and rigorous philosophical position that includes a personal cosmological vision or, as Jung would say, a personal *Weltanschauung*. Jung could not identify with any of the traditional Confessions, even though he was culturally a Swiss Reformed Protestant. This kind of faith— sheer belief—Jung could not claim for himself, and indeed he often expresses hostility and defiance if pressed to accept authorative teachings about transcendent or metaphysical teachings about God. But he did *respect* the religious traditions, all of them, and he learned a good deal from many. For him they were loaded with archetypal symbolism and taught him about the contents of the collective unconscious. He did not subscibe to their ontological and metaphysical claims, however, and so he did not have "faith" in any of them. One could say that he looked at all of them from the outside with an unprejudiced gaze, and from this perspective all were of equal value—for psychology. If he could replace "faith" with "respect," he was content. He did have genuine appreciation for religious thought and experience of all kinds.

But how "modern" was Jung, really, if we define "modern" as the absolute rejection of anything numinous, spiritual or transcendent? He is very hard to pin down and capture in the familiar terms we use nowadays to categorize historical types of attitude and thinking—"pre-modern," "modern," and "post-modern." In contrast to what he says in this letter to Victor White just quoted, Jung *was* quite capable of expressing intuitions of transcendence—a kind of

---

[5] A. Lammers (ed.), *The Jung-White Letters*, p. 119.

faith statement, I would argue—as they came to him spontaneously or through the channels of personal, and especially of numinous, experience. For instance, in a letter to Victor White just prior to the one quoted above, he writes: "Whoever has clearly understood, what it means: *"Qui fidelis est in minimo"* ["He that is faithful in that which is least" (Luke 16:10)], is overwhelmed with the dura necessitas [hard necessity] of submission and discipline of a subtler kind than the regula S. Benedicti [Rule of St. Benedict]. I don't want to prescribe a way to other people, because I know that my way has been prescribed to me by a hand far above my reach."[6] Jung's caution here about giving advice to others is based on the sense that his own life has received direction and shape, indeed commands of a sort, from "a hand far above my reach." From this statement it seems quite evident that he had given himself over in full submission to a "higher power" which, in other letters to White, he would freely refer to as God. Recall, too, the Delphic oracle inscribed over the doorway of Jung's own home: *Vocatus atque non vocatus Deus aderit* ("Called or not called, God is present"). Here stood a constant reminder, as he entered his home day in and day out, of "Deus." Although it is hard to pin down precisely what this means, *Deus* is certainly a reference to a transcendent factor of which Jung was constantly reminded.

It is of this type of awareness of a "way" that "has been prescribed...by a hand far above my reach" that I wish to speak in considering here the issue of faith and the practicing analyst. It is not faith in the conventional meaning of "belief" in traditional doctrines about God, but it is more than the neutral meaning of faith as simply trust in anyone or anything. It is faith rather in the sense of 1) owning up to having an implicit or explicit recognition of Being that is more complete and comprehensive than our focused knowing can in principle ever comprehend or exhaustively understand, 2) trusting in the occasional glimpses we do have of this "hand far above my reach," and 3) submitting to its greater vision,

---

[6] A. Lammers (ed.), *The Jung-White Letters,* p. 117.

wisdom, will, and power. No more than Jung are most of us ready to accept without question authoritative teaching delivered from pulpit, mosque, synagogue, or cathedral. We value our freedom to think and to experience life for ourselves too highly for that. But do we go as far as he did in owning up to, trusting, and submitting to a "hand far above [our] reach"? I mean this as a challenge.

Leaving a specific, revealed God out of the picture, let's say that "faith" is defined as a kind of intuitive cognition, with strong emotional under- and overtones, of a realm of being beyond our conscious grasp (awareness of "a hand far above my reach"), and that it is forward-looking with trust ("the assurance of things hoped for"). Karl Jaspers used the neutral phrase "the Comprehensive" to speak of this realm toward which we would direct our attention in an act of faith.[7] The person of, or with, faith would put trust in such intuitive cognitions and, I would add, would do so because of personal experiences that suggest this totality is a Truth, a totality that exceeds the self of the individual person and is a kind of Self of selves, an all-encompassing Self.

Question #2: "Have *I* faith or a faith or not?"

To this second question, each of us must give an individual and personal answer, quietly, inwardly, drawing on a personal anamnesis (to follow Eric Voegelin's example in establishing his noetic certainty and varieties of transcendences of consciousness[8]). We have to consult our memories, look back at the unfolding patterns in our life, reflect on the question of meaning in the seemingly accidental twists and turns of our personal history (the synchronicities), and recall the "miracles."

Speaking personally, therefore, I have to say that I have asked myself this question often and have answered it in different ways at various times in my life. As a child I was exposed to religious faith

---

[7] K. Jaspers, *Way to Wisdom*, pp. 28-38.
[8] E. Voegelin, *Anamnesis*, Chapter 3.

in our home. I grew up with the Bible and became familiar with many of its stories and figures. Later, I studied Christian theology formally and intensively. And so, throughout my life I have had many phases of being with and without, in and out of faith in the religious sense, depending on the phase of the individuation process I was in.

As I enter the later decades of life and ask myself this question, I find myself now drawing on a wealth of specific and what I call primary experiences, including important dreams, scenes and events from active imagination, and several astonishing synchronicities (I think of them as miracles) that have shaped what I would now call my "faith platform." Of course, my reading in a wide variety of literatures has been important as well, but the primary experiences are the crucial elements. Considering these experiences, I can find also what Jung called respect for the religious traditions and for what people in them experience when they speak of faith, but my own platform of faith is somewhat apart from the planks laid down by my own background religious tradition, Protestant Christianity.

Put into a few words and rather abstractly, my faith platform is that *time and eternity intersect and assure the transcendent value of certain numinous experiences, which in turn offer a deep sense of meaning for life.* I do recognize this as a variation on the notion of incarnation as affirmed in Christian faith, where an infinite God and a limited human consciousness unite in a specific historical moment. The element of numinosity in this moment is key. In my experiences, however, the Deity who is present in this moment is not always specified as the biblical one, although for me the symbol of Christ remains central.

Sometimes these numinous experiences of transcendent value have taken place in the *vas bene clausam* of analysis with my analysands. These are indelible "transformational moments"[9] for consciousness, and they have been recognized as such by both of

---

[9] I thank Linda Carter for this phrase in her article, "Countertransference and Intersubjectivity."

us in the process. The intuition of an intersection or interpenetration of time and eternity, the finite and the infinite, the concrete and the symbolic is the essence of this experience. It has a feeling of timelessness, and it communicates a sense of meaning that can be trusted for the present and the future. The hand behind the timing and exact location of these intersections is hidden in the Great Mystery. It is the "hand far above my head," as Jung says.

A satellite or derivative of this platform is the article (also of faith) that the individual human soul/psyche/self is of infinite value. Why? Because each finite person is a suitable subject for reception of the infinite. To my mind, this is what Jung meant by "the Christification of many" in his late work, *Answer to Job*. Everyone is called to incarnate the infinite in this life; everyone is capable of receiving intuitions of the Divine, and of finding ultimate meaning in life as lived concretely in each and every human context on the planet. Such Gnosis is freely available to every single person on earth. The human self is an *imago dei* and therefore related to the Deity itself and graced with ultimate value. Whether the person realizes this or not, lives a short or a long life, individuates consciously or not, the value remains. So we "meet the Buddha" or "the Christ" in ourselves and in all the others we may encounter in our brief lives on earth. Rabbi Leo Baeck affirms the same basic value from a Jewish perspective in his powerful essay, *"Individuum Ineffibile,"* delivered at the Eranos Tagung in Jung's presence in 1947.

This also means that the human encounter with others, as we experience it in analysis for instance, is of infinite potential. The horizontal interpersonal relationship, with all of its transference and projections, illusions and disillusionments, love and hate and other dramas, is intersected by a vertical line of infinite value and potential for meaning that extends beyond the two empirical humans in this joint venture. In this we can trust.

Question #3: Does the presence or absence of faith on the part of the analyst make a difference for the course and outcome of analytic work?

Obviously this makes a difference! Everything the analyst brings to the therapeutic relationship makes a difference if the analytic process becomes transformative. The analyst's attitudes, temperament, cultural biases, complexes, personal development—all of these factors make a difference for the course and outcome of analysis because in the end they all enter into the process, participate in the "field" and influence the client. But maybe it is useful to look more closely at how precisely this factor—faith, as I have defined it above—might make a crucial difference.

An analysand asked me recently at the beginning of a session and more or less out of the blue: "Do you believe we can change our fate, our destiny?" It was not clear to me where this question was coming from or why it was an issue. It is of course an impossible question on a scientific or rational level. What is destiny, fate? Do they really exist? To hold that each life has a destiny or a fate is itself a statement of faith and must be answered on the same level. And why would one want to change it? In reflecting on this question, I have to confess that I don't think we can interfere with an individual's destiny if that is what Jung meant by "a hand far above my reach." But we can come to accept it, even to love it (*amor fati*). For the analyst to take this position, however, requires an act of faith, namely that each individual's destiny is of value, even of ultimate value and meaning. Without this attitude engendered by faith, the analyst might be tempted to play God and try to help a person change their destiny. But where would that leave them? One thinks of the famous so-called Serenity Prayer by Reinhold Niehbuhr: "Father, give us courage to change what must be altered, serenity to accept what cannot be helped, and the insight to know the one from the other."[10]

---

[10] https://yalealumnimagazine.com/articles/2709-you-can-quote-them

"Only when God is there may one cease to be obliged to be God," wrote the German psychoanalyst and theologian Eugen Drevermann. It's a brilliant insight. For analysis to work properly, it seems to me, the analyst must not be cast in the role of God, but for this to be the case it is necessary to have a sense that the Transcendent is present in the room apart from either of the human participants, yet with them, among them, for here "two are gathered." Analysis takes place in the presence of the Divine and so participates in the sacred aura. In such a setting even a very difficult fate can be accepted, appreciated, and found to be of ultimate value.

In this perspective, I often think of Jung's statement: "... the fact is that the approach to the numinous is the real therapy and inasmuch as you attain to the numinous experiences you are released from the curse of pathology. Even the very disease takes on a numinous character."[11] When even a disease— depression, anxiety, addiction, borderline disorders, perversion— takes on a numinous character, it must mean that it has been placed within the infinitely containing perspective of faith.

What I would caution against is settling for something that sometimes, perhaps even often, happens when in classical Jungian terms faith in the spiritual and religious sense of its meaning is translated simply as knowledge of the (invisible) archetypal world and the contents of the collective unconscious and trust in the self's processes. Jungian analysts routinely do employ this type of thinking when they treat patients, especially the challenging and difficult ones. They have faith in the psyche's wisdom, in the self's operations, even when these are opaque and hidden from view. From their training, they have some positive knowledge about the invisible world of the unconscious—they know of complexes and archetypal images and patterns of thought and behavior. They know about the self and about the ego's relativity with respect to the objective psyche. Without this knowledge it would be difficult to proceed in many cases. But this falls short of faith as

---

[11] G. Adler (ed.) *C.G. Jung Letters*, p. 377.

it is understood in the stronger sense, which implies knowledge of and trust in transcendent factors that lie entirely beyond the psychological realm and extend into what Jung called the psychoid dimension, and even beyond that to altogether trans- or non-human material and spiritual dimensions of reality. Faith in this sense speaks of territory beyond the discernible ends of the specturm that Jung uses as a metaphor to describe the human psyche, with the infrared shading off into the soma and the material world and the ultraviolet passing into the spiritual. Faith of this far reach passes beyond the personal, the causal, the rational and looks to realms that Jung calls "the beyond" (*Jenseits*) in *The Red Book* and later discusses as the basis of synchronicity. The horizon of rationality of whatever kind is breached and opens out into the transpersonal and the cosmic. An image of such a glimpse into the cosmic world is depicted in the famous picture of the alchemist poking his head out of the globe and gazing at the supercelestial firmament of the stars, a firmament beyond even the physical stars. It is from here that our fate and our destiny is drawn. Our psyche is an *imago Dei*.

For modern people (like most of us) this is the sticking point: Is such knowledge possible, is it credible? For traditional religionists, it is possible only because of divine revelation, hence Anselm's famous sentence: "*Neque enim quaero intelligere ut credam, sed credo ut intelligam. Nam et hoc credo, quia, nisi credidero, non intelligam.* " ("Nor do I seek to understand that I may believe, but I believe that I may understand. For this, too, I believe, that, unless I first believe, I shall not understand.") But after Kant's critiques, we have become appropriately cautious about such certainties.

Yet Jung, quite sensitive to the Kantian caution, could also say, quite boldly, at the conclusion of his Terry Lectures at Yale in 1937: "… if the spiritual adventure of our time is the exposure of human consciousness to the undefined and indefinable, there would seem to be good reasons for thinking that even the Boundless is pervaded by psychic laws, which no man invented, but of which he has 'gnosis' in the symbolism of Christian dogma."[12] Clearly he was intent on exploring beyond the bounds of the purely psychological realm, and of course this attitude entered into his practice as an analyst.

Faith provides a quite specific perspective on the therapeutic process, in that it trusts that if the psyche/soul opens to the unconscious (which is without limit and cannot be defined exhaustively by the conscious mind) the necessary developments and movements for individuation will emerge. There is implicit trust that what is happening, however peculiar or bizarre at times, has potential for meaning. The effect of this attitude on the part of the analyst is that analysands gain a sense of faith in themselves (in the self within themselves). The faith of the analyst, I would suggest, is subtly communicated and taken up in time by the analysand. The analyst's, "I have faith that your psyche has infinite potential," becomes translated into: "I have faith that my psyche has contact with the infinite and with its potential for meaning in my life."

Of course, in this era of evidence- (and not faith-) based medicine and psychotherapy it is necessary to offer studies and research that demonstrate results, that show that our methods work, that people benefit and get better, become more trusting of themselves, of their own feelings and intuitions. We need to be able to show that faith is communicable, that it passes from "I trust in you" to "I trust in the Self."

It is a moving scene in Dante's *Divine Comedy* when Virgil, who has accompanied the poet through Hell and Purgatory, takes his leave of Dante. He says to him:

> "My son," he said, "you now have seen the torment
> of the temporal and the eternal fires;
> here, now, is the limit of my discernment.
>
> .....
>
> Expect no more of me in word or deed:
> here your will is upright, free, and whole,
> and you would be in error not to heed

---

[12] C.G. Jung, *Psychology and Religion*, *CW* 11, para. 168.

whatever your own impulse prompts you to:
lord of yourself I crown and mitre you."[13]

Dante is now on his own as he makes his way onward toward Heaven. His guide, Virgil, has faith in his ability now to trust his own impulses, which have been cleansed and made conscious in the journey through Purgatory. He can now rely on his own connection to the Self. This does happen, too, in analysis, *Deo concidente*.

When faith is called for in analysis

There are phases of analysis, sometimes longer, sometimes shorter, when the analyst's faith in the process is tested. Jung writes about this quite explicitly and graphically in his essay, "The Psychology of the Transference." In reference to Pictures # 6 and of # 7 of the *Rosarium Philosophorum*, titled "The Ascent of the Soul," which he discusses at length in his work, he writes:

> This picture corresponds psychologically to a dark state of disorientation. The decomposition of the elements indicates dissociation and the collapse of the existing ego-consciousness. It is closely analogous to the schizophrenic state, and it should be taken very seriously because this is the moment when latent psychoses may become acute, i.e., when the patient becomes aware of the collective unconscious and the psychic non-ego. This collapse and disorientation of consciousness may last a considerable time and it is one of the most difficult transition the analyst has to deal with, demanding the greatest patience, courage, and faith on the part of the doctor and patient. It is a sign that the patient is being driven along willy-nilly without any sense

---

[13] Dante, *The Divine Comedy*, "*Purgatorio*" XXVII 127-143.

of direction, that is, in the truest sense of the word,
he is in an utterly soulless condition...[14]

What the analyst needs in this moment of the analytic process is, as Jung says, "faith." But faith in what? This is faith in the archetypal individuation process that is going through a passage of transition in which death and rebirth are the guiding powers. Death appears strikingly in the analytic setting, either as loss of energy or confidence, or as depression that things are not improving but rather are getting worse, or as phantoms and dreams of death actually appearing to the patient's consciousness in an astonishing way and with the force of conviction. Patients are convinced they are about to die! Or they feel the presence of Death in their lives. Here the analyst must hold on to the faith in individuation as an archetypal process. The analyst must be knowledgable about the death-and-rebirth archetype. But this must be Gnosis, i.e., knowledge based on the analyst's own experience, otherwise it is not effective or strong enough to hold the analyst's confidence and trust in the process.

There are three typical types of crises that we as analysts face in our work with patients: a crisis of identity (shadow confrontation with accompanying shame and guilt); a crisis of "loss of soul" (anima disappears and leaves behind a cold and empty void); and a crisis of "loss of meaning in life" (animus flies away, leaving a blank space in cognition). Each one calls for a process of death-and-rebirth. And each one can challenge the analyst's faith in the individuation process.

Often all three crises fall together in one dramatic period of life: the death of a close loved one with accompanying feelings of shame and guilt; the loss of social and/or professional status; a signficant failure in business (bankrupcy) or relationship (divorce); a catastrophic medical diagnosis that suddenly presents the prospect of a short time to live or requires extreme medical treatment with limited chances of survival. As psychotherapists, we live constantly in the shadow of failure and death. We,

---

[14] C.G. Jung, "The Psychology of the Transference," *CW* 16, para. 476.

too, are challenged to maintain a constructive attitude and a sense of meaning in what we do as caretakers of the soul.

If we look at how Jung came to his faith in transformation and personal Gnosis as described in *Liber Novus*, we see many encounters with the Dead and even with Death itself. In *Liber Novus*, Chapter vi of Liber Secundus is titled "Death." Jung describes his encounter with a "figure" standing "on the last dune... wearing a black wrinkled coat: he stands motionless and looks into the distance... he is gaunt and with a deeply serious look in his eyes."[15] Thereafter follows a vision of a multitude of the dead rolling down the hills into the sea, and Jung witnesses the horrors of the Great War to come. He himself descends into the cold valley of the shadow of death, where he loses all hope in new life afterwards. And then there comes the grisly experience of rebirth: "*Inter faeces et urinas nascimur*" ("We are born between faeces and urine" – St. Augustine): "For three nights I was assaulted by the horrors of birth. On the third night, jungle-like laughter pealed forth, for which nothing is too simple. Then life began to stir again."[16] Jung speaks of his Phoenix-like rebirth: "When I comprehended my darkness, a truly magnificent night came over me and my dream plunged me into the depths of the millennia, and from it my phoenix ascended."[17]

It was from experiences of the death-and-rebirth archetype such as this that Jung and many other analysts following his leadership have forged their Gnosis. This is the experiential/existential ground of the analyst's faith in the individuation process.

---

[15] C.G. Jung, *The Red Book*, p. 263.
[16] *Ibid.*, p. 268.
[17] *Ibid.*, p. 265.

References

Adler, G. and Jaffé, A., (eds.). (1973). *C.G. Jung Letters*. Vol. 1: 1906-1950. Princeton, NJ: Princeton University Press.

Carter, L., (2010). "Countertransference and Intersubjectivity." In M. Stein (ed.), *Jungian Psychoanaysis*. Chicago, IL: Open Court Publishing Company.

Alighieri, D., (2003). *The Divine Comedy*. J. Ciardi, (Trans.). New York: New American Library.

Jaspers, K., (2003). *Way to Wisdom*. New Haven, CT: Yale University Press.

Jung, C.G., (1946/1966). "The Psychology of the Transference." *CW, Vol. 16*. Princeton, NJ: Princeton University Press.

_____. (1970). *Psychology and Religion. CW, Vol. 11*. Princeton, NJ: Princeton University Press. (Original work published 1938)

_____. (2009). *The Red Book. A Reader's Edition*. New York: W.W. Norton & Co.

Lammers, A., (ed.). (2007). *The Jung-White Letters*. London and New York: Routledge.

Voegelin, E., (1978). *Anamnesis*. Columbia, MS: University of Missouri Press. (Original work published 1966)

Social Turmoil: A Moment of Social Change for our Communities and Nation

"The problem of opposites, as an inherent principle of human nature, forms a further stage in our process of realization. As a rule, it is one of the problems of maturity."
(Jung, 1953, para. 88)

"We cannot change anything until we accept it. Condemnation does not liberate, it oppresses."
(Jung, 1958, para. 519)

Introduction

The evolving and terrifying pandemic reached the United States in early 2020. By 2022 hope for an end to it was continuing to build, with the availability of vaccines and the increasing number of people receiving them. As noted in the introduction to Part 1, people were beginning to look past the pandemic toward a return to normalcy. In terms of the pandemic and its variants, a small path forward was slowly emerging.

At the same time, an intense period of social change and uncertainty was continuing. Social issues and concerns include:

❖ Polarization in the United States
❖ Political violence and unrest
❖ Engagement with equality
❖ Increased gun violence

At the community level, it is still a time of strife and dread. We are being challenged by upheaval, isolation, anger, exhaustion, and grief. These are issues that are not going to be resolved immediately. We are in a time of social change and development. The issues focused on in this section are similar to the individual challenges we are all facing but from a community, collective perspective:

- Living with polarization and having to develop alternative ways of thinking about and working with these complex social issues
- Managing fear, anxiety, and discontent in the face of these tensions
- Living with anger and with increasing gun violence
- Facing the war in Europe

Each concern outlined above is, like the ongoing pandemic, likely to be with us for a long time. Underlying these issues and affecting the resources available to individuals to respond to this increased and long-standing uncertainty is the reality that we are in a time of cultural paradigm shift or, in Jungian terms, a major archetypal shift. This deep cultural and social change process, where old forms of structure and support have lost their power and new archetypes are emerging, is not visible as part of daily life, yet the process has a subtle, important impact on how we manage in our uncertain times.

The Jungian perspectives in this section will recognize and articulate what is happening, offer ways to understand current social pressures and develop personal options to manage ongoing uncertainty, and show various ways to think about the important social and environmental issues confronting us.

The three essays in this section will go a long way toward helping with the development of an individual approach for living more comfortably with ongoing social and political uncertainty.

Donald Kalsched: *Democracy and Autocracy in the Individual and the Collective: Reflections on Psychological Factors at Play in Our Polarized World*

Sean Fitzpatrick: *Thorns in the Spirit: Sustained Engagement in Racial Justice*

Thomas Singer: *Psychological Responses to the Uncertainty Principle in the Individual and Group Psyche*

References

Jung, C.G., (1966). *CW, Vol. 7: Two Essays in Analytical Psychology.* Princeton, NJ: Princeton University Press. (Original work published 1953)

_____. (1989). *CW, Vol. 11: Psychology and Religion: West and East.* Princeton, NJ: Princeton University Press. (Original work published 1958)

Inner and Outer Democracy and the Threat of Authoritarianism: Reflections on Psychological Factors at Play in our Polarized World

Donald Kalsched, Ph.D.

Introduction

I am a Jungian psycho-analyst in private practice for more than 50 years, and also a proud citizen of the United States, having lived through almost 8 decades of its history from 1943 to the present. These two identities have always existed comfortably inside myself—not only because I love my profession on the one hand and my country on the other, but because the *inner democracy of the psyche* with which I work every day informs and deepens my understanding of and appreciation for American democracy in manifold ways. Over the years I have come to appreciate that both healthy individual psyche and healthy community psyche require free, open, and honest communication among all the diverse—sometimes oppositional—parts of the whole. Authoritarian factors, operating out of fear in both the inner and outer psychological landscapes—conspire against such integration, and make demo-cracy difficult.

I have been an enthusiastic student of American democracy and the American experiment in general—ever since I began to learn about the history of our country in a 9th grade history class. The book that thrilled my young adolescent soul at the time was *Rebels and Redcoats: The American Revolution Through the Eyes of Those who Fought and Lived It* (Scheer & Rankin, 1957). The book is advertised by the publisher as a record of "the first great war of principle." And the reader soon discovers what that principle is, namely—the equality of all citizens as carriers of God-given rights. In the immortal language of the Declaration of Independence, "We hold these truths to be self-evident, that all men are created equal and are endowed by their creator with certain unalienable rights...." (United States, 1776).

As a 14-year-old, I had no idea what a radical idea this was—that all men and women on this earth are equal because they are all created in the image of God, i.e., we are equal because we contain something sacred. Nor did I understand at that time how the exclusion of one half of the population (women) or 4 million enslaved (Black people) or millions of Native Americans, severely compromised and undermined the core principle of democracy being articulated and fought for in our War of Independence.

It would take another 30 years, and the discovery of C.G. Jung to help me understand the principle at the core of the American experiment. Jung's psychology helped renew and consolidate my love for democracy and my appreciation for what he called the *democracy of the psyche*. For Jung, outer democracy was the healthiest political polity in the world because it was the only political structure to expect and encourage an open conflict among the opposites and the inclusion of all opposing factions in one national deliberative body. In the same way, inner democracy, he felt, actualizes a healthy psyche by encouraging all the parts of the self, especially conflicting feelings, to suffer through an integration in the service of greater wholeness: *e pluribus unum*.

In both cases, Jung believed, democracy—in its inclusiveness, diversity, and insistence on the suffering of honest conflict—is an organ of consciousness-generation. The outstanding question, left unanswered by Jung, is *do we want to become conscious or not?* As I have discovered, there are very powerful forces in the psyche and world that can become organized to prevent us from becoming conscious. We call these anti-consciousness factors, dissociative defenses, and they exist in all of us as a barrier to the diversity and inclusiveness on which democracy depends.

Terry Tempest Williams (2004, p. 143) once said that "the human heart is the first home of democracy." And while I think this may be true in one sense—certainly the human heart is the place within us where we wrestle with our most painful emotional conflicts, and where the human soul is fashioned through conscious suffering—nevertheless, I doubt whether the human heart is the first home of democracy. We know it takes a long time and much psychological work to develop what Bruno Bettleheim (1971) called an "informed heart," where a democratic struggle with our inner conflicts becomes possible. Democracy is an achievement, not a given. And the psychological work necessary in its creation is a true *opus contra naturam*. The human heart is not naturally and irresistibly drawn to democracy. On the contrary, the human heart is often the source of authoritarianism, fascism, and extremism of all kinds. The human heart can be broken by warring opposites and archetypal antinomies, in which case democracy becomes a distant dream.

Currently in the United States, democracy is under assault. We live in a dark and polarizing time where partisan extremes of every stripe are shouting at one another. Social media algorithms radicalize people, feeding them content that provokes polarized emotional reactions. People are arming themselves with guns and buying ammunition at a rate never before seen in our history, and militias are proliferating. Death threats on social media are sent regularly to election workers in certain states. Mass murders in our schools and synagogues are now frequent occurrences.

David Brooks (2020) described this polarization in a New York Times essay titled "Trump and the Politics of 'Mean-World.'" Mean-world thrives, says Brooks, on fear....

> and perpetuates itself by exaggerating fear.... Its rhetorical ploy is catastrophizing and its tone is apocalyptic. ... The larger threat is that we're caught in a polarization cascade. Mean world fanatics— on the left and the right—are playing a mutually beneficial game.... Trumpian chaos justifies and magnifies the woke mobs on the left. Woke mobs magnify and justify Trumpian authoritarianism on the right. The upshot is the obliteration of normal politics, the hollowing out of the center and the degradation of public morality. Under the cover of this souped-up, screw-or-be-screwed mentality, norms are eviscerated, truth is massacred, bigotry is justified and politics turns into a struggle to culturally obliterate the other side.

Why is this the case? Why is the center of our democracy— the principle of equality that our founders fought for—being hollowed out by paranoia, splitting, and a regression to polarization and extremism in our time? Why is William Butler Yeats' poetic lament 100 years ago so painfully descriptive a century later? The first stanza of Yeats' (1920) poem, *The Second Coming*, reads as follows:

> Turning and turning in the widening gyre
> The falcon cannot hear the falconer;
> Things fall apart; the centre cannot hold;
> Mere anarchy is loosed upon the world,
> The blood-dimmed tide is loosed, and everywhere
> The ceremony of innocence is drowned;
> The best lack all conviction, while the worst
> Are full of passionate intensity.

Yeats wrote this poem during the 1918-19 Spanish flu pandemic that killed millions of people. As he wrote it, his pregnant wife Georgie Hyde-Lees lay mortally ill with the virus, near death. Her chances of surviving were slim because the highest death rates of the pandemic were among pregnant women—around 70%. Fortunately, she did survive, and during her convalescence, Yeats wrote his famous poem. This was also just a year after the most violent, disillusioning war in history had begun. A war that was supposed to end all wars, but that simply set the stage for the most violent and destructive century in the history of humanity. So both world-wide violence and a terrifying illness were the oppressive realities swirling around Yeats as he sat down to write this poem. With Covid-19 having ravaged our modern world in the last several years, these are our realities also.

"Turning and turning in the widening gyre, the falcon cannot hear the falconer." What might this image mean as applied to our current situation? A gyre is a whorl or spiral; in this case, one in the sky made by the gliding motions of a falcon circling the falconer. In falconry, when the falconer releases his falcon, the bird ascends into the blue sky and begins to glide on fixed wings in wide circles or gyres, looking for game. When the falconer wants to end the hunt, he blows a whistle and the falcon hears it, ends his hunting, and returns to the falconer's outstretched, gloved hand. Yeats' image describes a bird, flying free, circling above and the falconer, fixed in a central location on the ground. And in between them a communication in sound carried on the wind that connects them in a relationship, an invisible tether that makes the enterprise a meaningful whole.

So who's the falcon and who's the falconer? The way I'd like to think about this image is that we the people are the falcon. In a functioning democracy, we are tethered to a grounded spiritual reality both in ourselves and in our nation. This grounded spiritual reality is that principle referenced by the writers of *Rebels and Redcoats* and at the core of the American experiment, that "all men are created equal, and endowed by their creator with certain unalienable rights." This (and the institutions that serve as vehicles for its implementation) is what makes our diversity and inclusivity possible. Without this principle holding us together, the centrifugal forces, or vehement primitive emotions, of the gyre will pull us apart into extremes, hollowing out the center and potentially destroying the whole enterprise in a regression to authoritarianism.

Authoritarians impose a center from above and it is always identical with the tyrannical personality of the leader who gets his power through domination. Democrats allow a center to develop from the bottom up so to speak, i.e., through a process involving the diversity of the people expressing themselves freely through a regular voting process.

How might we help restore the missing center of our democracy? How might the primitive emotional forces of the gyre be mitigated? If our American experiment is, as Abraham Lincoln said in his 1862 message to Congress, the "last best hope of earth," this is no small question! In addressing it, we will need to understand the psychological conditions under which democracy is possible—and the psychological factors that weaken or strengthen that invisible tether that holds falcon and falconer together—both for the individual and the group. In approaching these inner psychological factors, we will find illuminating insights from C.G. Jung, who spoke extensively and eloquently about both inner and outer democracy and their requirements.

Authoritarian Threats to Democracy in America

Many commentators on our political scene, especially since 2016 and the election of Donald Trump, have written eloquently about the threat posed by fascism and authoritarianism to our American democracy. Three are especially noteworthy: Ann Applebaum's *Twilight of Democracy: The Seductive Lure of Authoritarianism* (2020); Steven Levitsky and Daniel Ziblatt's *How Democracies Die* (2018), and finally Astra Taylor's *Democracy May*

Not Exist, But We'll Miss It When It's Gone (2019). All three give important insights into how various social, economic, and political factors in our modern world have eroded the basic foundations of equality and inclusion that are a part of what democracy really means: Power, *kratos, demos*, to the people.

All these writers highlight the existential insecurity of our time and the various cultural threats that contribute to it: the threat of immigrants to our national borders; the painful realities of climate change, leading to starvation and displacement of increasing segments of the world's population; increasing inequality of rich and poor around the world; rising U.S. gun-violence in American culture, and finally, increasing awareness of racism, sexism and rising abuses of power all over the world.

While these writers focus on the economic, social, and political factors behind the new authoritarian threats to democracy, there is also a well-known tradition in Journalism that explores underlying psychological factors of authoritarianism. Perhaps best known is Theodore Adorno's 1950 book *The Authoritarian Personality*. Profoundly shaken by the rise of fascism in Nazi Germany, Adorno, Frankel-Brunswick and their collaborators were at pains to discover whether something like fascism could ever reemerge in the culture and under what conditions. And they wanted to understand how apparently "normal" individuals could get drawn into radical-right authoritarian movements. So they tried to uncover personality traits that made people susceptible to fascist propaganda. Their original Fascism-scale included 77 questions to test for a person's tendency to rely upon outside authority— of parents, teachers, institutional representatives—and they discovered that the relationships children had with such authorities over their lifetime had a profound effect on their susceptibility to authoritarianism.

When the original 1000-page study first came out it rocked the academic world. But it soon fell out of favor during the post-war economic boom when democratic optimism ran high. The election of Donald Trump changed all that and the book has been reissued (Adorno, 2019) on its 70th anniversary with a new introduction by Peter E. Gordon, professor of history at Harvard University, who notes how timely it is and emphasizes how "extraordinarily fragile democracy is as a political form." While the original study demonstrated high authoritarianism on both the left and the right, with a healthy middle ground, new research indicates an emotionally driven partisan divide with the highest measures of authoritarianism on the political right and a hollowed-out middle ground. One researcher (Macwilliams, 2016) discovered that authoritarianism, as measured by the F-scale, was the most significant variable in differentiating Trump-supporters from those supporting other candidates in the field.

A second effort to explore the psychological factors was Richard Hofstadter's (1964) *The Paranoid Style in American Politics*. Hofstadter notes that American politics has often been an arena for angry minds, angry outrage often gathering around extreme right-wing causes but not only on the right. "I call it the paranoid style," says Hofstadter, "simply because no other word adequately evokes the sense of heated exaggeration, suspiciousness, and conspiratorial fantasy that I have in mind" (1964, p. 3).

Hofstadter discovered that the paranoid style is not confined to our own country and time; it is an international phenomenon. This fact was illuminated for him by British historian Norman Cohn (1957) whose acclaimed and distinguished work, *The Pursuit of the Millennium*, described a "persistent psychic complex" made up of certain preoccupations and fantasies:

> [T]he megalomaniac view of oneself (and one's race or class) as the Elect, wholly good (innocent), abominably persecuted, yet assured of ultimate triumph; the attribution of gigantic and demonic powers to the adversary; the urge to purify the world through the annihilation of some category of human beings imagined as agents of corruption

and incarnations of evil; the refusal to accept the ineluctable limitations and imperfections of human existence, such as transience, dissention, conflict, fallibility whether intellectual or moral; the obsession with [conspiratorial] prophecies . . . systematized misinterpretations, always gross and often grotesque" (Cohn, pp 309-310)

Cohn's work emboldened Hofstadter to suggest that the tendency to see the world in this way "may be a persistent psychic phenomenon, more or less constantly affecting a modest minority of the population," and that "certain historical catastrophes or frustrations (class conflicts for example) may be conducive to the release of such psychic energies, and to situations in which they can more readily be built into mass movements or political parties." Hofstadter concludes:

….the paranoid disposition is mobilized into action chiefly by social conflicts that involve ultimate schemes of values and that bring fundamental fears and hatreds, rather than negotiable interests into political action. Catastrophe or the fear of catastrophe is most likely to elicit the syndrome of paranoid rhetoric. (1964, p. 39)

The current pandemic of Covid-19, having killed well over one million Americans is clearly a major factor in exacerbating our national fear and encouraging the "paranoid disposition."

Fear and Defenses Against Fear

The role of fear in setting the groundwork for the mobilization of the paranoid disposition is emphasized by Adorno, Hofstadter, and Cohn. Fear leads to anxiety and paranoid insecurity which leads to anger at the source of the fear, which leads to counter-violence, which creates more fear which leads to more violence, in what we might think of as a Fear-Anger Cycle. This has been confirmed by many investigators. The quickest way to end fear and the suffering of anxiety is to get angry at whomever is making you feel afraid. This is the most common form taken by those psychological defenses we call dissociation. Commenting on the extremists in the South during the 1930s, W.E.B. Du Bois once said:

> Back of the writhing, yelling, cruel-eyed demons who break, destroy, maim and lynch and burn at the stake, is a knot, large or small, of normal human beings and these human beings at heart are desperately afraid of something. Of what? Of many things, but usually of losing their jobs, being declassed, degraded, or actually disgraced; of losing their hopes, their savings, their plans for their children; of actual pangs of hunger, of dirt, of crime. (1935 p. 677)

Dubois makes a clear link between fear, the threat of humiliation, and the hate that spills over into societal chaos, creating more fear and more violence. How the leaders of a nation handle this fear and outrage is a distinguishing feature of democracy vs. authoritarianism. It was Franklin Roosevelt who famously said, as the US was going to war with two nations at once, "we have nothing to fear but fear itself" (1933). And this was the message the American people needed to hear from their President. Today, many politicians and media moguls in the country stoke the coals of fear and fan the flames of outrage in an effort to release the extreme emotions that fuel dark apocalyptic narratives and conspiracy theories, justifying hatred and creating more fear. All this is aided and abetted by social media, AI, and the echo-chambers of chat rooms.

From 2016 and 2020, instead of a commander in chief, we had a divider in chief as our President. Instead of holding the opposites and helping to promote a center where we might start to explore our differences, Trump's extremism helped to discharge emotion, creating grievances and leading to the "mean world" cycle that David Brooks noted above. The result was an increasingly hollowed-out center in our democracy where the core principle on which the country was founded, the moral center of equality and diversity enshrined in our Declaration of Independence, was largely forgotten.

Psychological Considerations

One of the reasons that the current conflict between democracy and authoritarianism in America and the world interests me, is because there's so much primitive psychology in it! By "primitive psychology" I mean a regression to what Jung described as the deep mythological, archetypal stratum of the collective unconscious that underlies the personal layer of ego functioning occupying the "higher" cortical centers in the triune brain. Readers of this essay will recognize that one of Jung's major contributions to our understanding of the human psyche was to point out that as it receded into the unconscious depths, it took on more and more religious dimensions, or mythological features. These features, Jung proposed, derived from archaic and typical (archetypal) powers that populated the deepest and most primitive stratum of the psyche, the collective unconscious.

The hollowed-out center in our democracy creates a vacuum, and as Jung made clear, this vacuum will always be filled from below, i.e., from the more primitive totalistic powers of the archaic psyche. All archetypes are binary. Hence the powers in this collective layer contain primordial opposites—polarized, binary extremes—the antinomies of the archetypal psyche—us vs. them, good vs. evil, justice vs. injustice, the purity of innocence vs. the corruption of sin. These fundamental thought-forms get their energy from extreme and vehement emotions and these emotions are also binary, for example love vs. hate, hope vs. despair, etc.

For Jung, such regression to the primitive level of mythology was something he found in his psychotic patients, but also in the disturbing manias and possessions that followed the

Nazi phenomena in Europe, where fear had spread through the population:

> …until 1933 only lunatics would have been found in possession of living fragments of mythology. After this date the world of heroes and monsters spread like a devastating fire over whole nations, proving that the strange world of myth had suffered no loss of vitality during the centuries of reason and enlightenment. (Jung, 1959, para. 67)

Jung held Christianity responsible for this regression with its tendencies to split good and evil and the way the Church had commodified and corrupted the true (democratic) message of Christ by turning the Church into an authoritarian institution designed mostly to protect the power of the priesthood.

> The end result is a true antimimon pneuma, a false spirit of arrogance, hysteria, woolly-mindedness, criminal amorality, and doctrinaire fanaticism, a purveyor of shoddy spiritual goods, spurious art, philosophical stutterings, and Utopian humbug, fit only to be fed wholesale to the mass man of today. That is what the post-Christian spirit looks like. (Jung, 1959, para 67)

It is hard not to recognize ourselves in this mirror that Jung holds up. The question is how to understand it psychologically and how to imagine ways of restoring the lost center in ourselves and in our country where democracy is being hollowed out almost daily by the extremes that thrive in the paranoid style of political discourse swirling around us.

My Own Contributions: The Self-Care System

For the last several decades, I have been studying the inner world of a special population of patients in whom fear and the threat of humiliation are prominent features, patients who have suffered severe early childhood trauma. These patients have not had the luxury of living in emotionally supportive environments where their primitive emotions (including fear) could be slowly transformed into manageable feelings they could talk about and use in the course of everyday living. Instead, their vehement emotions—including their existentially threatening childhood vulnerability and dependency—had to be regulated and controlled by a system of primitive defenses that we call dissociation. Needless to say, this regulation and control is authoritarian in nature. Hence, the inner world of the traumatized psyche, hollowed out by fear, is dominated by an authoritarian system.

I call this system of defensive structures and emotional dynamics the Self-Care System, hereafter abbreviated SCS. The system consists of an interlocking set of self and object-representations—often appearing in primitive archetypal form, together with the powerful polarizing emotions that belong to such archetypal powers. The major figures in this three-part system are a vulnerable inner child on the one hand, and its protective or persecutory guardians (Kalsched, 1996, 2013) on the other. These inner personifications often appear in dreams when early trauma has been triggered by something in the patient's life or in the therapy relationship. The major parts of this system are as follows:

1. Violence: The Persecutor

Because the SCS is a dissociative system, and because the splitting involved in dissociation requires violent energy, the major player in the SCS is primitive aggression and violence. This violence is directed at perceived outer threats, but mostly at inner parts of the psyche that threaten the host personality with the impossible pain of a traumatic past. The violence in the system involves what Wilfred Bion (1959) called "attacks on linking." Such attacks constitute an effort on the part of dissociative defenses to kill the connections among the components of whole experience.

While intended to regulate and control how much of the child's traumatic experience is allowed to become conscious in the ego, the violent inner system represents an authoritarian dominance of the weaker (i.e., more vulnerable) parts of the personality and therefore an attack on the *democracy of the psyche.*

A persecutory and violent inner figure in the SCS is the first daimonic personification I discovered in my work with the victims of early trauma. In dreams I have analyzed over the years, this violent entity has cut the dreamer's head off with an axe, brutally raped the dreamer, petrified the dreamers pet animals, buried a child alive, seduced the patient into performing sado-masochistic sexual favors, trapped the dream ego in a concentration camp, tortured the patient by breaking his knees in three places, shot a beautiful woman in the face with a shotgun, and performed a variety of other destructive acts the purpose of which seem to be nothing less than driving the patient's terrified dream-ego into a state of horror, anxiety, and despair.

And yet—and here is an irony of psychological life that may help us understand the outer violence in our world today—this inner terrorist is actually a lesser evil than the black hole of madness at the center of the traumatized psyche. The inner terrorist gives archetypal anxiety a face. It turns it into fear and keeps the fragmentation-prone ego in being, ever vigilant, driven to survive in a real or imagined hostile environment in the face of which it can mobilize heroic defenses. Simone Weil (1987) once said:

The true God transforms violence into suffering.

The false God transforms suffering into violence. (p. 65)

To turn violence into suffering requires a capacity for conscious feeling and, because feelings are often complicated, this means holding conflict inwardly without expelling one side of it through dissociation. The psychoanalytic term for this is affect-tolerance—the ability to tolerate and witness intense emotions and especially conflicting emotions such as negative and positive feelings--love and hate, joy and sorrow, excitement and shame—

without identifying with one side and dissociating the other.

In personal development this requires a loving relational container for the child, within which strong opposing affects can be held and entertained in the child's relation to a parent. The earliest childhood affects come in the form of titanic eruptions—880 volts direct from the brain stem. These archetypal storms of emotion must be slowly transformed into feelings, from 880 to 440 to 220, and eventually to 110 where the energy can be utilized for adaptation and true-self living. This happens in any relational container where the overpowering affects are co-regulated in the infant/mother dyad. The result is the development of an ego where feelings find words and a relational container, leading to a central ego strong enough to hold the center. It leads to a capacity for conflict and a democracy of the psyche where all feeling-parts can be entertained. Where such holding and witnessing are missing in a child's life, the optimal co-regulation of affects gives way to regulation by defenses. These inevitably lead to dissociation, a hollowing out of the center, and to a takeover by the centrifugal emotional forces of violence, extremism, and authoritarianism.

2. Illusion: The Protector

Alongside the persecutory inner object just described, a second major power often appears in the SCS and this figure represents a less violent, protective form of dissociation. This figure helps in the encapsulation and numbing of psychic pain. Owing to its archetypal origins, it can cast spells or put the ego in a trance. Emily Dickinson (1961) describes the inner activities of this guardian figure in her famous poem:

> There is a pain so utter
> That it swallows substance up
> Then covers the Abyss with Trance—
> So Memory can step
> Around – across – upon it
> As one within a Swoon –

Goes safely – where an open eye
Would drop him – Bone by bone.

Trauma is about pain so "utter" that it swallows up normal developmental processes, leaving an "abyss," or "basic fault" (Balint 1979, 18) between self and world outwardly and between the ego and the unconscious inwardly. Fortunately, the story doesn't end with this cleavage because the human psyche has enormous self-curative powers. It "covers the abyss with trance" so that life can go on.

The benign protective powers of the SCS can throw an invisibility cloak over a traumatic memory and help the trauma survivor simply "forget" what happened or create an alternative reality for the survivor to live in. This power specializes in altered states such as psychic numbing, states of oblivion, forgetting, spacing out. While the Persecutor represents violence, the Protector specializes in illusions. Both help the trauma survivor to dissociate from an impossibly painful and terrifying reality. The whole system is a defense against fear and yet exacerbates fear as it operates. Hence, the traumatized psyche is self-traumatizing.

Our current outer collective situation in America contains many examples of how the activities of the inner Protector/Persecutor bleeds through into a fear-ridden culture. "Fake news!" says the Protector to the host personality. "It never happened! The News media is conspiring to mislead you. It's all a lie! You didn't lose the election! It's been stolen from you." Or when more than 20 children were murdered in their Sandy Hook elementary school by a teenage boy, the inner Protector (in this case personified and channeled by the delusional Alex Jones) says, "It's all a hoax. It's a false flag operation, actors pretending to die, conspiring to mislead and alarm the public to help the anti-gun lobby. It never happened!" In South Dakota during the height of the Covid Pandemic (Doering, 2020), dying patients on ventilators were angrily channeling their inner persecutory voices, shouting at their nurses that they had been misled by a conspiracy of the government, vehemently denying the reality of their own sickness while angrily claiming they were innocent victims of a disinformation campaign by the government. And they could find plenty of "evidence" for their illusions on social media.

Such is the way that archetypal defensive processes, designed to protect us from trauma we can't bear, lead us into the oblivion of Mean-World. Troubled citizens in our nation who are confused by all the suffering and moral complexity of modern life, may long for rescue by such a protective guardian angel. Unconsciously they search for someone upon whom to project this powerful psychological factor. And Donald Trump, with his blonde hair, Midas-like wealth, and golden tower in the sky makes an easy target for such archetypal projections.

3. Vulnerability and Innocence: The Child

Perhaps the most important symbolic figure in the SCS is an inner image of the survivor's inner childhood self. I have come to think of this child in two ways. First as the wounded empirical child of the patient's outer life, carrying the historical injuries of traumatic abuse or neglect in his/her small body. On the other hand, this child represents the trauma-survivor's innocence—the pre-traumatic core of the personality, carrying the divine spark of vitality and the instinct for life—now menaced by the great powers of Violence and Illusion. Both these powers and the system they supervise, are dedicated to the proposition that this dual child (both wounded and innocent) must never be violated by reality again.

Because innocence is an archetype, it can be recruited as a part of a dissociative defense and this frequently happens. Innocence is often placed in the service of violence and illusion. Trauma survivors know they are not innocent and often feel overcome by deep feelings of badness, shame, and sin. Nonetheless, their innocence remains a sustaining implicit assumption of the defense-organization and frequently is exploited by the inner forces of Violence and Illusion to create grievances that contribute to the host personality's sense of being unfairly victimized by others, giving them further reasons to be angry at the world. Christopher Bollas (1995) describes such "malignant innocents" who insist on the absolute innocence of the self throughout life (vs. the generative innocence of origins), and who participate in what he calls the "contemporary festival of victimology" (p. 201). Such people can't bear to take responsibility for their own destructiveness and must project it onto objects that are beneath contempt. The unholy defensive alliance between the innocent child in the SCS and the caretaking guardians of Violence and Illusion leads to the infamous tyrannical infantilism typical of the Borderline Personality Disorder sometimes referred to as the 'King-Baby' or 'Queen-Baby' syndrome.

I have frequently witnessed the exploitation of the patient's generative innocence in the service of illusions provided by the archetypal Protector in the SCS. Such a combination makes for a frequently sentimentalized and melodramatic self-narrative built around a victim/perpetrator dynamic. This narrative justifies all sorts of inflated entitlements and unrealistic expectations from others. In our national collective scene, this kind of malignant innocence can be found on the radical right in its convictions about American goodness and exceptionalism vs. what Donald Trump (2018) called "shithole countries." The same mentality would ban textbooks that teach about sexuality or Critical Race Theory in our schools. On the radical left, we often find an unholy alliance between the life-sustaining illusions of the archetypal Protector in the SCS and the personality's innocence in the cancel culture that exists on some college campuses and online. In these situations, discomfort is often confused with abuse and people lose their jobs for discussing controversial subjects or using the wrong word. Safe zones are now required on some campuses, lest the allegedly fragile psyches of students be traumatized. This is another form of malignant innocence paired with violent exclusion.

Summary

To summarize, I have discovered in my work with a certain group of trauma-surviving patients, an authoritarian regime in the inner world of the psyche. This regime lives in the unconscious of everyone, but is especially activated and inflamed in the inner worlds of people who have suffered severe early childhood trauma— or, more generally, at times of acute crisis and existential threat to the collective psyche, such as we are going through in the post-pandemic America. Because trauma and its dissociative defenses are universal, the authoritarian system is universally present underneath our civilized selves and is triggered by vulnerable, painful, or fearful feelings. We are in a continual battle with these centrifugal forces. These vehement emotions are part of us, and need representation in a democracy of the psyche, just like they need representation in true democratic political systems in the outer world.

Practicing Democracy: Nazis at the Swimming Pool

Practicing democracy is a daily affair for most of us. When my wife and I lived in Santa Fe, New Mexico I frequently went to our local athletic club which had an Olympic-sized swimming pool with three lanes. Before Covid-19, I would show up there, wait for a lane, swim, take a shower and go home. After the Pandemic started, however, everyone had to call for an appointment and show up at the appointed time and swim in the appointed lane. The rules stated that you did not go into the pool area until the time of your appointment.

On this particular morning I arrived at 5 minutes to 9 a.m. Waiting at the outer door was a young woman swimmer who I knew. Looking through the door at the empty pool I asked her if she wanted to join me and go in. "You can try," she said, "but the Gestapo will stop you." Looking through the door I saw a staff member Barbara, who I knew was a stickler for rules, but with whom I'd always gotten along just fine. By now it was 3 minutes to 9 so I said, "well, I can't imagine she'll make a fuss over 3 minutes." So I opened the door and started towards the check-in desk.

Whereupon Barbara erupted from behind the desk and

walked aggressively toward me with both hands extended, "NO NO NO—it's not time yet—you don't belong here!—back out! back out! back out!" I did. "See what I mean?" said the young swimmer who had waited outside. By this time I was fuming. This was ridiculous! Two minutes! And besides, the pool was empty! Yet properly chastised and put in my place, I waited until 5 minutes after 9 when Barbara finally came out. "OK," she said, "you can go in now…just don't forget, there are rules!" I couldn't contain myself any longer and muttered something underneath my breath. Barbara stormed off. I stormed in, shaking my head and fuming. Violence and its ever-faithful companion innocence had just taken over.

My swim that morning was unusually vigorous, steam coming off the water one lap after another. My eruption of anger had immediately catapulted me into a defense. I now hated Barbara and began playing over in my mind various nasty dialogues with her: such as "Hey Barbara, you missed your calling. You should have been a traffic cop—or maybe a prison guard—you like rules so much, what're you doing here?" Then another lap. "You would have made a great soldier in the Germany during the Second World War, Barbara!" Another lap. I imagined lodging a complaint about her with the management. I was a paying member of this club like everybody else—who was she to treat me like this?

Then as I got dressed I reflected on this interchange and I started to feel shame about myself. "What are you DOING?" I asked myself. I realized that I had skipped right over the most important feeling I had experienced that morning and that was the feeling of shame at being made "bad." Feeling innocent, I went right to my anger and my anger made her bad, so I got rid of my own inferior feelings and put them on her. She was a thoughtless bitch. I was an innocent customer. End of story. No hurt to deal with, just righteous anger and resentment. I now felt badly about our interchange and sorry that I had snapped at her.

So on the way out I stopped and talked with her. I apologized for all the fire in my belly earlier and said that I was triggered by her rules. She nodded. I said I was sure her job of always enforcing the rules wasn't an easy one especially with Covid-19 threatening everyone, and that I had probably made her job more difficult that morning. "You have NO IDEA!" she replied. And then she unloaded on me about how many people seemed to resent the rules and how entitled they were and how she had always tried to be nice about it but that sometimes she just reached the end of her rope, like with me that morning. We commiserated about our mutual tendencies to reach the end of our ropes. And we parted friends. In the weeks that followed I actually looked forward to seeing Barbara. We had created something together that went deeper than our previously superficial nice acquaintance. A tiny act of democracy after an authoritarian eruption on a sunny morning in Santa Fe.

Jung on Democracy vs. Authoritarianism

Jung was a champion of inner and outer Democracy because he saw both as arenas where greater consciousness could be generated. Jung frequently spoke about our binary tendencies under the topic of the opposites and he was clear that without a struggle between opposing feelings in the psyche, and between opposing powers in the world, you don't become conscious. For Jung, to struggle with the opposites was to struggle with the most primitive archetypal affects and powers: powers of love and hate that lay at the evolutionary beginning of the human psyche as well as at the evolutionary beginnings of human civilization. To dis-identify from these archetypal powers was to humanize them, and this meant sacrifice of our inflated identification with them and a descent into our full and flawed humanity. Democracy facilitates this descent. Autocracy resists it.

When Norman Cohn described the Paranoid Style as "the refusal to accept the ineluctable limitations and imperfections of human existence, such as transience, dissention, conflict, fallibility whether intellectual or moral" he was describing this refusal to embrace the inner conflict that keeps democracy centered in the all-too-human realities (limitations) of human existence. This is our common reality as flawed and mortal people, the *"demos"* in democracy.

Power from and to the people is a relatively new phenomenon on the face of the earth. When Abraham Lincoln (1862) spoke at Gettysburg about the possibility that "government of the people, by the people, and for the people" might perish from the earth, he was highlighting just how fragile our experiment in democracy was.

It would be fair to say that in the beginning of our history as a species, the people had no power in the way society was organized. In fact, at the dawn of civilization there were no democracies. There were small bands or tribes of people led by a chief patriarch, later a King or Queen. This chief was not elected and he was elevated to quasi-divine status with virtually unlimited power. There was no voting and few individual liberties. Usually the chief rose to power because of special capacities: physical strength in battle, charisma, intelligence, or, if he was a medicine man or shaman, uncanny spiritual powers connected to the collective unconscious. Because of these powers, the leader was understood to have a special relationship to the divine. He had a vertical connection to the divine and ruled from the center of the community. Individual members of the tribe had their relationship to a supportive spiritual reality through the great individual who was their leader. Erich Neumann articulates these dynamics around what he calls the "great individual."

Every good for the individual in this pre-democratic system depended on a subordinate relationship to the monarch and, through him, to the divine authority. That is what we would call an authoritarian system. It's like a beehive where everything is organized around the central authority, the Queen. Individual workers have no autonomy. They are simply units in a collective dynamism with the Queen as center. Eventually, at least in the West, the monarchy lost some of its power, became secularized, and the special connection to the divine came to be vested in the Church and the authority of the Priesthood. That was the beginning of the separation of church and state, which is another hallmark of healthy democracies. There are no theocracies in the democratic West. In the Catholic system, the head of the Church was the Pope who had the direct connection to the divine; secular authority was required to retain a special relationship with the Pope in order to retain his power.

Slowly, societies grew more complex. Additional centers of power and authority developed (business and commerce were the first) and these new centers of power began to vie for power with the monarchy and demand representation in the court of the King or Queen. Slowly more representative polities evolved, and the people began to get some form of representation through representatives that served in the King or Queen's court or parliament. Eventually there were revolts against the monarch's power altogether, such as in the American Revolution which established a democratic republic.

Jung was unique in understanding that democracy was a developmental achievement over early authoritarian systems, inwardly and outwardly. In all his writings Jung sees both democracy and individuality as salutary developments in the gradual evolution of the psyche away from collectivism, or the group mind, and toward interiority. He saw this evolution happening slowly, over eons of time, and one of its most dramatic steps, he felt was the Protestant Reformation. Here's Jung (1964, para. 326):

> The Reformation shattered the authority of the church as a teacher and thereafter the authoritarian principle itself began to crumble away. Recall that the Protestant Reformation rebelled against the idea that individual people were only sacred to God through the "Church and the Priesthood." Protesting this idea, the Reformers claimed there was an individual vertical relationship between the soul of

each person and the divine. This broke the authority of the Priesthood and the Papacy as necessary mediators to the divine, and left each individual to be saved by Faith, and through the Word of the Bible which was now suddenly available to all literate people. The inevitable consequence was an increase in the importance of the individual, which found expression in the modern ideals of humanity, social welfare, Democracy, and equality.

So Jung was a champion of dynamic political forms, institutions, and structures that made the expression of opposites possible. Such institutions, he said, provided containers within which opposing emotions can be spoken and explored. Commenting on his own country's democracy, Jung (1964, para 455) once said:

> In Switzerland we have built up the "perfect democracy" where our warlike instincts expend themselves in the form of domestic quarrels called "political life." We fight each other within the limits of the law and the constitution and we are inclined to think of democracy as a chronic state of mitigated civil war. We are far from being at peace with ourselves; on the contrary, we hate and fight each other because we have succeeded in introverting war.

And then Jung (1964, para. 456) describes the inner psychological corollary of outer democracy, a democracy of the psyche in which we have an ego strong enough to hold and witness conflict:

> We psychologists have learned through long and painful experience that you deprive a man of his best resource when you help him to get rid of his complexes [with their violent affects]. You can only help him to become sufficiently aware of them and to start a conscious conflict within himself. In this

way, the complex becomes a focus of life….It is surely better to know that your worst enemy is right there in your own heart. Man's warlike instincts are ineradicable….True democracy is a highly psychological institution which takes account of human nature as it is and makes allowances for the necessity of [inner] conflict….

Conflict means holding conflicted feelings. Love and hate for example. Melanie Klein (1952) made the capacity to love and hate the same person the major psychological accomplishment of childhood. She called it the "depressive position," and saw it as an immense step beyond the "paranoid/persecutory" position where good and evil were dissociated. This developmental milestone involves a kind of democracy of the heart. It takes courage to hold opposing feelings and to realize as Jung says that "your worst enemy is right there in your own heart."

In a true democracy, people can admit that they were wrong… they can admit that they are not innocent. They can admit they lost an election. On the other hand, the immature and insecure ego, puffed up with archetypal energies, cannot bear to take responsibility for its own shadow qualities and must eject anything "bad" or "inferior" onto an outer object which is then scapegoated or suppressed—and rigidly controlled, eliminated or in our modern culture-wars, canceled. People with this kind of ego are "authoritarian personalities" and governments based on these assumptions are "authoritarian states."

According to Jung, "a democracy of the psyche requires that a man realize that the conflict is in himself, that the discord and tribulation are his riches, which should not be squandered by attacking others" (Jung, 1955, para. 511).

If the projected conflict is to be healed, it must return into the psyche of the individual, where it had its unconscious beginnings. He must celebrate a Last Supper with himself, and eat his own flesh and drink

his own blood; which means that he must recognize
and accept the other in himself. (Jung, 1955, para. 512)

Recognizing and accepting the other in ourselves is an act of psychological courage and maturity. It means we are not identified with an idealized image of ourselves. We are not pure. We are not innocent victims at war with evil perpetrators. We are not innocent progressive Democrats at war with evil Republicans. We can see the value in the positions of the enemy party and we can subject our values to a larger process of adjudication called a majority vote. We are willing to lose and we are not made less by losing. For these and other reasons, a democracy of the psyche leads to psychological health in a person.

So inner and outer democracies, through the inner conflict they encourage, are always breaking down fundamentalistic, totalistic, and absolutist categories into relativistic, contingent and human ones—always transforming 880 volts of affect into usable feelings. Democracies, in this sense are to the collective polity what healthy families are for bringing up civilized human children. They are transformational containers. They are projection-eating machines. They take in evil, digest it, and give it back—first as hate—and finally as civil disagreement. They mitigate the polarizing centrifugal forces of our time and hold the center.

Final Reflections on the Center: Churning of the Sea

In the great Indian epic, the *Mahabharata* from the 4th century BC, there's a creation story about how the great light and dark forces of the universe joined forces to "churn the milk ocean" in order to create order and civilization (cosmos) out of chaos (Moon, 1991, p. 34). Uprooting a huge mountain as the central churning stick (axis mundi) and attaching it to the back of a great tortoise, the Gods on one side and the Demons on the other, pulled back and forth on either end of a huge serpent, Vasuki, wrapped around the axis. On the top of the turning pillar sits the God Vishnu. From the back and forth movement of their struggle, the great axis turned and churned the milk ocean like a giant butter churn. Slowly, various elixirs arose out of the milk: the white horse of the sun, the great elephant Airavata, a magic cow, and finally the elixir of immortality itself, which the Gods kept for themselves, establishing their sovereignty.

The image gives us a wonderful metaphor of what it takes to create and maintain a relationship between the light and dark forces of the psyche, and hence, a center. In the image, the archetypal extremes in the universe (Gods and Demons) are engaged in an *agon*, a great contained struggle that eventually produces benefits for mankind. Jung once said that life without binary opposites would be boring. "Opposites are not to be understood as mistakes but as the origin of life" he said (McGuire, 1990). In our image, the struggle between the opposites produces the life-giving boons of civilized living. But there's a proviso to Jung's statement. In order to energize life's vitality, the opposites must be brought together in something other than a complete clash, something like a rope pulling contest between the Gods and Demons. This is what democracy does. It makes a place for the meeting of opposites and ultimately for a *coniunctio oppositorum*.

Our recent mid-term election in the United States was a classic example. Despite catastrophic fears and predictions by the press, the centrifugal forces of polarization pulling in opposite directions, resulted in an effective election. The center held and our society was re-vitalized.

In the psychotherapy process, this is equivalent to the struggle to convert a dissociative psychology into a conflict psychology....., to get the light and dark forces—the loving and hating feelings—in the patient's inner world talking to each other. When these archetypal forces are related to and allowed a human voice, they start to transform. They "slough off their mythological envelope" as Jung would say (1960, para. 384) and start to become human. This is a sacrifice (to make sacred) that slowly transforms violence into suffering. The elixir of democracy begins to precipitate out of the churning. Archetypal aggression becomes effective ego agency. Archetypal love becomes more related, and less possessive of the beloved.

In our image, the central pillar, the *axis mundi*, has a God sitting on top of it, Vishnu. I think this is significant. It points to the something more that is created when the opposites are brought together on a level playing field. A third is created and Jung felt that this intermediate reality portended something transcendent. He called it the transcendent function. I think the American experiment in democracy, and all others in the world, contain this transcendent something more.

The Transcendent Third in American Democracy

Over history, the men and women who have been able to hold the tension among factions in our society without vilifying one side or the other, "with malice toward none, with charity for all," as Abraham Lincoln said in his Second Inaugural, are the great peacemakers of our world. They have the courage to live in conflict, thereby holding the center, and for that reason they are universally venerated. We carve their visages into stones, like Mount Rushmore. They actualize in the suffering body of an individual human being what Jung meant by the central archetype of the Self—the *coniunctio oppositorum*, the holding of the opposites—and through that holding, the creation of something ineffable that we all recognize as meaningful and good.

For extremists, integration is the worst imaginable thing. The dangerous other gets too close to the center and anyone who stands for a dynamic peace among the opposites threatens the fragile self-esteem of the authoritarian personality and must be eliminated. Witness the murder of Abraham Lincoln, Anwar Sadat, Martin Luther King Jr., Yizhak Rabin—all killed by extremists who could not bear to allow the diversity of otherness into the center. All these men were peacemakers, reaching out to the previous enemy in peace. Extending a hand through the space between the opposites to touch the other. They were all killed by extremists who couldn't bear the conflict created when opposing sides began to embrace one another and create a center, a One out of the Many. This is how difficult democracy is.

In our own American history there are many examples of brave men and women who have resisted the centrifugal forces of extreme emotion and held the center in our democracy. Jon Meacham gives examples of this courage in his 2018 book *The Soul of America*. These men and women did not cater to the forces of fear and division. Though sometimes they had to be dragged into the center by the responsibilities of the Presidency itself—like Harry Truman. A descendent of enslavers who loved Robert E. Lee and hated Abraham Lincoln, he used racial slurs in private and once wrote to his wife Bess that he was "strongly of the opinion that negroes ought to be in Africa, yellow men in Asia and white men in Europe and America." (Meacham, 2018, p. 255). Then Truman witnessed a brutal attack in South Carolina. A Black soldier just back from war was beaten and blinded by police in South Carolina. "My God!" said Truman "I had no idea it was as terrible as that! We've got to do something!...Whatever my inclinations as a native of Missouri might have been, as President I know this is bad. I shall fight to end evils like this" (Meacham, 2018, p. 256).

And he did. Truman's 1948 message to Congress outlining his civil rights program, explicitly forbade lynching, integrated the military, and strived for fairness in voting, employment, housing, criminal justice and public accommodations. Southerners were aghast and fought it all the way but lost on most counts. Another step in the direction of democracy, inclusion, and the creation of a center of unity between the extremes.

Even George Bush, who was not otherwise noted for his peaceful qualities, struck a healing note after the terrorist attacks of 9/11/01. Three days after the terrible attack on the World Trade Center, Bush climbed the steps at Washington's National Cathedral and found the center in his faith: "This world God created is of moral design, he said. Grief and tragedy and hatred are only for a time. Goodness, remembrance and love have no end. And the Lord of life holds all who die and all who mourn" (Meacham, 2018, p. 262). Bush knew that something larger than a binary view of this tragedy was necessary if our injured democracy was to be healed and a center re-established.

For Bush, it was God. For Barack Obama, it was a song. Late in his presidency, in 2015, after a young white supremacist had entered a Bible study group at the Emanuel African Methodist Episcopal Church and opened fire with a .45 caliber pistol, murdering nine innocent parishioners, Obama met with members of the grieving congregation. As he eulogized one of the ministers, he spoke of grace, "...out of this terrible tragedy, God has visited grace upon us for he has allowed us to see where we've been blind. ....We may not have earned it, this grace, with our rancor and complacency and short-sightedness and fear of each other, but we got it all the same; He gave it to us anyway" (Meacham, 2018, p. 263-4). And then through his tears, Barack Obama started to sing. Into the center of this fractured congregation—into the center of our democracy—both hollowed out by hatred and extremism, parched and dry from lack of feeling, he poured a song.

Amazing grace! How sweet the sound,

That saved a wretch; like me?

I once was lost, but now am found,

Was blind, but now I see.

Suddenly there was a center again, what had been hollowed out by violence and extremism, now occupied by one man who was brave enough to hold and suffer both his love and hate in one place, and pour a song into the middle. Suddenly my falcon could hear the falconer again!

References

Adorno, T., Frankel-Brunwik, E, Levinson, D. and Sanford, N. (1950). *The Authoritarian Personality,* New York: Harper and Brothers.

Adorno, T., Frenkel-Brenswik, E., Levinson, D.J., & Sanford, R.N., (2019b). *The authoritarian personality.* New York: Verso Books.

Applebaum, A., (2020). *Twilight of Democracy: The Seductive Lure of Authoritarianism.* New York: Doubleday.

Balint, M., (1979). *The Basic Fault: Therapeutic Aspects of Regression,* Evanston, IL: Northwestern Universities Press.

Bettleheim, B. (1979b). *The informed heart: Autonomy in a Mass Age.* New York: Avon.

Bion, W., (1959). "Attacks on Linking," in *Second Thoughts,* New York: Jason Aronson, pp. 93-109.

Braun, B.G., (1988). The BASK model of dissociation. Dissociation: Progress in the Dissociative Disorders, 1(1), 16-23.

Brooks, D. "Trump and the Politics of Mean World," *New York Times* Opinion Page: August 27, 2020.

Cohn, N., (1957). *The Pursuit of the Millennium.* London: Secker & Warburg.

Dickinson, E., (1961). *The Complete Poems of Emily Dickinson,* Thomas H. Johnson (ed.), New York: Little, Brown & Co.

Doering, J. "Some Patients Dying of Covid-19 Still Think it's a Fake, Says a South Dakota Nurse." November 17, 2020. https://www.self.com/story/covid-19-patients-dying-still-think-its-fake.

Du Bois, W.E.B. (1999). *Black Reconstruction in America, 1860-1880.* Free Press, p. 677.

Hofstadter, R. Harpers Magazine, 1964, November Issue. "The Paranoid Style in American Politics," adapted from the Herbert Spencer Lecture, delivered at Oxford University in November, 1963. pp. 3-40.

Jung, C.G., (1955). *CW, Vol. 14: Mysterium Coniunctionis,* New York: Pantheon Books: Bollingen Series XX.

_____. (1959). *CW, Vol. 9:ii, Aion: Researches Into the Pheno-menology of the Self,* New York: Pantheon Books; Bollingen Series XX.

_____. (1964). *CW, Vol. 10: Civilization in Transition,* R.F.C. Hull transl., New York: Pantheon Books; Bollingen Series XX.

_____. (1973). *Letters, Vol. 1,* (Gerhard Adler, Edtr), London: Routledge.

Kalsched, D., (1996). *The Inner World of Trauma: Archetypal Defenses of the Personal Spirit,* New York: Routledge.

_____. (2013). *Trauma and the Soul: A Psycho-Spiritual Approach to Human Development and its Interruption,* New York: Routledge.

Levine, P., (2015). *Trauma and Memory: Brain and Body in Search for the Living Past,* Berkeley, CA: North Atlantic Books.

Levitsky, S., and Ziblatt, D., (2018). *How Democracies Die.* New York: Broadway Books.

Lincoln, A., (1862). Annual message to congress - concluding remarks. https://www.abrahamlincolnonline.org/lincoln/speeches/congress.htm.

_____. (1862). *The Gettysburg Address.* https://www. abrahamlincolnonline.org >speeches.

MacWilliams, M., (2016). *The Rise of Trump: America's Authoritarian Spring.* Amherst, MA: Amherst College Press.

McGuire, Wm. (Edtr) (1990). *Analytical Psychology: Notes of the Seminar Given in 1925 by C.G. Jung,* New York: Routledge.

Meacham, J., (2018). *The Soul of America: The Battle for our Better Angels,* New York: Random House.

Moon, B., (edtr) (1991). *An Encyclopedia of Archetyal Symbolism,* Boston and London: Shambhala Press.

National Archives: *America's Founding Documents: Declaration of Independence: A Transcription;* www.archives.gov/ founding-docs.

Roosevelt, F.D., (1933). *First Inaugural Address:* https://www. fdrlibrary.org/first-inaugural-curriculum-hub.

Scheer, G., and Rankin, H., (1957). *Rebels and Redcoats: The American Revolution Through the Eyes of Those who Fought and Lived It,* New York: Da Capo Press.

Taylor, A., (2019). *Democracy May Not Exist, But We'll Miss It When It's Gone,* New York: Henry Holt and Company.

Trump, D., (2018). www.nbcnews.com/politics/white-house.

Williams, T.T. "Engagement," *Orion,* July-Aug. 2004, p. 143.

Weil, S., (1987). *Gravity and Grace,* London: Ark Paperbacks.

Yeats, W.B. *The Second Coming:* first published in both The Nation and The Dial in November 1920; https://www. poetryfoundation.org/poems/43290/the-second-coming.

Thorns in the Spirit: Trauma and the Uncertain Personal Work of Racial Justice

Sean Fitzpatrick

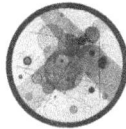

This book addresses the topic of experiencing and living with uncertainty. As has been discussed, we are living with continuing uncertainty on many levels: personally, in the face of social change, with the continuing shift in Covid-19, the environment, and the reality of war. This chapter will explore how we, collectively, engage with racial justice issues, and address how exposure to the overwhelming suffering of others can paralyze as well as galvanize the observer. I will sketch a possible path toward changing that experience of paralysis in the context of racial justice engagement. We should also begin by acknowledging the most important first step when we describe trauma: preparing to care for ourselves. Below, I will describe events involving trauma to others, which may or may not already be familiar to you from media reports. Take time to notice how it affects you, and do not hesitate to step away from the text to return to the present if you feel overwhelmed. As we will discuss, hearing narratives of trauma can be traumatic events in themselves.

How We Observe, and How It Affects Us

Every time we access our screens, we open ourselves to powerful forces. We choose this willingly, though we can make a good case that we have far less control over the choice than we think we do. I write this in late 2022, after nearly three years of extraordinary social turmoil and individual suffering spurred in great part by the emergence of a tiny virus into the human bloodstream. Covid-19 has both revealed the breadth of our connectedness and radically interrupted and altered our ways of connecting. In most of the developed world, screens have been essential in creating and maintaining relatedness.

Have you done any doom-scrolling lately? Like many of us influenced by C.G. Jung and the creative communities of analysts, psychotherapists, scholars, writers, artists, and healers inspired by his work, words fascinate me, and I am interested in the lives they have led before we picked them up. Words often have images at their hearts, and those images engage and express parts of us that extend beyond, around, and underneath concepts and rational thought. Each of us is more than can be contained in written or spoken language. To the best of my knowledge (by which I mean, the knowledge Google is curating for me this particular moment), doom-scrolling emerged into language five years ago, as a way of describing something many of us were doing: helplessly reading news story after news story, viewing image after image, encountering terrible facts and worse possibilities. Crucial to the experience is the feeling of helplessness. No matter how scared or angry we feel, how much sleep we lose or time with loved ones we miss, we cannot look away.

This is by design. Specifically, the design of companies using psychological research to determine how best to keep us using their products. This is by no means new; as long as we have had commerce, we have had sales tactics. What does feel different during these times is the way intense, even overwhelming, emotional experiences can be evoked at will to exert control over our lives, to render each of us into endless streams of data that can then be used to generate revenue, political choice, and social change. It is amoral, which is different from being immoral (though certainly I experience much of it to be immoral, too); it occurs outside of morality, ungoverned by it, though individual actors within these processes are undoubtedly guided by their understandings of what is right and wrong, what is humane and what is dehumanizing.

Doom has its etymological root in judgments of right and wrong. In its earliest usage in Old English, it meant simply a decree, an expression of justice, equity, or righteousness. Over time it gained darker connotations, as an expression of a final condemnation by the Christian God. Scrolls, too, evoke written decrees, a single continuous piece of paper or animal skin on which long documents were captured. I cannot help but think that when we are doom-scrolling, our moral imaginations are active and anxious, expecting punishment long deferred and finally coming due, without possibility of appeal.

Of course, this too is at least partly by design. Increasingly moralistic characterizations of ourselves and others have been part of our cultural discourse over the last decade at least. As he mentored leaders who would serve as senior advisors in the Trump White House, conservative writer David Horowitz taught them hope and fear are the greatest forces in American politics, but that fear is more powerful. This is not new, either, and it leads in predictable human directions. Those with whom we disagree become existential threats, subhuman and malevolently superhuman enemies whose destruction is both morally justified and necessary for our survival. I write this the day after a hammer-wielding assailant brutally attacked the husband of Democratic Speaker of the House Nancy Pelosi in their home in San Francisco. Five years ago, Republican Representative Steve Scalise and three others were shot by a left-wing extremist while playing baseball in a Washington, D.C. park.

Political violence has been with us throughout time. These current violent outbursts unsettle us, though, because they seem to be increasing along ideologically extreme lines. They are not confined to high-profile officials. According to the FBI, hate crimes in the United States jumped 20% between 2010 and 2020. We are all traumatized by them. Some of us are survivors of hate and bias incidents. Some of us know others who have been victimized. Almost all of us encounter them through our screens. And witnessing the suffering of others can hypnotize and paralyze us as well as galvanize us into action. *How do we change what is too painful to hold in our awareness and feels far larger than any one of us?*

Encountering the effects of psychological trauma

Trauma, too, carries images within it. A Greek word meaning "wound," trauma emerged in a medical context in the Middle Ages as a way of describing physical injury. At least in English, it seems to have come into use in a psychological sense at the end of the 19th Century, as European psychologists struggled to make sense of a strange set of symptoms found primarily in women. These psychologists used the term *hysteria* to describe the behavior of these women: everything from seizures to paralysis with no physical cause to intense emotional expressiveness to delusions and hallucinations. Reasons for this set of behaviors shifted over time and culture. Four millennia ago, Egyptians first described the effects of a "wandering womb," which required intervention to return to its normal place.

Under the sway of Christian theology, this experience became the work of Satan and the effect of sin. Sigmund Freud, with his colleague Josef Breuer, landed on a different cause. They noted that their patients (mostly women, though Freud applied the diagnosis to men as well) consistently reported sexual abuse in childhood. This was a truly new perspective, and Freud and Breuer expected that it would spark a revolution in patient care, one necessarily tied to social change. When they brought their findings to the medical authorities of the time, however, they were met

182

with stony silence. The white, male physicians could not accept that childhood sexual abuse was so prevalent. It took the passing of multiple generations for researchers—now including women—to affirm the root social cause of Freud's original theories. We know now that childhood sexual abuse is far more prevalent than those European men could accept. With no path forward but ridicule, Freud revised his theory, suggesting that it resulted from forbidden sexual urges and fantasy—not actual abuse.

But Freud and Breuer's original publications made their way to the brilliant American psychologist and philosopher, William James. He took them seriously. In an article supporting their findings, James referred to these experiences of childhood sexual abuse as "psychic traumata, thorns in the spirit, as it were" (1894, p. 199). James seems to be the first writer to apply the word *trauma* to the human psyche. That image, thorns in the spirit, captivates me. It makes intuitive sense as a way of imaging the overwhelming experiences that one cannot see the way one can see a broken arm, and yet can be seen everywhere once one's perspective allows it. And it also suggests a path toward addressing those experiences over time.

By applying the word *trauma* to psychological phenomena, James gave us a new, rich imaginative field in which to explore and treat psychic injury. Certainly, the thorns we receive are not limited to sexual abuse in childhood. In the late 1990s, the CDC and Kaiser Permanente conducted a groundbreaking study linking ten events in childhood, which they labeled Adverse Childhood Experiences, to a range of long-term negative behavioral, mental, and physical outcomes. Physical, emotional, and sexual abuse; neglect; and a range of experiences in the household, including the abuse of parents, drug use, mental illness, and incarceration of family members, all correlated strongly to poor outcomes in adulthood. The theorization of trauma and its effects also depended on the treatment of military veterans over the course of the 20th

Century. If we return to the image James gave us, we may find new and useful ways of understanding the path forward.

Thorns in the Spirit

Thorns are organic, parts of plants that serve a protective function. They protect by wounding creatures that encounter them. We are used to thinking of the wound as a puncture, a small, but deep, breach of our own protective surface, our skin. But, of course, thorns can also tear the surface without penetrating deeply.

Likely the most famous thorns in Western history are woven into the crown that was placed on Jesus' head during his execution. This story is particularly relevant for us because William James connected thorns with the spirit. Our words *spirit* and *spirituality* share a common root with our word *respiration*. Breathing is a two-part process. We breathe air into our lungs, where we take in oxygen. And we breathe out, so we can rid ourselves of carbon dioxide and other waste. It is no mystery that many spiritual practices focus on our breath, like meditation or centering prayer. When James used the word *spirit,* the Christian origins of that word was a strong part of the context, although James himself was not a traditional Christian.

In the Biblical passages that describe the crown of thorns, it is used as a way to mock Jesus. But not just Jesus. The Roman soldiers called him "King of the Jews." Remember that the Romans were an imperial power who controlled Israel and exploited the Jewish people. The crown of thorns was meant not just to humiliate Jesus. It was also a symbol of imperial domination. To the Romans, Jesus was a ridiculous king, and the Jews were ridiculous to think they could rise up and defeat them. The thorns of Jesus' crown did not just pierce the flesh of Jesus' head. They were also meant to pierce the dignity of the Jews, and their spirit, their relationship to God. In this sense, thorns are taken from their original, organic context of self-defense and twisted into a tool of domination by others.

This distinction may be useful for us to keep in mind. We can be wounded by natural events. We will encounter thorns in the world. We can be wounded accidentally, or by a force acting with the intention of self-defense. Each of us has our own thorns pointed outward that can wound accidentally or as ways of protecting ourselves. We can wound with criticism, by withholding our attention, with emotional violence, as well as with our fists. But we can also receive wounds that are misuses of this self-defense system. As noted above, larger forces can manipulate the fears of others to inflict great suffering on us. The thorns of others can be turned into crowns that humiliate and dehumanize us.

The wounding power of trauma extends to us as witnesses. Embedded in the etymology of *witness* is a social expectation: we testify to what we have observed in some public way. Observing does not necessarily lead to acts of witnessing or make us witnesses.[1] Whether we witness or simply observe—perceive—the wounding of others, we can experience pain, confusion, and disruption to our lives because of our capacity for empathy. When we choose to perceive the wounding experiences of others, we must go slowly, and we must learn ways to calm ourselves and end the experience trauma evokes in our bodies and souls. For those of us who do not personally experience these wounds but observe them in person, through image, video, and audio, or listening to the experiences of the traumatized, the need to escape our own suffering can end any chance that we might work to change the conditions that led to the trauma. In short, if we want to be allies to those who are wounded, we need ways to stay engaged without shutting down and turning away.

---

[1] The classic trauma triangle model of victim-perpetrator-bystander sometimes uses witness in place of bystander, which would depart from the understanding of witness I've described. Bystanders do nothing to change the situation and risk complicity through inaction. We will discuss this model further below.

Working with Observing Participants

We might think of the kinds of trauma exposure we face as observers in three ways:

- Secondary exposure through observation of others' trauma at a distance in time and space, as we do through media and in hearing stories after the fact;
- Secondary exposure through observation in person, in real time —what we might call observing participation[2];
- Direct, personal experiences of primary trauma, as observers of our own wounding.

Each of these positions of observation come with pain, both for the observer and for how their experience as an observer may cause, or at least not prevent, wounding in others. I will now focus on the thorns carried by observer participants.

In 2020, early outbreaks of Covid-19 in New York City led to awful expectations placed on the healthcare workers in the region. The surges of cases overwhelmed the care infrastructure, and individual physicians and nurses worked exhausting hours with limited supplies and little effective treatment for the stricken. Dr. Lorna Breen, the emergency room director at New York-Presbyterian Allen Hospital in Manhattan, became one of the most visible casualties as she completed suicide. Her death started a national conversation on the effects of Covid-19 care on the caregivers.

Not long after that surge in New York ended, its effects on healthcare workers appeared here in Houston. Our county public health department invited me to lead psychoeducational trainings and conversations with their staff about self-care and the personal

---

[2] The reader may be reminded of a similar term from anthropology, which inspires its use here. Anthropologists conducting fieldwork understand that their presence in any community under study affects that community, and their technique of participant-observation is a way of acknowledging the interactions that occur between the researcher and those being researched, and how knowledge is acquired through their inclusion, however temporary, in the community being studied.

costs of their work. I continue to feel profoundly privileged at this opportunity. As we spoke in one of the early sessions, one nurse became increasingly aware that the worst-case effects I was listing described her reality. Devoted to the needs of the stricken, she, along with many like her, followed the surges across the country. She left the suffering and death of New York to help with the emergent surge in Houston. She struggled to sleep. She was plagued by images of her previous patients. She found herself drinking far more than she had before Covid's emergence. And she was worried that Dr. Breen's fate might become her own. Covid presented a direct threat to her life, a primary psychological trauma. But more affecting was the cumulative experience of witnessing, and caring for, the traumatized.

We live in a culture in which many of our difficult growth tasks are outsourced to others. For the last eight years, I have given variations of the same presentation to frontline human service workers. A group of social workers at a local hospital asked for a presentation on the ethics of self-care, a notion I'd never considered before. These caregivers worked with children, sick and wounded children, sometimes dying children. It is emotionally hazardous work, but unlike the nursing teams who wear personal protective equipment when treating infectious diseases like Covid-19, the protection for caregivers exposed to trauma is minimal. This particular group of social workers convened their own monthly self-care lunch, supplying parking tokens and Starbucks gift cards to presenters out of their own pockets. They understood that their capacity to treat children and families competently depended on their own well-being. How they attend to their own needs is an ethical matter.

Not long after that initial talk, one of those social workers invited me to present to their new team, the forensic investigators of Harris County. Forensic investigators work with medical examiners to determine cause of death. Their workplace is the worst day of someone's life, at the location of the body, within ninety minutes of its discovery. I've been privileged to continue to work with them, meeting for many years in monthly circles in a conference room across the hall from the morgue. They witness the effects of grievous trauma every day, the worst in human nature. Burnout is a given; the question is not whether they will leave the work but how long it will take.

These circles connected me with the fundamental human reality of physical death uncontained by the antiseptic clinical space and perspective of the hospital or funeral home, but at a degree of separation from it. I spent a day in the field with the investigators, an experience I expect will be with me for the rest of my life. I'm grateful for it, and I do not want to repeat it.

The experience of being wounded by the trauma of others is now often called *secondary traumatic stress or vicarious trauma*. If disruptive enough, these wounds can result in more formal diagnoses, such as acute stress disorder and post-traumatic stress disorder. While these terms are relatively new, the core insights they reflect are not. In her classic *Trauma and Recovery,* Judith Herman related that repeated exposure to the graphic depiction of victimization results in challenges to basic faith, pervasive distrust of others' motives, and pessimism about the human condition (1992, p. 141). Those exposures happen through narrative and through the unspoken, unspeakable affect in which the therapist and patient sit in the consulting room. But not only the consulting room, of course.

In every presentation, I cite a haunting paper by Smith (Hatcher, et al. 2011) which studied educators in the juvenile justice system. These are English, math, science teachers whose only encounter with the trauma narratives of their students is in the natural course of teaching in the classroom. Of the three then-current diagnostic criteria for PTSD, more than 80% of these educators exhibited clinically-significant symptoms of one; more than half (55%) met two criteria; and nearly 40% met all three criteria for diagnosis with PTSD. The researchers controlled for outside events in the teachers' lives; these symptoms resulted from exposure in the classroom. Just by teaching these youth, the teachers were wounded.

Any of us can be affected the ways these teachers were. They were bystanders, witnesses only to the stories and to their evident effects in the lives of these youth. Empathy can motivate us to act on behalf of others. It also can, and will, wound us.

Thorns in the Racial Justice Movement

The ways in which we witness trauma have been affected by advances in technology, which have brought new exposures to secondary traumatic stress. Smartphones have profoundly changed contemporary conversation about police-involved violence toward others despised for their origins or the color of their skin. We might step a bit further back in history, to the surreptitious video camera that recorded the police beating of Rodney King in Los Angeles in 1994, for the origin of viral videos of police-involved violence. But when smartphones emerged, providing many of us with high-quality video recording and transmission devices, our ability to document and watch these traumas through social media channels has made observers, if not witnesses, of us all.

In the United States, we know the names Rodney King, Philando Castile, and George Floyd; each was killed through acts of police brutality. We may be less familiar with George Holliday, Diamond Reynolds, and Darnella Frazier, though Ms. Frazier won a special Pulitzer Prize for her agonizing video of George Floyd's death in police custody. Among others, these three citizen journalists opened our eyes to the physical trauma hidden deliberately through the historical marginalization of the communities of the victims. These courageous acts resulted in the kind of emotional and mental distress described above.

The effects of these graphic depictions of violence against Black bodies have been wide ranging and deeply affecting. Ms. Frazier's video of George Floyd's death drove the growth of the

Black Lives Matter movement, expressed in widespread mass protests throughout the world during the summer of 2020.

What does it mean to witness these traumas? The profound Black writer and activist James Baldwin understood it to be an essential act in bringing about social change. Princeton scholar Eddie Glaude summarized Baldwin's charge to us this way: "Tell the story. Make it real for those who refuse to believe that such a thing can happen/has happened/is happening here. Bring the suffering to the attention of those who wallow in willful ignorance. In short, shatter the illusion of innocence at every turn and attack all the shibboleths the country holds sacred" (Glaude, 2020, p. 53). Witnessing also can be a necessarily painful path to psychological growth.

These videos capture unutterable human suffering. Ms. Reynolds began broadcasting live video on Facebook from her car, immediately after her boyfriend Philando was shot next to her, with her four-year old daughter in the back seat. Anyone with an internet connection can watch this moment of ineffable personal horror. The New York Times integrated her video with surveillance and police footage that contextualizes and amplifies the horror. In 2021, Ms. Frazier described the profound impact of her video of Mr. Floyd's death on her life: "I couldn't sleep properly for weeks. I used to shake so bad at night my mom had to rock me to sleep. Hopping from hotel to hotel because we didn't have a home and looking over our back every day in the process. Having panic and anxiety attacks every time I seen a police car, not knowing who to trust because a lot of people are evil with bad intentions. I hold that weight" (Hernandez, 2021).

We can hear James Baldwin calling us to become like Mr. Holliday, Ms. Reynolds, and Ms. Frazier. We might call them *engaged observers* of trauma, which disrupts the roles in what has been called the *trauma triangle*. This useful, enduring model describes a repeated loop that keeps trauma present and unhealed. The victim is powerless. The perpetrator is not, nor is the bystander.

In some iterations of the model, the role of bystander is replaced by that of rescuer, who likewise retains power while the victim remains powerless. We want the traumatized person to move from victim to survivor, and one model for this—by no means the only one—is to help the survivor create safety in their environment and psyche, so they can slowly accept the trauma story to end ongoing responses to the trauma that maintain their suffering and difficulties functioning in the world.

Engaged observers make the darkness conscious. They do not rescue, but they do not deny or avoid, either. They are compelled to participate by documenting the experience. They do this at great risk. Ms. Reynolds was arrested; some of the most difficult footage in the New York Times piece comes from the camera inside the squad car, as her four-year old daughter attempts to comfort Ms. Reynolds, handcuffed and unable to hold her child. The trauma is primary—Ms. Reynolds and her daughter were both at great risk of harm. Ms. Frazier reasonably feared reprisal by police. She also witnessed a murder firsthand; her descriptions of panic, anxiety, and sleep disturbance are consistent with primary and secondary trauma.

I watched the New York Times piece once. I still vividly remember it. And I wrestle with how I continue to relate to it, what constructive value it might have in my life, holding those heartrending images of grief and terror. It remains a thorn in my spirit, calling me to be an engaged observer. The work of making the darkness conscious can liberate us from our frozenness, guilt, and terror.

Accepting and Removing our Thorns

We have looked deeply into the effects of trauma on observers from several angles. The experiences of those engaged observers who recorded and shared the incidents with us have resonances with those of us observing their courageous work. Though we may feel quite secondary, saved from the choices these engaged observers had to make in a moment, we are not so distant from their dilemmas and their thorns as we might imagine. Watching their acts of video witnessing, we are called to change not that traumatic moment, but the conditions that created it and that will inevitably create others like it. How do we navigate that call? And how do we relate to and manage the real pain that comes from our observation?

While some of us may have direct, personal experiences of trauma, most of us experience secondary exposure as we try to remain conscientiously informed through the range of media we access about our communities and the larger forces at work in our world. As noted at the start of this chapter, we are all being deluged with bad news, uncertainty, and fears for the future. We are besieged by social concerns, the impacts of climate change, war, and the ongoing challenges of living with Covid-19. Most of us are feeling overwhelmed, vulnerable, and uncertain, and we are struggling to adapt to the changes around us. We could all use tools and approaches that can help us navigate these troubled times.

Secondary trauma is a fact of our lives, though serious psychological disruption does not have to be. Remaining conscientious citizens requires us to see what we do not want to see. Doing this essential work of remaining connected, however, has to take into account the very human need to disconnect and protect ourselves when we are overwhelmed. How can we deal with our own overwhelming responses to the images we see every day and answer the call to be engaged observers?

Opening oneself in a sustained way to the traumatic experience of others involves a conscious choice to suffer. It also risks losing contact with the fullness of the experiences of those others, another reduction to an object with which relationship is forever foreclosed. What I propose is a path toward empathic engagement for us all that leans on curiosity and mutual support rather than shame and judgement, while not saving us from either.

When we encounter the trauma of others, we can lose ourselves in doom-scrolling or turn away out of pain and fear. Both of these paths are human, but they are also inevitably unconscious, automatic. The work of making the darkness conscious, of engaging what is hardest to accept in us, does not have to be self-destructive or overwhelming, though. As allies, we can choose how and when we engage, and we can develop an ongoing practice that relieves us of our thorns and transforms our souls. Here is one path to take on this challenge.

The Work Begins with Us

Jung's insistence that we all have parts of ourselves we do not want to acknowledge, our shadow, and that our healthy development depends on exploring our shadows, makes him an ideal guide for these times. He noted that:

> As any change must begin somewhere, it is the single individual who will experience it and carry it through. The change must indeed begin with an individual; it might be any one of us. Nobody can afford to look round and to wait for somebody else to do what he is loath to do himself. (Jung, 1988, p. 101)

The work begins with what is closest to us: our own experience. Jung elsewhere told us that "every psychic process is an image and an imagining," (Jung, 1969, para. 889) which reflected his insight that we experience the movements of our souls through our imagination. It's worth saying that, by using this term, we do not simply mean a visual experience. Those of us who are vision impaired do not lack imaginations. What we mean is a field of creative possibility within that encounters the world accessed through our senses. So, when we reach for resources from Jungian thought, the first place to start is with how we work with these experiences of imagination, our images.

We have already done this, earlier in this chapter, as we reflected on James' image of thorns. I collected associations – my first impressions of an image. Then I began to imagine more broadly, collecting some key cultural associations. This is not a scientific process, but a creative one. What we are hoping to do is to open up the possibilities in each image so that we can create new ways of understanding ourselves and our context. It is useful to note at the outset that we are our best guides regarding the potential to be overwhelmed. As we begin this work, start with images that are not intensely charged with emotion for you. Respect for their power to wound is essential to this work, even as we understand that opening ourselves to unpleasant experiences is part of the work as well.

I invite you to choose an image to work with, something close to your experience. This is part of what is often described as shadow work: we consciously allow something that is troubling in our psyches to return to our awareness. This may be an image from a dream, or perhaps something from a moment when we were mildly upset or frightened. The goal here is simply to begin the work of acclimating to what is difficult within us, not to charge to our deepest traumas, which likely will be counterproductive, if not paralyzing or overwhelming. We will work with this image in a simple, three-step process:

1. **Associate.** Allow yourself to notice the immediate qualities of the image: color, shape, weight, size, presence. What other images connect to it? In what context does it appear? And, crucially, what feelings emerge as we give it our attention? We are simply looking for what comes up within us. Resist the temptation to interpret or assign meaning to your experience. When I was working with the image of thorns earlier, I noticed the action of thorns: puncturing or tearing, one of their functions to protect an organism; and some of the broader cultural context of thorns, in the Christian tradition, as part of the drama of Jesus' execution.

2. **Resonate.** After you have collected some associations, let yourself notice how you feel about those associations and, especially, the intensity of those feelings. Some of those feelings may be unpleasant. What matters here is how

strongly you feel; some of that feeling may be aversion. Those feelings are potent guides. Some of them may not be pleasant, and we want to resist the temptation to ignore those or deny they are ours.

3. **Contain**. Focusing on these emotionally-charged associations helps us to move closer to interpretation, which is always an evolving process. Notice how your experience of the original image has changed. What has been added? What layers revealed? What can you feel now that you could not before? Again, to use the example of the thorns: as I return to the associations, I'm struck by my own reaction to the crown imposed on Jesus. What is used by others in defense can be twisted into new forms, as tools of domination and ridicule. It is not hard to see the armor and weapons wielded by Derek Chauvin, the police officer who killed George Floyd, as ostensibly defensive tools used by an individual and by broader cultural forces to dominate and ridicule Mr. Floyd and his community. Containing these associations deepens my awareness of the sociopolitical dimensions carried within William James' image. It is part of me now, part of my perspective on trauma and on Mr. Floyd's murder.

This emotional engagement with our images can make healing possible. It may seem paradoxical, but increasing our capacity to draw closer to what is most difficult within us and in society strengthens us and leaves us less vulnerable to being overwhelmed in the future. Out of this work may come a clearer sense of why we were overwhelmed and a better understanding of how to regulate our future experience of woundedness. We may also find that actions flow from this new, deeper understanding of what we observe.

A starting point for this kind of practice is C.G. Jung's belief that "one does not become enlightened by imagining figures of light, but by making the darkness conscious" (Jung, 1953, para. 335). What we do not know about ourselves, what we are afraid to know, what we have avoided, what others have not allowed us to see or to live, is what we most need to grow and to live grounded, meaningful lives. Not all of what is hidden from us is trauma, but trauma by its nature hides in plain sight. It is that which is overwhelming in our experience, that which has split our psyches so that we might be able to survive, at great cost. We constantly work around the fractures within us in partial, inefficient ways. Removing the thorns in our spirits involves seeing them first. And this of course is as true in a community as it is in a single psyche.

That sentence from Jung is well known and well-worn. But the sentence that follows it is not: "The latter procedure, however, is disagreeable and therefore not popular" (Jung, 1955, para. 335). By "the latter procedure," of course, he means the process of making the darkness conscious. Why would we take it on? It may be morally honorable, but rather than frame it that way, we should understand it as a practice for spiritual growth, one that acknowledges the pain it evokes and reveals, one that understands that learning how to hold that pain sustainably is integral to our development.

How We Can Engage, and Stay Engaged, with Our World

Building on the inner work described above, I would like to offer a process of five simple, but not easy, steps by which we can stay engaged with what is most difficult and painful in the world without becoming paralyzed, hypnotized, or avoidant. And we can think of it as a spiritual process, though not one tied to any specific religious tradition. Sometimes spirituality is framed as an expression of our yearning for transcendence, and that yearning can take psychologically problematic form. In recent years, the counseling profession has developed the term *spiritual bypass* as a way of describing spiritual beliefs and practices that we use to avoid dealing directly with the real difficulties in our lives, praying to God to save our relationship, for example, without doing the hard work ourselves. With his metaphor of thorns in the spirit, William

James is guiding us to see spirit as embodied, tangible, vulnerable, and capable of healing.

Here are the steps:

1. Listen, with humility, to the voices of directly affected people.
2. Observe what emerges within us.
3. Accept what we find in our experience.
4. Connect with others.
5. Act in the world.

Listening with humility to the experience of directly affected people involves learning how to ground oneself. Humility shares a root with our words *ground* and *humus*. We use "grounding" as a technique in trauma care, a way of returning the survivor from the trauma to the body in the present. So, this kind of listening depends upon developing the capacity to leave the paralysis of trauma and return to this moment, this present body.

This can happen in many different ways. The simplest is to pause, breathe deeply, and notice three things in the room about you that you can see. Then notice three things you hear. Then three physical sensations. This kind of exercise reminds us that we are here, safe, in this moment, and not in the car with Ms. Reynolds, or in our own past wounding. *What is also crucial here is that we listen to the firsthand experience of those affected, and not rely on the representations or interpretations of others.*

When we observe what we find within us, we attend to the body. All of our images, affects, thoughts are embodied. We notice the tension, discomfort, pain, excitation before we contain it with names. We may find things in our reverie and fantasy that are deeply uncomfortable. Our experiences of the narratives of directly affected people may live in us, intrude in the way that memories of trauma intrude on survivors. Without a containing process, this intrusion of the experiences of others in our psyches can become so disruptive as to be diagnosable, as acute stress disorder or post-traumatic stress disorder. This work of observation helps us to keep our attention in the present, to gently leave the world of the trauma and focus on our own experience now, where we are physically safe.

Accepting what we find is not integration. Perhaps the better metaphor is holding, not racing away from difficult experiences to easy shelter, but also not denying what may begin to emerge as a path toward further engagement. It involves acknowledging the pain we experience, and then soothing it. And acknowledging urgencies to act, numbness, intellectualizing, avoidance, and the moral judgments that can lead to paralysis. This is also an act of allegiance with the people who have experienced trauma. Not denying what is real within us contributes to the collective work of not denying what is real in the world that wounds and marginalizes the bodies and minds of others.

Connecting with others is crucial. Trauma isolates us. But communities that share these experiences can hold them together. Mutual accountability requires mutual support. This process makes possible action in the world that emerges from empathy and relatedness, from a foundation of self-examination. Acknowledging how difficult this work is, without making our experience more important than that of the traumatized, makes it more sustainable. This process of connecting with other observers may be the most difficult part of the work. Finding people who are committed to this process or others like it may take persistence. But simply finding a compassionate, empathetic friend who can listen to our experience without judgment will be profoundly helpful.

Acting in the world seems to be the social result. This is where change happens, we imagine. It can look like calling out a xenophobic joke. Making a donation. Campaigning for a candidate. Standing with the target of a hate incident. Any of these actions can of course happen without engaging in the broader process I've described. It may lead to a kind of false release from responsibility. Taking our action, we can judge ourselves free and miss ourselves still unhealed, still caught in a cycle that does not change.

What this process does, though, is to connect the inner with the outer. By making our own darkness conscious, by uncovering what is difficult for us to experience in ourselves, by locating our thorns, we make sustained engagement possible and root social change within our sphere of control. And we recognize, with Jung, that our world is collectively imagined. What is outside is always already inside or, the distinction we make between what is inside and what is outside is much more complex than we think. Social movements are ongoing acts of imagination that are personal and collective at once. How we imagine matters, and we will change the world if we allow ourselves to fully see it, hold it within us with care for its effect on us, and let it transform us. Then action becomes natural, powerful, and sustainable.

Suggestions for Further Reading

These helpful, accessible works are intended for those newly learning about trauma:

deBecker, G. (2021). *The gift of fear. Survival signals that protect us from violence.* New York: Back Bay Books.

Kalsched, D. (2013). *Trauma and the soul: A psycho-spiritual approach to human development and its interruption.* London: Routledge,

Van der Kolk, B. (2014). *The body keeps the score: Brain, mind, and body in the healing of trauma.* New York: Penguin.

Winfrey, O., and Perry, B. (2021). *What happened to you? Conversations on trauma, resilience, and healing.* New York: Flatiron Books

References

Al-Hlou, Y., (2017). Philando Castile, Diamond Reynolds, and a nightmare caught on video. *New York Times,* June 23, 2017. https://www.nytimes.com/video/us/100000005181340/philando-castile-diamond-reynolds-and-a-nightmare-caught-on-video.html.

Federal Bureau of Investigation. (n.d.). Crime data explorer. https://crime-data-explorer.fr.cloud.gov/pages/explorer/crime/hate-crime.

Felitti, V., Anda, R., Nordenberg, D., Williamson, D, Spitz, A., Edwards, V., Koss, M., Marks, J., (1998). Relationship of childhood abuse and household dysfunction to many of the leading causes of death in adults. *American journal of preventive medicine, 11:4, pp. 245-258.* Doi: https://doi.org/10.1016/S0749-3797(98)00017-8.

Gross, T., (2020). 'Hatemonger' paints Trump advisor Stephen Miller as a case study in radicalization. *Fresh Air with Terry Gross.* https://www.npr.org/2020/08/24/905403716/hatemonger-paints-trump-advisor-stephen-miller-as-a-case-study-in-radicalization.

Herman, J., (1995). *Trauma and recovery,* New York: Basic Books.

Hernandez, J., (2021). Read this powerful statement from Darnella Frazier, who filmed George Floyd's murder. *National Public Radio,* May 26, 2021. https://www.npr.org/2021/05/26/1000475344/read-this-powerful-statement-from-darnella-frazier-who-filmed-george-floyds-murder.

James, W., (1894). *Psychological Review, Vol. 1*. London, UK: Forgotten Books. (Republished 2018).

Jung, C.G., (1967). *Alchemical Studies,* Princeton, NJ: Princeton University Press.

_____. (1969). Foreword to Suzuki's "Introduction to Zen Buddhism." *Psychology and religion: West and east. CW, Vol. 11* (pp. 538-556). Princeton, NJ: Princeton University Press (original work published 1939).

_____. (1988). *Man and his symbols,* New York: Anchor Press.

Knoll, C., Watkins, A, and Rothfeld, M., (2020). 'I couldn't do anything.' The virus and an E.R. doctor's suicide. *New York Times,* July 11, 2020. https://www.nytimes.com/2020/07/11/nyregion/lorna-breen-suicide-coronavirus.html.

Psychological Responses to Uncertainty in the Individual and Group Psyche

Thomas Singer

Uncertainty has become an everyday reality and overarching theme of contemporary life. It is both on the surface and beneath the surface of consciousness in many of the exchanges that we have with the inner and outer world. This chapter will explore the theme of uncertainty in terms of its presence in recent times, as well as the psychological responses that we have to it. I have written this chapter in the spirit of Olga Tokarczuk, the Polish, Nobel Prize–winning novelist, who states in *Drive Your Plow Over the Bones of the Dead:* "It's a good thing that God, if he exists, and even if he doesn't, gives us a place where we can think in peace. Perhaps that's the whole point of prayer—to think to yourself in peace, to want nothing, to ask for nothing."[1]

I hope this chapter might be a place to think about the uncertainty that floods the world today just as uncertainty is built into Tokarczuk's universe. God may or may not exist, but either way the idea of God allows us to pray, which Tokarczuk sees as a place to "think in peace." Our current world is swamped with

---

[1] Olga Tokarczuk, Drive Your Plow over the Bones of the Dead, trans. Antonia Lloyd-Jones (New York: Riverhead Books, 2019), 233.

uncertainty and overstimulation, each fueling the other. This easily leads to the feeling that our current time is unlike any other in that the combination of pandemic, climate change, changing abortion laws, mass shootings, war, the impact of the internet, and any other number of less dramatic but equally powerful changes seem to be overtaking us at an unparalleled, exponentially amplified pace and intensity.

A Very Brief History of Uncertainty in Modern Times

I was stunned, upon rediscovering Anne Morrow Lindberg's seventy-year-old *A Gift from the Sea*, that her sense of being overwhelmed by contemporary events in 1955 resonates with a freshness of vision that gives expression to what many of us feel and care about most deeply today:

> The search for outward simplicity, for inner integrity, for fuller relationship—is this not a limited outlook? Of course it is, in one sense. Today, a kind of planetary point of view has burst upon mankind. The world is rumbling and erupting in ever widening circles around us. The tensions, conflicts, and sufferings even in the outermost circle touch us, reverberate in all of us. We cannot avoid these vibrations. But just how far can we implement this planetary awareness? We are asked today to feel compassionately for everyone in the world; to digest intellectually all the information spread out in public print; and to implement in action every ethical impulse aroused by our hearts and minds. The inter-relatedness of the world links us constantly with more people than our hearts can hold. Or rather—for I believe the heart is infinite—modern communication loads us with more problems than the human frame can carry. It is good, I think, for our hearts, our minds, our imaginations to be stretched; but body, nerve, endurance and life-

span are not as elastic. My life cannot implement in action the demands of all the people to whom my heart responds. I cannot marry all of them, or bear them all as children, or care for them all as I would my parents in illness or old age. Our grandmothers, and even—with some scrambling—our mothers, lived in a circle small enough to let them implement in action most of the impulses of their hearts and minds. We were brought up in a tradition that has now become impossible, for we have extended our circle throughout space and time.[2]

That was in 1955. I don't know if Anne Morrow Lindberg felt the same uncertainty that we do about the continuing existence of life on the planet as we know it. I wrote a paper on Extinction Anxiety that may have had less relevance to her than it might to many of us today.[3] At the same time, she was living in a time of great uncertainty as evidenced by the rise of existentialism after the catastrophes of the early twentieth century that witnessed two World Wars, the Great Depression, and the explosion of the atomic bomb.

Soren Kierkegaard, a mid-nineteenth century Danish theologian, anticipated and embraced the angst of uncertainty that would overtake modern humans. His fearless, stark vision cuts to the bone:

And this is the simple truth—that to live is to feel oneself lost. He who accepts it has already begun to find himself, to be on firm ground. Instinctively, as do the shipwrecked, he will look around for

---

[2] Anne Morrow Lindbergh, Gift from the Sea (50th Anniversary Edition) (New York: Pantheon Books, 2005), 215–217.

[3] Thomas Singer, "Extinction Anxiety: Where the Spirit of the Depths Meets the Spirit of the Times, or Extinction Anxiety and the Yearning for Annihilation," in Vision, Reality, and Complex: Jung, Politics, and Culture (London: Routledge, 2021), 101–107.

something to which to cling, and that tragic, ruthless glance, absolutely sincere, because it is a question of his salvation, will cause him to bring order into the chaos of his life. These are the only genuine ideas; the ideas of the shipwrecked. All the rest is rhetoric, posturing, farce.[4]

And in the twentieth century, Sartre and Camus, the two most celebrated existentialists who followed in Kierkegaard's footsteps shared in his sense of the utter dislocation and of potential liberation that comes from the awareness that the known order of the world had collapsed, and that meaning is not a given in existence. This was summarized in a phrase that Sartre coined in 1945: "Existence precedes essence." One way to understand Sartre's formulation is that there is no inherent preordained meaning or purpose in being human or, for that matter, in the universe itself. Again, the collective experience of the two World Wars and the Great Depression shattered in many the belief that meaning was inherent in human existence and in the universe. This turned upside down the very foundations of millennia of traditional religious beliefs that the universe as God's creation has structure, meaning, and purpose. Camus proclaimed the universe "absurd": "The absurd is the essential concept and the first truth."[5] Uncertainty is at the heart of the existentialist experience of the world.

I remember attending a small Jungian conference at the Greystone Lodge in New York City in 1967 when I was a young medical student and would-be Jungian. I raised the question of the twin foundational existential assertions that the universe was absurd and that "existence precedes essence." In my memory, I was chastised by no less than Esther Harding, an early analysand of

---

[4] Soren Kierkegaard, "The Sickness unto Death," in Fear and Trembling and the Sickness Death, trans. Walter Lowrie (Princeton, NJ: Princeton University Press, 2013).

[5] Albert Camus, The Myth of Sisyphus (New York: Knopf, 1955).

Jung's, pioneer of the American Jungian tradition, and author of *Women's Mysteries: Ancient and Modern.* Harding responded to me in no uncertain terms (which is not the same as uncertainty) that the existentialists were "superficial" and "didn't understand anything." From her perspective, the notion of the archetypes can be seen as affirming that there are preexisting structures in the psyche, and therefore, it can be reaffirmed that essence precedes existence. The Jungian notion of the Self took the destroyed belief in the inherent meaning from out in the universe and placed it back inside the psyche where it would be safe from the attack of those who find the universe "absurd" and without intrinsic meaning.

My point is that uncertainty is not new to our age. In fact, it is age old. But we experience our uncertainty as if the world has never witnessed the crisis of uncertainty that we are currently experiencing—and, in one sense, that is true. But it is also true that the only certain thing about the topic of uncertainty is that there is nothing new about it.

Uncertainty in the Twenty-First Century

It now seems as though the timing of the World Trade Center and Pentagon attacks was no accident. That date, September 11, 2001, ushered in the twenty-first century's version of uncertainty, which includes everything from increasing uncertainty about practical day-to-day realities to a pervasive, profound underlying uncertainty about the fate of human existence and the planet as we know it—not to mention the fate of all the other plants, animals, and creatures that share the planet with us.

We cannot be sure what the price of a gallon of gas will be; we cannot be sure if we can obtain a safe abortion if need be; we cannot be sure when the pandemic will end, or another will begin; we cannot be sure if there will be enough water for our crops or too much water for them to survive. We cannot be sure when we enter public spaces whether someone with an assault weapon is on a mission of death and destruction. We cannot be sure if democracy

207

as we have known it will survive the uncertainty of a world lurching toward authoritarianism. We cannot be sure about what is true and what is untrue in a world deluged with misinformation and conspiracy theories and a growing awareness of the relativity of truth—as well as everything else. Do we, as Jungians, have anything to offer to this crisis of uncertainty—either in terms of understanding the causes of our uncertainty or in terms of offering some approaches for dealing with the uncertainty of our current situation?

We are such a prescriptive culture that a common response to uncertainty is to embrace simplistic diagnoses and remedies with fanatical devotion. This undoubtedly contributes to the rise of fundamentalist beliefs of all kinds—whether it be in the form of dogmatic religious ideas or the convictions of conspiracy theories. They have an answer. It apparently doesn't make a difference whether the answer is right or wrong, as long as it is embraced with a fanatical emotional devotion. Kierkegaard had the heads up on this human tendency when he observed: "There are two ways to be fooled. One is to believe what isn't true; the other is to refuse to believe what is true."[6]

The alternative to embracing beliefs that provide certainty is to embrace uncertainty as a precondition of being alive. Our practical and progress-oriented culture has trained us to think in terms of bullet points—both in terms of describing problems and prescribing solutions. Although that doesn't work very often, we learn to believe in the bullet-point approach to life and its problems. Jungians are often no exception to this tendency and sometimes I think we should create a Jungian Center for Wish Fulfillment where our unflappable beliefs in transformation can be preached. Jungians love the promise of transformation that is embodied in the title of Jung's transformative book, *Symbols of Transformation*. How do you prescribe transformation and who made the promise

---

[6] Soren Kierkegaard, Works of Love (New York: Harper Perennial, 1962), 23.

that transformation is the inevitable result of hard psychological work? Transformation is our tradition's seductive promise and prime mantra that is chanted endlessly. Transformation is offered as our tradition's antidote to the stress of living with uncertainty.

A Tentative Model of Psychological Stages of Collective and Individual Responses to Uncertainty

In an attempt to find some frame for approaching the topic of uncertainty in the individual and group psyche, I found myself imagining a schema that takes bits and pieces from several well-known contributors to psychological theory: Elisabeth Kübler-Ross's studies of the stages of grief and loss, Norman Cameron's study of paranoid psychotic processes, Melanie Klein's contributions to object relations theory, the Tavistock Institute's studies of group processes, and, finally, some of my own thoughts about the mythopoetic imagination. This model has three stages, or, as Melanie Klein preferred to call them, "positions." I think of this as a hybrid and tentative hypothesis about varying individual and group responses to uncertainty.

I must acknowledge at the outset that many properly warn of the dangers of taking the insights of depth psychology about individual development and applying them indiscriminately to the psychology of the collective. I am uncertain about the danger of my doing that in this chapter but feel it is worth the risk of being psychologically, if not politically, incorrect in the wish to give some broad strokes toward understanding the different phases of responses to uncertainty. I am engaging in metaphoric thinking here and do not want the model I am suggesting to be taken too literally. I offer, instead, a kind of imaginative, intuitive thinking perspective.

For instance, Kubler-Ross's stages of grief are often taken too literally, as if one passes through each stage in a linear progression. Of course, this is not how it happens and certainly not how it is experienced. One cycles through each again and again and the movement is anything but linear. I would urge you to think of the model I am proposing as being similar—that one cycles and recycles in and out of each stage or position in a nonlinear progression.

I am proposing a model for how both the individual and collective psyche responds to the "uncertainty principle"—a psychological variation on Heisenberg's original theory in which he stated that "we cannot know both the position and speed of a particle, such as a photon or electron, with perfect accuracy. The more we nail down the particle's position, the less we know about its speed and vice versa."[7]

It seems as if the Heisenberg uncertainty principle has overtaken every aspect of modern life, not just the movement of physical particles. We live in a world of relativity and the knowledge that what we think, feel, and say is heavily influenced by our point of view, which can shift depending on a variety of circumstances. Notions of any absolute truth or objectivity are subject to immediate doubt from ourselves and others. Uncertainty has become an integral part of our zeitgeist. In a way, we have all become accustomed to living with uncertainty. Nevertheless, uncertainty can be a real threat both to the individual and group sense of security and stability. In this model, I am suggesting that there are various stages of our reactions to the threats posed by uncertainty.

Attitude One: The Paranoid-Schizoid Position

Klein posited that a healthy development implies that the infant has to split its external world, its objects and itself into two categories: *good* (i.e., gratifying, loved, loving) and *bad* (i.e. frustrating, hated, persecutory). This splitting makes it possible to introject and identify with the good. In other words: splitting in this

---

[7] "What Is the Uncertainty Principle and Why Is It Important?", Caltech Science Exchange, https://scienceexchange.caltech.edu/topics/quantum-science-explained/uncertainty-principle.

stage is useful because it protects the good from being destroyed by the bad. Later, when the ego has developed sufficiently, the bad can be integrated, and ambivalence and conflict can be tolerated.[8]

In the paranoid-schizoid position, the frustrating, hated, persecutory bad "object" is split off and projected outside of the infant (or the "infantile" group mind). It protects the good from being destroyed.

This sounds so familiar when we think of how different groups in the United States and around the world are currently relating to one another. It feels as if much of the world is in a paranoid-schizoid position, not that there aren't real forces of brutal destructiveness.

I would like to combine Klein's notion with Norman Cameron's brilliant description of the origins of paranoid processes in the disturbed individual, which is not necessarily the same as what Klein described as a "normal" position in the developing infant. Cameron describes a psyche that has become overwhelmed by uncertainty, confusion, and anxiety.[9] As a last desperate attempt to bring some order to the chaos, the psyche constructs a simple narrative explanation that offers clarity, even if it is a paranoid delusion or fantasy. The paranoid idea brings order to disorder, certainty to uncertainty. It doesn't matter whether the idea is right or wrong, true or untrue. What matters is that order and certainty have been created out of disorder and uncertainty.

What if the collective psyche works in the same way? When there is too much information that is overwhelming and confusing, the collective psyche can easily be captured by a simplistic idea that explains it all. In a contemporary context, QAnon is a perfect

---

[8] Wikipedia, s.v. "Paranoid-schizoid and depressive position," accessed December 1, 2022, from https://en.wikipedia.org/wiki/Paranoid-schizoid_and_depressive_positions#:~:text=5%20Notes-,Paranoid%2Dschizoid%20position,of%20development%20through%20certain%20positions.
[9] Norman Cameron, Personality Development and Psychopathology: A Dynamic Approach (Boston: Houghton Mifflin Company, 1963), 470–515.

example of a shared paranoid belief system in its assertion that the world is controlled by the "Deep State," a cabal of Satan-worshipping pedophiles, and that former President Donald Trump is the only person who can defeat it. It may be outrageous and paranoid, but it organizes the world into a comprehensible simple narrative of why things are so disordered and bad. Cameron also pointed to another main feature of the paranoid mind—it creates a so-called pseudo-community in that it lumps together in the mind of the paranoid individual (and I would add paranoid group) whole groups of people who have no real relationship to one another who are suddenly joined together in the mind of the paranoid individual or group as a "cabal of Satan-worshipping pedophiles." This creation of a false community of people creates an enemy and fulfills the second part of Klein's original formulation of the paranoid-schizoid position—namely the schizoid splitting off of the frustrating, persecutory bad "object."

It is not a stretch of the psychological imagination to appreciate the tremendous pull of a collective psyche fixated on a world of good and bad objects, good and bad groups. The whole world splits. There is a suction from the collective psyche that can easily swallow any of us into the paranoid-schizoid position as it creates certainty out of uncertainty in a world that has become more uncertain. And, of course, the consequence is that our world has become populated by multiple pseudo-communities in which whole large groups of people are seen as belonging to multiple bad, persecutory evil "objects."

Another way of thinking about how the paranoid-schizoid position can be reflected in the group psyche is in the notion of *cultural complexes*. Many cultural complexes are built around the nidus of an original and recurring group trauma. This is certainly true for Jewish people, Black people, women, and many other groups that have been discriminated against for centuries. There is an original profound and often continuing trauma of violence against the group, and the cultural complex accumulates self-affirming memories that continually validate the fixed conviction and deep emotion surrounding the primal wound of that violation and violence. A cultural complex can know in the depth of that group's psyche that it has been the victim of systematic discrimination and the complex can develop a paranoid-schizoid position that has its own built-in certainty—and certainly lots of objective reasons to see the world that way. But the complex can't allow the uncertainty of not feeling discriminated against or the uncertainty of realizing that everybody from an enemy group is not an enemy. The cultural complex can't tolerate uncertainty and posits its own certainty in simplistic ways.

Attitude Two: The Depressive Position

Klein saw the depressive position as an important developmental milestone that continues to mature throughout the life span. The splitting and part object relations that characterize the earlier phase of the paranoid-schizoid position are succeeded by the capacity to perceive that the other who frustrates is also the one who gratifies. Schizoid defenses are still in evidence, but feelings of guilt, grief, and the desire for reparation gain dominance in the developing mind.

In the depressive position, the infant is able to experience others as whole, which radically alters object relationships from the earlier phase.[10] "Before the depressive position, a good object is not in any way the same thing as a bad object. It is only in the depressive position that polar qualities can be seen as different aspects of the same object."[11] Increasing nearness of good and bad brings a corresponding integration of ego.[12]

---

[10] Melanie Klein, "Notes on Some Schizoid Mechanisms," in Envy and Gratitude and Other Works 1946–1963 (London: Hogarth Press and the Institute of Psycho-Analysis, 1946/1975), 3.

[11] James S. Grotstein, Splitting and Projective Identification (New York: Jason Aronson, 1981), 37.

[12] Wikipedia, s.v. "Paranoid-schizoid and depressive position."

If the paranoid-schizoid position offers the certainty of a fixed idea and strong emotional conviction in knowing that one's self or group is good and right and just and the rest of the world is wrong and bad and persecutory, the depressive position in the individual and the group may be a developmental achievement but it comes at the cost of having to tolerate the knowledge that good and bad exist in all of us and in all groups. This tolerance of ambivalence and a level of uncertainty often means living with the burden of a depressive mood. In my mind, the dystopian mood that has overtaken much of the world in response to seemingly insoluble problems and unending conflicts is one of the most disheartening and disturbing aspects of contemporary life.

I think of this dystopian mood as the group equivalent of living in the depressive position. It may be a psychological achievement to see oneself, one's family and friends, and the greater world community as being a mix of both good and bad and not split into good and bad. But living with that painful truth and reality can leave one in a state of disillusioned resignation to the uncertain fate of a world in rapid decline. A natural consequence of the dystopian mood is for the individual and the group to withdraw from active engagement in the world.

This withdrawal can take many forms and different degrees—from just giving up on any meaningful commitment at all in a nihilistic resignation to a more moderate disengagement with the broader world and a sharpened focus on what is in one's immediate surroundings. As in Lindberg's 1955 statement that the world has become too much to take it all in, the increasing moves to a more local focus of many—from food production to shopping habits to friendship circles to isolationism from involvement in greater world issues and conflicts—can be seen as a consequence of narrowing one's vision to what is manageable in a highly uncertain world.

What concerns me most about the rise of the dystopian mood as a reflection of the depressive position is that it kills whatever capacities we have to imagine a positive future or any future at all. It freezes everything and the resulting stasis is a calcifying killer. Perhaps a current example of such stasis, paralysis, and calcification is the state of the polarized United States and our Congress, which seems to be a mirror of that frozen collective psyche in its paranoid and depressive attitudes, immobilized from effectively considering a shared future among all our citizens.

Attitude Three: Reflective Thinking in Peace, Social/Political Engagement, and The Mythopoetic Imagination

"From the living fountain of instinct flows everything that is creative; hence the unconscious is not merely conditioned by history, but is the very source of the creative impulse."[13] The tendency to cycle through the paranoid and depressive positions as natural responses to uncertainty in the world can kill the capacity to imagine a better future or to feel in touch with what Jung called the *creative unconscious*. The paranoid-schizoid position and the depressive position effectively block access to the creative unconscious in the individual and in the group. It is true that paranoid fantasies in individuals and groups can seem quite creative in their imaginative distortions, but they rarely move the psyche forward in a way that is more than defensive, retaliatory, and persecutory.

I have become increasingly convinced that the most positive way to deal with uncertainty is to find access to the enormous energy and spirit that belongs to "the creative unconscious." We cannot will ourselves into a good or open relationship with the creative unconscious. But we can cultivate a receptivity to its energies that flow through different people and groups in various ways, depending on temperament and typology.

---

[13] C.G. Jung, "On the Structure of the Psyche" (1927/1931), in The Collected Works of C.G. Jung: Vol. 8. Structure and Dynamics of the Psyche (Princeton, NJ: Princeton University Press, 1969), para. 339.

I will outline three separate ways in which we can experience a breakthrough of the gridlock hold that the paranoid-schizoid and depressive positions can exert on the creative energies of the psyche.

- "Reflective thinking in peace"
- Social/political engagement
- The mythopoetic imagination

These three modes of responding to uncertainty are hardly prescriptive or suitable to bullet-point application. But when they knock on the door of the psyche of the individual or group, our task is to respond to them, to open the door and let them break through the logjam and paralysis of the dystopian mood.

We can cycle through each of these different modes of expression of creative energies, or we may find that one mode particularly suits our individual styles of taking the world in and responding to its conflicts, demands, and opportunities. In whatever form these energies emerge, it feels like a gift to sense them flowing, especially after a long period of stasis such as during the Covid-19 pandemic. The following descriptions of these ways of responding creatively to uncertainty are accompanied by examples from my own recent experience. I imagine that each of you can come up with examples from your own experience.

"Reflective thinking in peace"

This is the mode of responding creatively to the uncertainty of our times that Olga Tokarczuk so elegantly models in her writing. Although it may not be at the top of many peoples' lists of how to respond to uncertainty and is undervalued as not being active enough in the world, how can we respond creatively to uncertainty if we do not take the time and effort to understand its origins. Once again, I turn to Kierkegaard who noted: "People demand freedom of speech as a compensation for the freedom of thought which they seldom use."[14]

---

[14] Soren Kierkegaard, Either/Or, trans. David S. Swenson and Lillian Marvin Swenson (Princeton, NJ: Princeton University Press, 1944), 19.

For instance, we can rail at the absurdity of those drawn to Trump's promise of Make America Great Again. But it may be better to spend some time trying to understand what might motivate people to embrace such patently false and simplistic premises. Are they unconsciously possessed by their own deep anxieties and uncertainties, yearning for a strong leader who promises to make the world safe and prosperous? Although we seem to always favor the quick fix, "reflective thinking in peace" allows for new ideas to percolate and emerge. Here are a couple examples in which I have had the privilege of sharing with others this way of responding to uncertainty in the world, a way that values probing the origins and causes of uncertainty on any number of issues in the mode of Olga's prayer.

The first example of collectively gathering to engage in "reflective thinking in peace" occurred at the Analysis and Activism/Presidency Conference hosted by the C.G. Jung Institute of San Francisco just prior to the 2020 US Presidential Election.[15] Presenters and participants from around the world gathered virtually to engage in "reflective thinking in peace" on a variety of the most urgent issues facing the world.

And, in the same mode, we gathered a group of leading experts to consider the relationships between psyche and politics in the *Mind of State* podcast series that encouraged thoughtful reflection on the most vexing problems of our times https:// mindofstate.com). In both examples, we created a space to exercise a clear mind, lively intuition, deep feeling, and attention to sensate detail that became a kind of prayer, whether there is or isn't a God or gods.

---

[15] Thomas Singer and Andrew Samuels, eds. The Reality of Fragmentation and the Yearning for Healing: Jungian Perspectives on Democracy, Power, and Illusion in Contemporary Politics, https://aras.org/analysis-and-activism-2020-us-presidency-conference-1.

Social and Political Engagement

Many people find creative expression through much more direct action to bring change to a world stuck in the paralysis and inertia of a dystopian mood, even when the fueling conflicts seem intractable and overwhelming. Both the paranoid-schizoid position and the depressive position tend to freeze such engagement, although there are certainly times when people are motivated to act out of their paranoid-schizoid fantasies. I have witnessed in our own Jungian tradition a growing awareness for the need of social and political engagement as part of the psyche's natural creative expression in the world.

Within the Jungian tradition, most prominent in this mode of expression has been the Analysis &Activism Group that originated with Andrew Samuels and Emilija Kiehl in London. This group has rallied around it the more socially and politically active Jungians from across the world. Of course, this social and political engagement is by no means limited or unique to the Jungian tradition, or for that matter to psychological traditions, and can be seen in many different arenas from business communities to religious communities to environmental groups. But no one in contemporary times has embodied more fully the mode of social and political engagement as a way of breaking through the stasis of the defensive reactions to uncertainty than the president of Ukraine Volodymyr Zelenskyy.

Just when democracies seemed most bogged down in ineffective paralysis with the autocrats threatening to take hold of the reins of power around the world, Zelensksyy has come to symbolize a spirit of activism that had seemed moribund in this time of authoritarian tyrants such as Putin. That much of the world has rallied to the support of Ukraine and reaffirmed the spirit of democracy has felt like a miraculous breakthrough, a true *enantiodromia* that has at least for the moment turned the tide of a dangerous drift to authoritarianism. Internationally, Ukraine's surprising resilience in the face of a brutal Russian onslaught, and the suggestion that more moderate forces in the American political psyche are effectively countering more extreme elements in politics, have given hope. Perhaps a shift in the Spirit of the Times is countering the defensiveness of the paranoid and depressive positions that have contributed to a deepening climate of dangerous uncertainty.

Mythopoetic Imagination

The third mode of responding to the toxic and paralyzing effects of the paranoid-schizoid and depressive positions that take hold of the individual and group psyche in response to uncertainty is what I have come to think of as the mythopoetic imagination. During the height of Covid-19, wildfires in California, and deadly stalemate in American political life—with Russia's invasion of Ukraine then on the uncertain horizon—I stumbled into several projects. Only retrospectively did I realize these were unbeckoned breakthroughs of the mythopoetic imagination into a dystopian mood and stasis that had taken hold of my psyche and most of those around me, within which we could hardly envision anything positive or creative in the present or the future.

These experiences of the mythopoetic imagination surprised me with a sense of delight and renewal, putting me on high alert to the importance of having an active capacity to smell when something soulful and spirited is breaking through the numbing fog of uncertainty, that has the effect of shutting us down to any signs of creative life-affirming energies. I want to mention a few of these projects and provide links to them where they can be viewed in their entirety. And, then I want to focus on one project in more detail to give a sense of what I mean by the mythopoetic imagination.

The first experience came to me courtesy of my wife who dragged me to a show of miniature rooms filled with puppets created by the set designer of a local theatre forced to shut its doors during Covid-19. I was stunned by the evocative, truly numinous awakening that I experienced in the presence of Steve Coleman's creative genius and felt a stirring inside that moved me to begin a series of discussions with Steve about the process of building the exhibit. Steve's mythopoetic imagination awakened in me and many others a sense of revelation and rebirth in the midst of the pandemic. I documented this experience in both *ARAS Connections* (https://aras.org/sites/default/files/docs/000145Singer.pdf) and *in Jung Journal: Culture & Psyche,* and eventually presented it in an evening performance at the theatre.[16]

Along with Jules Cashford, Craig San Roque, and Allison Tuzo, I also joined with ARAS to produce a series of six shows that focus on the mythopoetic imagination as a creative response to the climate change crisis and the deep uncertainty it creates about the very survival of our planet as we know it. *ARAS: Gaia Then and Now* focuses on the symbolic imagery that emerges in response to the threat to Gaia, ancient Greek Mother Goddess and name of the current scientific theory about the interrelatedness of all of Earth's beings, animate and inanimate. This mythopoetic outpouring is available in its entirety at (https://aras.org/newsletters/aras-connections-image-and-archetype-2022-issue-4).

The final example of the mythopoetic imagination breaking through the stasis, paranoia, and depression of contemporary culture focuses on the artwork of Millie Kutz who entered into a conversation about her work with Jean Kirsch, a San Francisco Jungian analyst, and me. As a senior in high school, Millie was home bound for a year because of Covid-19 school closures. All of her academic and social life was conducted on the internet. In the absence of the stimulation of the school and friendship environment,

---

[16] Thomas S. Singer, "A Portal to the Imaginal: Steve Colman, The Mill Valley Throckmorton Theater, and Ingmar Bergman's Fanny and Alexander," Jung Journal: Culture & Psyche 16, no. 1: 51–81.

Millie could have easily succumbed to the uncertainty of her daily and future life with a mixture of paranoia and depression. Instead, something in the creative unconscious got stimulated in this already talented young artist and the mythopoetic imagination broke through the isolation, fear, and all-pervasive dystopian mood. Millie embarked on a remarkable creative project—a series of drawings exploring the impact of the uncertainty and isolation imposed by the pandemic and accompanying increased dependence on the internet. The limits of this chapter only permit me to include a few of the images but a paper including many of them is available on ARAS at (https://aras.org/sites/default/files/docs/000146Kutz.pdf[17]).

I want to focus on three of the drawings that speak specifically to the psyche's responses to the impact of uncertainty I have outlined in my schema. Among the many things that impressed me about her series, which we called *Millie's COVID Fever Dreamscapes,* is the fact that Millie's mythopoetic imagination did not deny the paranoid-schizoid and depressive positions that overtook her at times. In fact, she faces them head on in her drawing. It is worth noting that Millie is not just being taken hold of by her own psyche but by the collective psyche and its cultural complexes as well.

Millie's Experience of the Paranoid-Schizoid Position

The first drawing is as good a representation of the paranoid-schizoid position overtaking the group psyche as we might find.

---

17 Millie Kutz, Jean Kirsch, and Thomas Singer, "Millie's COVID Fever Dreamscapes," ARAS Connections, https://aras.org/sites/default/files/docs/000145Singer.pdf.

The giant eye of the internet hovers over Millie
and all the people she knows.

About this drawing, Millie writes:

"This drawing represents my fellow clas-
smates and everyone I know who was engulfed by
technology. There are so many people, and they
go off into the distance, but you can still feel their
presence in a sort of infinite regression. They are not
all the same person but many different people. We
are all wearing the same colors as a way of saying
that we are all in the same situation. But they are not
all me. For instance, there are different kind of hair
styles, and they are not all wearing the hat. This time
it is a single eye rather than many eyes and I think
the single eye in this drawing is about technology
as a whole. I think this drawing is about how
overwhelming technology can be, about how tiny

and insignificant you can feel when confronted with this entire online world. With social media, there is a sense that you're constantly being perceived online by thousands of people. It is crazy to think that so many people can look at something at the same time. It's just so huge. I have Instagram and recently I got on to TikTok where I've been posting my art. It's weird to think that so many people can look at one thing, that you can be seen by so many people. I posted one video that got a hundred thousand views. It's weird to think that so many people can know you exist and perceive you in a certain way."

Millie's Experience of the Depressive Position

This was actually the first drawing that Millie did in this series. It is hard to make out Millie who sits cross legged and dark eyed in the bottom center of the drawing.

Bleak Reality

Here is how Millie describes this drawing:

"I think this was supposed to be like my reality—my mind—during those months of COVID isolation. It's sad now that I think about it. My reality was a lot bleaker than the imaginative worlds I was creating or dreaming about. That's why when I put all the drawings in a book I chose this as the first page. This is what reality was like. It was really bleak. A lot of people my age are getting addicted to this online world just because reality can be so bleak sometimes. When you have access to this very colorful, bright world that's at your fingertips, why would you choose to stay in bleak reality when you can do all this instead?"

Millie's Experience of the Mythopoetic Imagination

In this stunning fusion of religious and internet symbolic imagery, Millie's mythopoetic imagination allows us to see more clearly how easy it is to confuse an attitude of sacred worship with reverence for the internet.

Transcendent Reality and/or Dangerous Seduction

Here is the exchange between Millie, Jean Kirsch, and me about this drawing:

JK/TS: This almost has a priestly Zen temple quality to it.

Millie: Yeah. So, this one was supposed to represent technology as a religion. Technology comes in and takes over, replacing human connection. Rather than relying on other humans for entertainment or comfort or anything, we're relying on technology.

JK/TS: It has a wonderfully centered feeling to it. There's an altar and it's almost like a mandala and it's very centered. And then there's that seated figure who has a spiritual feeling. But I guess the feeling of it is not wonderful. But it has the quality of a spiritual practice in it, of making a connection with something that's transcendent. In a way, you're implying that technology in and of itself is transcendent.

Millie: Yeah, because I feel technology is almost like religion in a weird way. It's this very unknown world that's greater than ourselves.

JK/TS: You weren't thinking of a transcendent spiritual centeredness when you were drawing this? You were thinking more in terms of technology taking over.

Millie: Yeah, like technology replacing religion.

JK/TS: Well, if it's about technology taking over religion, it looks religious. So technology can wear the guise of religion, but one needs to be careful about it then.

Millie: Yeah, especially because there's a crowd at the bottom.

JK/TS: So you're really consciously playing with a spiritual image in a way that says technology can replace religion and worship. People can worship technology. So the drawing is sardonic?

Millie: Yeah. Because I think there is something seductive about technology. The online world is very structured and grid like as symbolized by the retro color bars. There is a tension between the orderliness of the technological world and the less orderliness of the human world. You can see how patterned and ordered the technological world is in this drawing.

Millie points to the orderliness of the internet as offering a most appealing analgesia to the disorderliness, bleakness, and uncertainty of living in everyday reality without virtual reality. Millie's ability to travel through the paranoid and depressive positions of her responses has as its foundation the vitality of the mythopoetic imagination with its capacity to clearly see the dangers and false promises, revealing through creative imagination that psyche can be objective about the brave new world. As opposed to the deadening of spirit and soul characteristic of an individual or collective psyche trapped in the paranoid and depressive positions, Millie's spirit shines through the very attitudes that could have paralyzed her. Her creative imagination allows her to transcend these positions even as it reveals them.

Conclusion

My beloved colleague, Jean Kirsch, in her own moment of giving expression to the mythopoetic imagination, takes us back full circle to Olga Tokarczuk's notion of prayer as a place to think in peace when she wrote rhapsodically about Millie's *COVID Fever Dreamscapes* (2022):

No matter what we name it, Millie has transported us through the medium of her intellect and her sizeable talent to a place of greater appreciation of what the British essayist Erich Heller calls 'the pure inwardness of human subjectivity.' We mortals with lesser talent suffer inchoately that which the artist can render into images with transcendent power. We gaze with amazement at Millie's work and are pitched into our own subjectivity, receiving the paintings each of us separately, finding individual meanings, yet we are united in awe. Perhaps even Millie, looking back at what she made in a fever of inspiration, stands mute and amazed.

With the global pandemic brought about by the Coronavirus and its numerous mutations, the now rampant wildfires of California, and almost daily news of calamity abroad, we have left all traces of Classicism and Romanticism in the arts behind us; we are no longer idealists of any political or economic ilk; and we feel with Yeats that, indeed, 'the centre cannot hold.'[18] Yet, we draw back from the nihilism which seems to beckon and we seek meaning as our guide and protector. We count upon a certain resilience of being. We are struck by some manifestation of matter inspired by spirit—a sunrise or a symphony, a painting or the way a drop of water hangs at the tip of a blade of grass—and we are held in awe. Such is our experience of the rare burst of creative genius that Millie so casually handed to us with her fever dream paintings. A once in a lifetime event, a way of painting she tells us is unlike her other work.

Perhaps Millie's struggle to put technology into its proper place as a tool, rather than succumb to its colorful allure, was lifted by wings of hope, that quintessential factor in our primal nature, and though we stand in the cold alongside her, we find

---

[18] From "The Second Coming," by William Butler Yeats, https://www.poetryfoundation.org/poems/43290/the-second-coming.

ourselves in a new situation through her art and with her can struggle on, as the pandemic gives way to an endemic. Maybe we are released from the direst prospects for tomorrow, but surely nothing more. Still, we give thanks.

My final point: we would all do well to become more alert to when the vitality of a soul or souls energized by the creative unconscious breaks through the deadening effects of our collective paranoid and depressive attitudes that freeze life and its flow, bringing to us a renewed sense of life's possibilities.

Challenges Facing Our World: Grappling with the Environment, the Pandemic, and War

"Just as there is a relationship of mind to body,
so there is a relationship of body to earth."
-Jung, 1957 para. 19

"We should know what our convictions are, and stand for them.
Upon one's own philosophy, conscious or unconscious, depends
one's ultimate interpretation of facts. Therefore, it is wise to be
as clear as possible about one's subjective principles.
As the man is, so will be his ultimate truth."
-Jung, 1954, para. 211

Introduction

As we noted in Sections One and Two, 2022 was a year of continued change on many levels. At the environmental level, it was also a time of strife and dread. Overarching our personal concerns about managing uncertainty and social disquiet, were a series of crises for our environment and our relationship to nature, our health, and the emergence of war. These environmental changes and the advent of war brought with them an additional intense period of social change and uncertainty. Environmental and physical issues and concerns include:

❖ Warming of the earth and rising sea levels
❖ New pandemics and illnesses
❖ Pollution of earth and the oceans
❖ Global effects of war

We are challenged by many environmental and natural emergencies. These are issues that are not going to be resolved immediately. These issues also raise similar questions to those posed in parts One and Two:

- How to develop alternative ways of thinking about and working with these complex environmental issues
- Managing new levels of fear, anxiety, and discontent in the face of these grave threats
- Living with ongoing disasters
- Facing the war in Europe

The Jungian perspective in this section will again acknowledge and articulate what is happening, offer tools for understanding current environmental pressures and developing personal mechanisms to manage ongoing uncertainty in these areas, and show various ways to think about the important environmental issues confronting us. These chapters will go a long way toward developing an individual approach for living more comfortably with nature and our environment.

In this part, the current environmental crisis is best described in our first chapter by author Jeffrey T. Kiehl. Our society is left with several vital questions that will be front and center as we come into our new ways to live. These include understanding and meeting our environmental challenges, learning ways to grapple with and grasp the opportunities and challenges that are being presented, and identifying what we as individuals can potentially do and, within that context, taking action.

The pandemic is another example of new issues caused by environmental changes. Climate change is creating a new relationship with viruses and the natural world. We are facing a new reality where new pandemics, diseases and natural events will continue to impact our lives and futures. Jan Bower in her chapter, *Three Horsemen of the Apocalypse of Our Time*, poses an interesting observation:

Jan delves into how and why communities and nations come together on an issue. She offers intriguing and important considerations and observation, as well as recommendations.

In chapter three, *Reconsidering Individuation in the 21st Century: When Archetypal Patterns Shift,* Joe Cambray brings us back to the nature of personal growth by posing the question: how is the signature Jungian concept of individuation, becoming as fully as possible, the person you are meant to be, interacting with the 21st century? He examines the concept of individuation in the context of new paradigms, such as complexity theory, which focuses on complex adaptive systems, synchronicity, and rhizomatic science.

References

Jung, C.G., (1954). *The development of personality* (R. F. C. Hull, Trans.). In H. Read et al. (Eds.), *CW, Vol. 17,* (pp. 165-186). Princeton, NJ: Princeton University Press. (Original work published 1934)

_____. (1970). *CW, Vol. 10, Civilization in transition,* Princeton, NJ: Princeton University Press.

The Nature of Uncertainty/The Uncertainty of Nature

Jeffrey T. Kiehl, PhD

"Western man has no need of more superiority over nature, whether outside or inside. He has both in almost devilish perfection. What he lacks is conscious recognition of his inferiority to the nature around and within him. He must learn that he may not do exactly as he wills. If he does not learn this, his own nature will destroy him. He does not know that his own soul is rebelling against him in a suicidal way."

—Jung, 1958 para. 870

"... for in all chaos there is a cosmos, in all disorder a secret order, in all caprice a fixed law, for everything that works is grounded on its opposite."

— Jung, 1959 para. 66

Introduction

I have been immersed in the works of C.G. Jung for over three decades including my own analytic journey and then work with my clients. In addition to my Jungian practice, I have worked as a scientist for over forty years, beginning in theoretical physics and then carrying out research in climate science. My love for science began at a very early age and has never really waned. To *do science* is itself a disciplined form of practice, requiring immersion in the languages of mathematics and measurement. The practices of Jungian psychology and science have provided me with meaningful guidance and orientation for much of my life. They form foundational parts of my personal cosmology or map for how I perceive, understand, and navigate life. This is not to suggest in any way that these practices have protected me from suffering. That is not the purpose of any practice or cosmology. What a working cosmology does is to help one find meaning in the very midst of suffering, or, at the very least, to ensure the suffering does not forever swallow one up.

Suffering emerges from the uncertainty and unexpectedness of life. We may be going along smoothly in life and then out of the blue we find ourselves facing unexpected, painful disruption. We are uncertain as to what to do. It is as though the stream of life hits an impediment and the flow becomes extremely turbulent. It is in such times we may become untethered and lack a guiding star that helps us reach a safer shore of certainty. It is inevitable such disturbances arise in life.

Uncertainty and suffering also occur on a larger collective scale. It has been a part of our lives for centuries. In our time, we have had to deal with great existential threats to humanity. In the 1930s and 1940s, the threat of dictatorships and the ensuing Second World War, in the 1950s and 1960s the global threat of nuclear annihilation. In the 1970s, we became aware of our many ecological crises, which now, in the form of climate chaos, threaten to disrupt the entire planetary life system. Of course, these were not the only existential crises over the past decades, racism, sexism, and authoritarianism have been ever present throughout this time. All these large-scale existential threats rife with uncertainties and filling us with fear and anxiety contribute to both personal and collective disorientation. Given the growing interconnected and complex nature of these issues, it is imperative we find ways of navigating the turbulent waters full of such immense uncertainty.

Personally, my scientific research in climate chaos has placed me in direct contact with an overwhelming sense of despair and uncertainty concerning our future. Anyone who works on the problem of climate chaos eventually experiences the challenge of holding and working with such overwhelming facts. After giving public presentations on climate chaos, I am often asked how I deal with such disturbing knowledge, how do I make it through the day? Quite frankly the only way I have found to deal with the feelings that well up within me involve the practices of science and Jungian psychology. I wish to share with you how these two practices, particularly Jungian psychology, have helped me work with the climate uncertainties we face for our future.

The natural environment as humanity has known it is currently going through a radical alteration. Such enormous change due to our actions has increased our sense of uncertainty about where we are and where we will be in the future. How will nature react to our continued assault against her? How will we deal with the rapid changes that are taking place in our environments, local and global? These tremendous uncertainties create universal states of fear, anxiety, and helplessness, particularly being felt by young people. It is not a question of whether the natural world will survive our destructive acts. Earth's history provides ample evidence that the planet is resilient. The more important question is: *what kind of a world will we bequeath to future generations?* Here I include not only human life, but the more-than-human world. Will we participate in ensuring a flourishing future for generations to come, or continue to create a collapsing climate system for generations to come?

From a Jungian perspective, the answers to these questions are deeply dependent upon the relationships we have with both inner and outer worlds, and the extent to which we experience the interdependence of these two worlds. In terms of Jungian psychology, our past and current crises arise from cutting ourselves off from the wellspring of archetypal numinosity residing in the depths of the unconscious. This cutting off involves a disconnection from nature herself. So, not only are we cut off from our inner world, but we are cut off from the world of nature around us. This is the root of our personal suffering, but also the root of our collective existential threats. Here cut off means not being in relationship. Life is multi-dimensional involving our inner world, the social world around us and the greater world of planet and cosmos. Living a full, balanced life involves being in relationship with all these worlds and feeling fulfilled. To begin the conversation, let us explore what we know is happening in the world concerning climate disruption.

Our Past and Present World

Generally, we feel most comfortable when the environment around us is predictable and nonthreatening. Human history is a story of how mankind used will, strength and knowledge to manipulate the local environment to create protective structures and reliable food systems to ensure our survivability. Mankind's transition to an agrarian lifestyle led to a rise in human population, which, in turn, created more need for food and more space to live. Thus, our story, as a species, is one of ever-growing numbers, migration across the planet, and increased consumption to support ourselves. These factors began to significantly affect the global environment with the onset of the Industrial Revolution around three hundred years ago. The discovery of coal and oil, as efficient energy sources, enabled mankind to grow at ever increasing numbers, fueling our consumptive habits. Such growth came with a tremendous cost to the extent and safety of the natural world, including coverage of forests, water quality, loss of species and an increasingly warming planet. These shifts have led to significant world-wide economic inequities. The irony is that the more we developed technologies to keep us safe from the wilderness "out there," the more our separation from the wilderness led to not only the destruction of the natural world, but also destruction of human lives. The appearance of Covid-19 is a perfect example of how human insurgency into the natural world created the worst pandemic in a century.

Of course, the other environmental catastrophe that looms large is the pollution of the world oceans. Toxic chemicals deposited into coastal regions are causing major loss of marine life, while the presence of microplastics is now present in the deepest parts of the oceans. Increased emissions of carbon dioxide from the use of coal and oil acidifies the oceans, which destroys the tiniest ocean lifeforms at the base of the global marine food chain. Numerous scientific assessments over the past decades have raised the alarm that we are literally fouling our nest to the point of a sixth mass extinction. No other mass extinction in Earth's 4.8 billion year history was caused by a single species, unlike the current one caused by *homo sapiens*. Given the disastrous impact we have had on the planet it is questionable whether we deserve the designation of *wise man*. Finally, the emission of carbon dioxide into the atmosphere through the burning of coal and oil has warmed the planet by 2°F (1.1°C) since since the mid 1800s. This seemingly small amount of warming—which historically is quite large—has led to a concatenation of catastrophic climate effects that are no longer occurring in distant lands but at the doorstep of every part of the planet. Increases in intense storms, raging forest fires, increased drought conditions, the melting of the Greenland and Antarctic ice sheets, and rising sea levels are accelerating at a phenomenally unprecedented pace. These climatically driven chaotic weather events are displacing millions of people and causing damages that cost multiple billions of dollars every year. Remember all these disasters are due to a 2°F (1.1°C) warming. Clearly, our behavior has strayed considerably from our original instinctual intent to keep our world(s) safe and predictable.

We hear daily stories about increasing anxiety, depression, and anger amongst the populace and in particular, young people concerning climate chaos. Dealing with stressors in life is nothing new. Most of us have had to deal with some form of disruption in our lives: early childhood upsets, frictions with parents, relationship issues, lack of vocational direction, or a loss of meaning in mid- to later life. In a sense these are the *predictable* dilemmas of a normal life and are viewed as the perennial problems we all face in our development process. Beyond these predictable obstacles of growing lie the more disruptive, traumatic stressors often leading to a life of deep suffering. Such severe disruptions often begin with early childhood trauma including neglect, rejection, psychological and physical abuse rooted in an unpredictable, fragmented family environment. Such beginnings precipitate an inability to establish stable relationships, and unpredictable outbursts of rage and/or self-loathing. In these situations, the world often appears unsafe and completely unpredictable. From a Jungian perspective these pathologies, the *logos* of suffering, provide a doorway to healing. Thus, chaos can lead to cosmos, or order in our lives. Through inner work we learn to live with the unpredictable forces in life.

Clearly something has changed over the past few decades given the reported dramatic rise in psychological suffering. *Pathos is on the rise, in lock step with global warming.* We have entered a new situation in which outer world chaos has become so intense and intrusive that our ability to deal with the personal disruptions in life—be they "normal" or "abnormal"—is being overwhelmed by an entirely new form of disruption. These disruptions are rooted in large-scale anticipated losses, which constellate within us, at the most primary level, tremendous fear and anxiety. Whenever I give public presentations on climate chaos, I ask people how they feel after listening to the facts around this issue. After a sustained moment of silence, inevitably individuals begin to express feeling toned responses of helplessness, hopelessness, fear, anger, guilt, numbness, and dissociation. No matter where or when I have asked this question, the same emotional responses are reported by the audience. Interestingly, all these affective responses are symptomatic of trauma. Thus, the very news of climate chaos causes traumatic symptoms, which then makes it difficult for people to take in and work with what is happening in their world. A popular term to capture the mood around climate disruption is eco-anxiety, which suggests the interdependence between ecology or ecosystems and our psychological awareness of their threatened existence. When I hear this phrase, I always feel compelled to not only recognize the anxiety felt by us, but the anxiety felt by the more-than-human world. *Suffering is reciprocal.* Whatever term you want to use, it is clear we have entered an entirely new age of collective suffering and are struggling to define and delimit its effects.

A Jungian perspective on psyche and the world is well equipped to deal with patterns of disorder like climate chaos for it is a psychology rooted in a framework recognizing the dynamic interplay of opposites. The fundamental opposite being the polarity of consciousness and unconsciousness. The dynamic interplay between these two realms determines how well we relate to each other and world around us. When the interaction between these realms is disrupted, we fall out of balance leading to chaotic outer world symptoms. Some argue we must focus all our attention on inner imbalances before attempting to address any outer world problems, an approach also maintained by certain spiritual communities. Such arguments are somewhat tenable when the outer world problems are limited in scope, but with a problem like climate chaos this approach guarantees catastrophic consequences for future generations. Why? To answer this, we need to consider the scientific dimensions of climate chaos and its relationship to time.

The Uncertainty of Our Future

Time is a central element to so many of life's processes. Earth as the living, complex entity Gaia contains a multitude of processes operating on a wide range of time scales. Our ability to simulate Earth's climate on supercomputers has improved greatly over the past few decades. We can now use these tools to ask how will the climate of Earth change in the future? The answer to this question involves many uncertainties. Indeed, understanding uncertainty in its varied forms is a central field of study in Earth System Sciences. There are uncertainties in quantifying and accurately representing fundamental physical, chemical, biological and ecological processes in the models used to project Earth's future climate. There are uncertainties in projecting future human behavior including population growth, consumption habits, energy needs and sources of energy. These manifold uncertainties may cast doubt on our ability to predict Earth's future climate. Those who doubt the human role in climate chaos often take this position. Yet, projecting aspects of Earth's future climate has been achieved with a great degree of accuracy.

For example, in the 1980s climate models were run forty years into the future to simulate how the climate would evolve over time. When scientists compare the predicted global heating over the past forty years with what really occurred, they find tremendous agreement between the predicted and observed heating. Thus, despite all the uncertainties implicit in the task of predicting future climate there is real skill in being able to make accurate predictions. So, science can provide a fairly accurate answer to our question about future climate change, which is where time plays a critical role.

The key uncertainty in answering this question is how much coal and oil we will burn in the future and when we will stop using these fuels. If we continue to rely on these fossil fuels as we have in the past, then within 14 years Earth will cross the 2.7°F (1.5°C) limit defined by the international science community as the safe limit to prevent catastrophic change, by 2053 we will warm the planet by 4°F (2°C), and within 80 years the planet will most likely warm by at least 7°F (4°C). I would also argue that these are conservative predictions given what we know about Earth's history and how it responded to high levels of carbon dioxide in the deep past. These may not sound like large numbers. After all the local temperature can change by more than 7 °F overnight. But the temperature I am citing is a global average. Perhaps the best way to understand the magnitude of this global heating is to perform an *anamnesis*, a remembering, of Earth's past. For example, the levels of carbon dioxide today are equivalent to where they were 3 to 4 million years ago, which was a warm climate. If we project out 80 years, then the carbon dioxide levels will be where they were around 40 million years ago. We know from various scientific studies that this was a time when Earth was very warm and there was virtually no ice at the poles and much higher sea levels. Of course, it took nature millions of years to reach such levels of carbon dioxide and associated warm climates then, while we are rapidly returning Earth to these past warm climates due to our fuel use. Based on geologic data we know with great certainty that the current rate of heating is unprecedented in Earth's history.

What I have described is a summary of the fundamentals of climate science. It is information that provides a foundation from which to carry out action. Note that the certainty provided by science helps us deal with what to do and when. Accepting the information rests on our ability to trust the science. We live in a time when special interest groups are attempting to sow distrust around the field of science, especially climate science. So, it is important to understand the value and meaning of science to society. Improved scientific understanding of climate chaos can help us grapple with the emotions associated with this issue. First, taking time to seek out the facts of climate change reduces our personal uncertainty around the issue. Numerous sources exist that clearly explain the science behind climate chaos. You do not need an advanced degree in the sciences to understand how the climate is being affected by our burning of fossil fuels. I provide a list of some of these resources at the end of this chapter. The more we know how something is taking place, the less surprised we will be when reading news stories about the climate system. There is power in knowledge. Second, I always encourage people to learn enough about climate chaos to become agents of change. Talk to your friends and family about the issue. Talk to strangers about it. Each of us can become a messenger of change. Form a local climate circle in your neighborhood, church, or school. These circles are foremost for the purpose of sharing your feelings around climate chaos. Sharing feelings within a small group creates a space for healing. Third, become familiar with where your local politicians stand on the climate issue and vote for those individuals who accept the scientific reality of the issue. Be especially aware of where local school board members stand on the climate issue. These three actions, rooted in your new knowledge of climate science, can help you grapple with and transform your feelings on the issue.

How much time do we have to move off coal and oil to avoid the worst scenario of heating? Unfortunately, we need to get off these fuels now. Postponing the transition anymore commits future generations to more and more heating. Let me be clear, 2.7° (1.5°), 4° (2°C) and 7°F (4°C) global heating over coming decades will lead to unimaginable suffering for all life on Earth. Many of the anticipated environmental changes are already occurring in places around the world and their impacts are intensifying. Experiencing these changes is heightening the felt sense of uncertainty and anxiety for our future. Young people are questioning whether to have children, mass migrations are underway among the poorer peoples of the world, while more affluent people are moving to regions less threatened by climate chaos. We don't know what to do, where to go, or what's going to happen to us and our loved ones.

It is imperative we act in time to avoid condemning our children and their children and all life on Earth to such suffering. We now face the greatest challenge in human history. Time is running out to prevent such destruction. *And here is the psychological dilemma: if we wait for a sufficient number of people to re-establish inner balance before acting on the issue, we will most assuredly commit the world to unimaginable suffering. So, a one-sided approach to addressing our collective dilemma is inadvisable.* Simply put, we need a both/and approach to collective problems like climate chaos. We must move off fossil fuels at the same time we do our inner work.

Our Inner Work

Outer world actions are a necessary part of addressing future uncertainties but not sufficient to holistically address the issues facing us. If we continue to adhere to old paradigms, perspectives, and worldviews, then our "solutions" come with hidden costs, cloaked within shadow. I am reminded of the apocryphal statement of Einstein's that, "We cannot solve problems with the same thinking used to create them." By itself this statement is too limited. I would rephrase it as, "We cannot solve problems with the same psyche used to create them" for thinking alone will not address our greatest threats and uncertainties. We need to embrace far more than thinking if we are going to create a flourishing future for life to come. We need a transformation of psyche. From a Jungian perspective, one-sidedness inevitably leads to neurosis, or an imbalance between us and the surrounding world. Living in neurosis means an inability to healthily relate to ourselves and others. Healthy relating involves valuing other dimensions of ourselves and those around us. Healthy relationships honor reciprocal interactions that go beyond egoic needs and wants. The root of the word health is to *heal*, or to make whole. Wholeness implicitly implies balance.

Interestingly, our inner imbalance is mirrored in the outer world as an imbalance in the flow of energy to and from Earth. Scientifically, a stable climate occurs when the amount of sunlight available to warm Earth is balanced by the amount of energy flowing out to space, which cools Earth. The disturbance of this balance by burning coal and oil alters the greenhouse effect leading to a decrease in the amount of energy leaving the planet. Less energy leaving Earth means more energy available to warm the planet. Our neglect of this scientific fact—one we have known for over a century—is a result of our inner psychic imbalance, for our inner imbalance prevents us from feeling a deep connection to nature. Without an ability to empathically connect to nature we exploit her for purely utilitarian purposes. From a Jungian perspective, our inner imbalance is a form of collective dissociation, an inner splitting of the psyche, which leads to alienation and insecurity and susceptibility to uncertainty. Our actions in the outer world are more likely to be in balance with nature when we are working on inner wholeness. A reestablishment of inner psychic energy is mirrored as a rebalance of the outer flow of energy to our planet.

How did we get to such a place of imbalance? Jung (1989) notes that, "… it is the special tragedy of man that in order to win consciousness he is forced into dissociation with nature" (p. 38). According to Jung, with the development of consciousness, in particular reasoning, humanity separated from nature and instinct. This process began early in human development and became firmly established during what's referred to as "The Age of Enlightenment." By this time the dominant belief was that reason alone could address the ills of the world and reveal all of nature's secrets. Reason and will became the foundations of our modern worldview, which led to an enormous collective shadow. Disregard and dismissal of other ways of knowing including feeling and intuition fell into the unconscious. It would be foolish to suggest we abandon reason and rational thinking and return to a mythical past. Doing so would be equally one-sided and impossible. It does suggest that we must retrieve what was lost over time. Jung states that,

> Western consciousness is by no means the only kind of consciousness there is; it is historically conditioned and geographically limited, and representative of only one part of mankind. The widening of consciousness ought not to proceed at the expense of other kinds of consciousness. (Jung, 1967, para. 84)

Jung is asking us to widen our consciousness to embrace other ways of knowing beyond just reason. Such ways of knowing are integral to many indigenous societies and were present in Western societies of the past (Bernstein, 2018). By integrating these other ways of knowing into consciousness, we create more comprehensive experiences opening multiple ways of holistically being present in the world. For example, feeling is essential for reciprocal relating to others; it opens us to truly valuing others. When someone or something is of little value to us, there is little interest in being in relationship with the other. Indeed, we can debase and even destroy the other if we view it as valueless. If we do not value nature and the more-than-human-world, then we can use and abuse it, which is what has happened and continues to happen in our world. Intuition is also often looked upon as an impractical and even untrustworthy way of relating to the other for it is difficult to concretize and pin down, it is mercurial by its very nature. Yet, modern psychology studies have shown that intuition is a powerful means for making decisions when faced with great uncertainties (McGilchrist, 2021, pp. 673-778). Intuition's ability to provide positive guidance connects us with emotions. By placing ourselves in a more open and flowing mood, intuition awakens in us and allows us to navigate the sea of uncertainty.

What I am arguing for, which is a core concept in Jungian psychology, is that we work towards balancing the functional ways psyche has in experiencing and knowing the world(s) in which we dwell so that we deal with uncertainties more creatively. The next time you read a news story about the latest ecological, economic, political, or social catastrophe try to be aware of which form of consciousness is engaging with the story. How would opening to other ways of experiencing the story shift your emotional response to what you are reading? Can you use a different lens to perceive this information? If so, how does your mood shift? An even more challenging, but greatly rewarding practice is to hold all four ways (thinking, feeling, sensing, intuition) of relating simultaneously.

In this way, we become more whole and address our state of dissociation or fragmentation. This integral approach to being in the world opens us to feeling more balanced and attuned with the stormy seas in ways hard to describe. The potential for such integral experiencing is within you.

Even more expansive ways of knowing and experiencing the world lie beyond the functional ways of relating. I call them expansive because they transcend the usual space-time realm of our phenomenal world. When I first read Jung's writings on dreams and synchronicity, I felt tremendous excitement for here was someone who recognized these two forms of experience as real. Unfortunately, mainstream science continues to deny the reality or relevance of these ways of experiencing the world. Since they defy controlled repeatability, they are deemed fanciful imaginations and, thus, irrelevant. Jung widened the definition of reality to include all empirical experience. In particular, dreams and synchronicity play an important role in our lives and how we relate to the world around us; most importantly they provide us with a sense of meaning. They even help us work with the uncertainties in life for given their transcendent nature they provide us with information unavailable through the usual ways of experiencing the world. Consider the following dream I had last year in which,

> I am underwater in scuba gear along with a Jungian colleague and friend. We are watching a woman – also in scuba gear – communicating with a manatee. Behind the woman lurk three threatening men in scuba gear, each holding a speargun. I am explaining to my friend that the woman is a marine biologist who is trying to save the manatee from extinction and that the three men behind her are trying to prevent her from saving the manatee.

The dream ended at this point. The next morning after recording the dream I went online to look up the manatee, an animal that I knew virtually nothing about at the time. In particular, I was looking to see if the manatee was threatened at all. None of the sites I visited suggested the manatee was under any kind of threat. However, six months after my dream, stories began to appear in the news about the manatee and how their existence was now under severe threat. Environmental groups were asking for help to improve coastal conditions to insure the survival of this species. At the time of this writing, it is not clear whether the manatee will survive the degradation of their habitat. What is clear to me is how my dream provided an early warning about the plight of these animals. I am quite open to viewing this dream as a message from the manatee. The presence of the female marine biologist provides an image of what is required to save the manatee, which is the active presence of thinking/sensation (biology) and feeling/intuition (the feminine). The three threatening men signify the masculine view of separation and dominion working to prevent the feminine from helping the manatee. This quaternity is quite representative of the collective domination of the masculine in our society and how this energy discounts and dismisses the value of nature. I note that the witnessing by myself and my friend is also interesting in that both of us are analysts committed to applying Jungian psychology to environmental problems. Currently, dream and synchronicity data play no role in addressing our collective problems, but they could make significant contributions if recognized for their psychological value. They could help us work with the uncertainty around the survival of species.

Ingrained habitual patterns of thoughts and behaviors also play a critical role in how well we deal with the reality of our changing planet. Many of our habitual patterns, or what Jung called complexes, form during childhood. We unconsciously take in family patterns of behavior and belief systems and they then live in us. They become the hidden feeling toned reactions that appear before we are even aware they are present. They are the faintly familiar voices that whisper to us when we are least expecting it, whispers telling us how we are less than, not good enough leading to feelings of insecurity and anxiousness.

In terms of our fractured relationship with the environment, the central complexes include, power, wealth, individualism, and growth, which are all interrelated. The power complex appears in our desire to control the natural world. We feel compelled to tame the wildness of nature. This power drive appears in the belief that we have been given dominion over nature. The wealth complex appears in how we define value or riches and is also known as our money complex. We are a society that values monetary riches over any other form of wealth including, well-being, health, or even the divine. Extreme individualism is also a powerful complex that plays a critical role in accepting the reality of climate chaos. We feel so separate from nature and others that we act in destructive ways. All of these complexes contribute to our current living myth of perpetual growth, which is perhaps the most destructive habitual belief in recent history. This belief is rooted in the unquestioned necessity for perpetual economic growth. Of course, unlimited growth is impossible given that we live on a planet of limited resources. This core cultural belief system also perpetuates global social and economic inequality, which then feeds back on environmental degradation, for the places of the poor are the dumping grounds for all manner of pollutants.

How do we work with a habitual destructive pattern of perpetual growth that is so deeply rooted in us and our culture? First, working with complexes requires an awareness that the complex, or habitual pattern is active in us. The telltale sign of an active complex is how highly emotional we become even to the point of extreme irrationality. We are literally seized by the complex and only after the fact become aware of its power over us. Second, having identified the complex we give it a particular form so that we can engage with it, the form could be of a person, animal, or even a physical object. This step can only happen when we are not in the grip of the complex. The third step is to query the complex as to its purpose. In this way we develop a relationship with the inner habitual pattern. Through relating we potentially release the strong hold the complex has over us. We at least become more aware of the presence of the complex in our life and how it is affecting us.

To summarize, the stages of complex work are awareness of its presence, giving a specific relatable form to it, and then engaging with the form, even to the point of challenging its purpose. One argument used to support perpetual growth is the belief that economic collapse would occur if we were to get off fossil fuels. This is a message used effectively by special interest groups to slow action on climate chaos. The message of economic collapse effectively taps into our wealth and individuality complexes. It creates uncertainty in us as to whether we should reduce our dependence on fossil fuels and we fall into fear and freeze, which is exactly what those who oppose action on climate change want to happen. The irony is that many studies have shown that moving off fossil fuels stimulates the economy and provides safer jobs for those in the energy industry (Way et al., 2022). Our strategy to work on this complex involves naming the presence of the complexes of money and individualism and giving them specific forms – personifying them. For example, picture our money complex as Ebeneezer Scrooge and then engage Scrooge in a dialogue concerning his love for money. Interestingly, Dicken's *A Christmas Carol* can be read as how one imaginatively deals with a money complex, in which Scrooge awakens to how this complex has constricted his life. We can carry out a similar process with our own inner Scrooge. What is this inner figure afraid of and where did this fear begin? One could personify the extreme individualism complex using the image of a rugged cowboy, an image deeply ingrained in the American psyche (Kiehl, 2020). Imagine facing this cowboy and asking him if he truly is completely self-reliant. Are there not others in his life upon whom he relies? How about his horse? Hopefully you get a sense of how to work with the habitual patterns that haunt our lives. Finally, I suggest that when grappling with cultural complexes, like the American rugged cowboy, you carry out this work with others. Gather a small group of people to work through the cultural belief system that is blocking action. Begin the group activity by naming the complex and constructing an image of it. Each person in the group could assign a specific characteristic to the image. Then go around the group and engage with the cowboy. Reflect on what feelings arise around this image. Can you see the cowboy's side of things? Bring in another image representing a different complex and engage with it. What unfolds is a rich narrative of how complexes affect us and our relationship to a collective issue like climate chaos.

A Cosmology for Climate Chaos

I have presented a cosmology, or map, to navigate through the seas of uncertainty surrounding our relationship to the natural world, a relationship which is fractured and leading to a destabilized climate. Imagine you are looking at this map right now (see figure 1), picture it as circular in form, like the antique maps of the world.

The rim of the map is comprised of the many manifestations of nature. Here you will find the sky, land, waters, and ice that make up our planet. Within each of these places are the living beings that populate Earth, birds of the sky, plants, reptiles, mammals on land, the polar bear and penguins living on ice, and the plethora of life in

the oceans. All the wonder and beauty of the natural world encircle us for this is a map of our relationship to Earth. Now imagine an inner circle of the map divided into four quadrants. Each quadrant represents a way of relating to the rim of nature. One way tells us that there is a world out there that can be experienced through our five senses. A second quadrant provides us with a way of categorizing and understanding the rim of nature. We can name and study the behavior of life. These two quadrants of experience provide the tools of scientific understanding. They allow us to quantify the uncertainties of nature. They provide the means to observe, theorize, and represent nature, which are the foundations of Earth Systems Science. Using these quadrants, we know how Earth's climate is changing and why it is changing. The third quadrant of our map tells us how valuable nature is, not just to us, but to all living beings. The fourth quadrant reveals the future potential inherent in nature. Our map integrates scientific knowledge with our deep feelings for Earth. Neglect of any quadrant leads to a less useful map, which may even limit our ability to relate to the natural world.

Now imagine a circle within the quadrants, here we find the deeper ways that our psyche relates to nature, the unconscious realm of relating through dreams and synchronicities. These are less predictable for they are not under the rule of the ego, but they are of great value. They can even inform the science world for we know of instances where great scientific ideas arose from dreams or synchronicities. Psyche wants us to know nature for the two depend on one another, so it is not surprising that the unconscious cooperates with nature. Again, if we neglect this realm of knowing, then we lose a soulful connection to nature. We are called to integrate this circle of knowing with the other circle. Imagine another inner circle that holds all our habitual patterns of reacting to the world, which have developed since birth. Some of these patterns open us to the beauty and wonder of the rim of nature, while others hinder our ability to experience this wonder. This is the realm of complexes that we need to identify and relate to in an intimate fashion. By working with these psychological patterns, we open new pathways to relating to the rim of nature. The cosmological map is almost complete, but what of the center? Our first thought might be that our ego forms the center for it is the center of consciousness. But this would be incorrect. Although we would like our ego to be at the center of the cosmos this is not the case. It is the grand illusion of ego to believe it is the center of everything. Jung's great discovery was that the center of psyche is not the ego, but the archetype of wholeness, or Self.

Archetypes are lenses through which we view and understand our relationship to both the inner circles and the outer rim of nature. Most importantly the lenses are shared by all living beings, since they dwell in what Jung called the collective unconscious. Although archetypes by their very nature are universal, the specific forms archetypes assume are determined by historical and cultural factors. Thus, the image of the archetypal mother has assumed specific forms in different regions of the world over time. Strong affect and intense numinous feelings accompany the experience of an archetypal image. We are deeply moved in the presence of an archetypal image. Reflect on the last time you entered a cathedral, an ancient sacred site, or an old growth forest and you will know what I am describing. We are moved to our very core in such moments. Interestingly, archetypes are bivalent for they can be either awe-filling or awe-full. Jung argued that archetypes are rooted in earth and nature. This being the case, an archetypal experience provides another pathway to relating to the rim of nature on our map. The archetype of wholeness, or Self, is the central organizing principle of our cosmology. It transcends space and time and connects everything. The paradoxical situation for our map is that the central core of Self includes the outer rim of nature. Our map extends beyond the phenomenal world of three dimensions. You could say it is multi-dimensional in space and time. It integrates, contains, and unifies the worlds of science and psyche providing a portal to a spiritual, meaningful experience of the natural world.

The Self or archetype of wholeness plays a critical role in healing our relationship with nature and grappling with the uncertainties of climate chaos. If we fail to connect to the center of our map, then we fall into a lifeless and meaningless life, or what Jung called a *provisional life*. We feel empty inside and look outside of ourselves to find fulfillment. We exploit the rim of nature and consume it to sate our inner emptiness. We consume Earth's resources beyond her capacity to provide for us and literally steal resources from future generations. The only way to avoid such destruction is to find an inner sense of wholeness, which does not depend upon how much we earn, own or can purchase. How do we find such inner wholeness? I can only speak from personal experience at this point for each person must explore this part of the map on their own. I will say that we are not alone in this search, for the Self comes to aid us, most often in the form of dreams. A reciprocal process occurs which has an emergent character. Our dedication to and interest in our inner search evoke a dynamic organizing principle that presents us with images of balance and wholeness. The images feel numinous and transcend our personal history. Honoring the presence of these images and concretizing the image through writing, drawing, song, or dance maintains the wholeness and creates a deep sense of meaning for life. Ultimately, we are dwelling in mystery. What results from finding the still center within is a union with the rim of nature. We experience a sacred connection to the natural world and from such a state our actions protect and preserve the natural world.

Conclusion

I have outlined a cosmology, or map, that opens us to our inherent manifold connections to the natural world. By exploring the many realms of psyche, we have created a way to orient ourselves in the world. Using our cosmology to navigate our lives includes science to learn more about the world we live in, working on the varied ways we experience the world, exploring our habitual patterns of thought and behavior, and opening ourselves to an emergent experience of wholeness. The map weaves together in a seamless fashion many threads of experiencing and knowing. The more we explore our cosmology of interconnectedness, the more we move from destructive stories of separation to creating a flourishing world for future generations. Ultimately, we enter this new cosmology out of love. Love for Earth and all her inhabitants. In the end we hope to reach the center of wholeness arousing an inner light of wisdom, a light that provides us with a sense of stability amidst great uncertainty. Our task is to embody this illumination and allow it to act through us. It is from this place of illuminated wisdom that actions heal our split with the natural world. There is no better time than now to explore this cosmology of wholeness. So let us begin the journey together.

In summary, here are the recommended practices to help you work with the uncertainties of climate chaos:

- Learn the fundamentals of climate change science and communicate with others

- Form a small group to share feelings around climate chaos

- Practice using the four ways of relating (thinking, feeling, sensing, intuiting) when reading news articles and discussing climate issues

- Record your dreams about climate chaos and share with others

- Practice on identifying, personifying, and engaging with complexes that arise around the myth of perpetual growth and climate chaos

- Open ourselves to the emergence of wholeness from within and without and concretize images of wholeness

- Embody and act from this place of wholeness

References

Bernstein, J.S., (2018). Different Realities: What is Reality and What Difference Does It Make? *Psychological Perspectives*, 61, 18-26.

Jung, C.G. (1967). *CW, Vol. 13, Alchemical studies* (pp. 1-56). Princeton, NJ: Princeton University Press. (Original work published 1929) https://doi.org/10.1515/9781400850990.1

_____. (1969). Psychology and religion. In H. Read et al. (Eds.), *CW, Vol. 11, Psychology and religion* (2nd ed., pp. 3-105). Princeton, NJ: Princeton University Press. (Original work published 1940) https://doi.org/10.1515/9781400850983.3

_____. (1969). Archetypes of the collective unconscious (R. F. C. Hull, Trans.). In H. Read et al. (Eds.), *CW, Vol. 9 pt. 1, Archetypes and the collective unconscious* (2nd ed., pp. 3-41). Princeton, NJ: Princeton University Press. (Original work published 1954) https://doi.org/10.1515/9781400850969.3

_____. (ed. S. Shamdasani) (1989/2012). *Introduction to Jungian Psychology, Notes of the Seminar on Analytical Psychology Given in 1925*, Princeton, NJ: Princeton University Press.

Kiehl, J.T., (2020). A Tale of Two Cultures: Climate Change and American Complexes, in *Cultural Complexes and the Soul of America* (ed. T Singer), pp. 257-274, UK: Routledge.

McGilchrist, I. (2021). *The Matter with Things, Vol. I*. UK: Perspectiva Press.

Way, R., Ives, M.C., Mealy, P., & Doyne Farmer, J., (2022). Empirically grounded technology forecasts and energy transition, *Joule*, 1-26.

Resources

Climate Change Science:

Henson, R. (2019). *The Thinking Person's Guide to Climate Change, 2nd ed.*, MA: AMS Books.

Climate Central: www.climatecentral.org

Jeff Kiehl, The Physics of the Climate System: https://www.youtube.com/watch?v=KFy0XSLHjIg

New York Times Climate Facts: https://www.nytimes.com/article/climate-change-global-warming-faq.html

Depth Psychology and Climate Chaos:

Fellows, A., (2019). *Gaia, Psyche and Deep Ecology: Navigating Climate Change in the Anthropocene.* London: Routledge.

Gillespie, S., (2020). *Climate Crisis and Consciousness: Re-imagining Our World and Ourselves.* London: Routledge.

Kiehl, J.T., (2016). *Facing Climate Change: An Integrated Path to the Future.* NY: Columbia U Press.

Mathers, D., (2021). *Depth Psychology and Climate Change: The Green Book.* London: Routledge.

Rust, M-J., (2020). *Towards an Ecopsychotherapy.* UK: Confer Books.

Weintrobe, S., (2021). *Psychological Roots of the Climate Crisis.* NY: Bloomsbury Academic.

Technology Solutions:

Hawken, P., (2021). *Regeneration: Ending the Climate Crisis in One Generation.* NY: Penguin.

Hawken, P., (2017). *Drawdown: The Most Comprehensive Plan Ever Proposed to Reverse Global Warming.* NY: Penguin Books.

Visser, W., (2022). *Thriving: The Breakthrough Movement to Regenerate Nature, Society, and the Economy.* NY: Fast Company Press.

The Three Horsemen of the Apocalypse of Our Times

Jan Bauer

In this chapter I'll be talking about what I call the three Horsemen of the Modern Apocalypse in the form of the war in Ukraine, climate change and the pandemic. In particular, I will be discussing the collective energy and attention that we as a species bring to each of the three archetypes and asking why are the levels of energy so different from one another. Why do we pay more attention to war than climate change or even to the pandemic?

To answer this question, I propose a couple of main ideas that I will develop throughout this chapter. They are as follows:

1. That the difference in degree of energy brought to each subject is very influenced by our ability to evoke or not a collective, ancestral memory around such an event. What do we remember about past war, past pandemics, past climate change?
2. Secondly I propose that we have a need to be able to evoke and name individual heroes who may have helped inspire human beings through the hard times caused by such disasters. Collective memory and heroes. Where are they, where have they been in the present apocalyptic situations mentioned above?

The chapter is divided into four main parts: an introduction and then an in-depth look at each of the three so-called Horsemen and the archetypes they emerge from.

Introduction: Experience of the Pandemic

To start out, I'd like to talk about the general experience of the pandemic and its consequences because it was reflections on this that led me to think about the whole question of collective energy and intensity and memory. We could certainly say, for example, that the pandemic caused startling changes in levels of collective energy and vitality as common public spaces were closed down and people were confined to their houses. And when all this took place, the unexpected change revealed a lot about what subjects unite us into unanimous action or not. On the one hand the virus itself was causing terrible things. It was causing fear, illness, death and uncertainty globally, everywhere. And yet, the Covid reality never managed to mobilize a majority of communities throughout the world into intense feelings of unanimous consent and effort for and by all. **Never.** Approaches to Covid remained very much the purview of individual countries, states, even cities. And they varied greatly.

Yes, some countries, some societies mobilized with more intensity than others. More autocratic ones like China forced closing down of their cities and spaces and freedoms. More collaborative and trusting societies such as Denmark and New Zealand, for a while, managed to stave off the worse of Covid-19 by creating a sense of unanimous agreement about the need for collective effort and sacrifice for the greater good. But this was rare. In most places there was no such unanimous groundswell of desire to make an effort together. More usually, within the same country, and among individuals and individual areas, consensus was varied, scattered, and there were areas very much for, others very much against measures proposed or imposed to fight the virus.

Yes, at the top level, most governments ended up looking for and finding ways to cope with the deadly virus. They scrambled to find rational ways of dealing with the unexpected visitor. They consulted the experts, imposed close-down measures, masking measures, distance measures. Pharmaceutical companies scrambled to find vaccines to protect against the virus. Health professionals of all kinds threw themselves into the fray and worked day and night for all of us. An intensity that cost many of them their health and even their lives. They were heroic, but who remembers their names today?

Just as important, the intensity of these actions emerged top down from rational studies of the threat posed by Covid-19, or as in the case of health professionals, in direct response to urgent cases while the rest of us were forced to stay home and wait. Intensity was not the norm for most of us. The norm for most of us was isolation, uncertainty, confinement, closing of public spaces, offices, no personal presence in sports, entertainment, shops, weddings, funerals or just the barbecue next door. These sudden and anti-social measures in the literal sense created, in my view, a kind of low-grade depression for most people and much higher levels of depression and anxiety for many.

To compensate, people undertook all sorts of new activities and ways of coping. Some threw themselves into baking, causing a temporary shortage of flour and a huge abundance of homemade cookies, evoking the cozy nourishing warmth of grandmothers both real and wished for. Others, feeling too alone and needing a reason to go outside, lined up at shelters and breeders to procure a dog. For the first time in history in North America, there were more people trying to get a dog than dogs available to be gotten. On the one hand, there was a good side to this. Finally, many rejected dogs got a second chance and in general people came to appreciate the world of having a dog. On the other hand, there was and is a lot of shadow in the new rush towards procuring a dog. Dog trafficking, over breeding, ridiculous prices, too many dogs given up a year or two later.

Let us look at the reasons surrounding the initial and ongoing collective energy to have a dog. It is said that the dogs were for companionship, to break the loneliness and isolation of the pandemic. Of course, they were, and they did their job for countless grateful dog owners. I would propose, however, that the dogs, cats, rabbits and hamsters were also mammal substitutes for the mammalian animal energy we were all lacking in our lives because of confinement. We know we are social creatures, sometimes we don't realize that as members of society we are also biological creatures. Daily interactions, walking, talking, working, playing with other humans also affords us actual biological energy, not just company. We breathe, touch, move, feel, and think in the company of others and all these activities begin in our bodies, meeting the energy of people doing the same in their bodies. Human mammals connect on a physiological level just like every other mammal species. If we are alone in pandemic confinement, energy flags without these daily mammalian connections. On the other hand, if we are confined with other people for too long, our mammalian tolerance grows shorter, fights begin, precious space is fought over. Like all mammals we need the right closeness and space with our own species to thrive. It's all about the instinctive level of our being, as Jung would say. And about seeking a way to get closer to nature as we huddle in our confined urban spaces.

Where was Collective Energy?

But to return to my theme of collective energy and where was it during the pandemic, while it would seem that low grade depression was widespread everywhere, one group that countered these feelings and stood out by its intensity consisted of those committed to both anti-vaxx and conspiracy theories. The QAnon group for example. There, we saw togetherness, passion, community banded together not for a cause but against one. Observing this, it occurred to me that the collective energy produced by these groups felt more related to the archetype of war than the archetype of illness. And that is the rub. That is why I decided to take a look at the three areas of present urgent human concern, three archetypal spaces that concern us all right now, and to compare the intensity that we humans bring to each of them. And ask why.

The basic archetypes I want to compare are those underlying illness, climate change/nature and war. All societies have and have had some transcendental representation of these realities.

The Archetype of Illness:

For illness, there are Gods of healing, medicine men, pilgrims on the way to Lourdes, or Compostela, and today seeking cures outside of mainstream medicine and online. Illness has always been with us, patients and healers, every society faces it differently. Every society has its beliefs and mythology around illness.

The Archetype of Nature:

The Archetype of Nature in this chapter is about climate change. We speak metaphorically of Mother Nature and Gaia today, but throughout human history in all societies, nature, and gods and goddesses of nature, have been much more than metaphors. They have had a central place in the human psyche. Mother Nature in various forms of positive and negative mother deities has been seen as the provider of bounty and life and the cause of unpredictable destruction and death. Nature was and has always been simply the source of life itself. It is the Earth, nothing less. Rain and sun, storm and calm that humankind could not control and needed to find ways to represent in the form of deities that must be appeased or fed.

The Archetype of War:

Our third archetype is represented by Ares and Mars in the classical world and manifold deities in other cultures. Along with these gods of war themselves come the heroes, the ones sung and remembered as part of our proud collective memory. All wars have heroes.

I'll be addressing these three archetypal forces that have always played a major role for humans everywhere, and I will be addressing them in the specific modern forms of pandemics, climate change and war in Ukraine. They are all dire today. They are in a sense our very own three Horsemen of the Apocalypse that threaten the end of our world as we know it. They all require urgent forceful intervention, yet not all receive the same attention. Why? I would propose that one thing that makes a difference in the energy that societies invest in these dire areas is a question, not of their actual importance, but of two other variables: collective memory and the presence of widely recognized heroes.

For example, regarding the war archetype in human history, everywhere we find collective memories of war and the presence of oft cited heroes in legend and stories. What about climate change? In spite of its urgency, climate catastrophes around the world, and imploring voices of notables such as Al Gore and David Suzuki, as a worldwide society, there is not yet enough collective energy to make the needed changes fast enough. Not enough energy to efficiently tackle the vested interests that refuse to acknowledge climate change. No collective memory. No statues of the very real environment heroes who have contributed to our knowledge and well-being.

As for pandemics, what collective memory might have been, and what heroes and heroines helped humanity through previous disasters, are either lost in time or were deliberately denied by leaders and hidden from society (as was the case for the closest major pandemic in history to us, the 1918 Flu). Let us now take these one by one and see up close why there is such a huge difference in the resources brought to bear on each.

The Archetype of War

Let's start with war. How can we not? The wanton criminal destruction of the country called Ukraine by another one has us all mobilized. At only a few months old, it succeeded in creating more social cohesion and shared emotions than three years of the Covid-19 pandemic, and many more of climate change urgency. Allied countries whose sense of collective global belonging seemed almost irrelevant during Covid-19, suddenly found themselves bonding together on all levels—governmental, military, political and personal. Citizens all over the world showed eagerness to help the fleeing Ukrainian people as well as the ones staying. As the Second World war brought an end to the Great Depression, the war in Ukraine seems to have brought an end not to Covid-19 itself but to our endless anxiety-ridden obsessions with it. We can now obsess over something far more directly inspiring, directly frightening, directly horrifying. And that is because we remember. We carry images of war in both our collective and personal imaginations. The psyche of everyone in the world remembers war. The gods of war, the language of war, the heroes of war. The arms trade, video games, books written, movies made, tales told of war. They are part of our human DNA, our collective memory no matter where we are born or what we have lived. In the Judeo-Christian tradition, the Four Horsemen of the Apocalypse include war in both Old and New Testament.

We know war. Our everyday language speaks of conquering illness, of battling cancer, of victory over polio and other scourges. All kids grow up knowing about war games, the good guys and the bad. Competition and sports are war games just a bit diverted. Military marches, music and honors are part of every culture's celebrations. Wars are collectively remembered as victory or defeat. Wars are remembered as the catastrophes that they are, catastrophes destroying millions of lives and great parts of civilization. We honor the dead, are reverent before the unknown soldier or black horse pulling the body of the fallen hero. We see the wounded, crippled, traumatized, and the rubble left behind. But we are less concerned with the climate changes caused by war, and the many illnesses unleashed.

As a child I remember being taken to a parade for the Fourth of July. There was a local band playing military music and I remember being surprised to find myself marching, knees high, something I had never done before. I don't think anyone noticed the small girl in shorts marching in step for the first time in her life. But I noticed and was surprised. Surprised to realize that a certain kind of music could actually make my legs move, my heart beat faster and experience a certain enjoyable feeling about it all. It was a first inkling that something bigger than me and my parents and friends could take me out of the moment, the first conscious awareness of being in the grip of a psychic force. I did not yet know that Jung and many others had discovered that before me.

All this to say that it is perhaps not surprising that the war in Ukraine has so shocked us and mobilized us and that we recognize it. We know war. We are part of a society that supposedly has spent 80 years trying to prevent wars officially and yet produces enough arms to destroy many globes. War as an archetype is present in every religion, us against them, the saved and the damned, good and evil. It is familiar, we know what to do, how to choose sides and take action. In his book called *A Terrible Love of War*, James Hillman explores this knowledge, collective memory and all-consuming intensity. He says,

> I base the statement 'war is normal' on two factors
> we have always seen:
> Its constancy throughout history, its ubiquity over
> the globe. These two factors require another more
> basic one: acceptability. Wars could not happen
> unless there were those willing to help them happen.
> There are always masses ready to join the fight and

others pushed into it. War drives everything else off the front page.[1]

His words evoke and confirm the fact that no human psyche can escape a collective memory of war. In Greek and Roman times, war was represented by the god named Ares or Mars. In Greece, Ares was born of two great gods on Olympus, Zeus the King and Hera the Queen. But they were a fighting couple, constantly vying for power and importance. And so, their son was a fighter. A god of war loathed by his father who said "thou are the most odious to me, for thou enjoyest nothing but strife, war and battles."[2] Ares was called a furious god, who was unpopular even among his peers, the Olympians, who for the most part had some norms of behavior to be respected. Athena meted out justice or withheld it, Demeter provided agricultural bounty or withheld it, Dionysius gave the freedom of alcohol and the loss of inhibition. Each god or goddess had their own domain to give and take, their own light and shadow, and they generally respected this. But Ares did not. He was not predictable, not containable. He was impulsive, he acted out all the time in a constant fit of rage. His thirst for brutality and blind violence made him a scourge of humanity. The names of his sons and helpers say it all: they were called Fear, Strife, drinkers of blood, destroyers of cities.[3] Ares was, in short, both a god and a thug seen with contempt by his fellow lofty Olympians, feared by humankind. And yet, as Hillman so rightly says, war is the one archetype ever present, ever intense.

I think that is partly true because of the deep paradoxical hold it has on us humans. It is hated and feared, and it is irresistible. It is not for nothing that soldiers speak of their service in war as the most memorable, the most missed sometimes, as well as the most awful time of their lives. And that is thanks to the other side of

---

[1] Hillman, 2004, back cover.
[2] New Larousse Encyclopedia of Mythology, pp. 124-125.
[3] Hillman, 2004, p. 125.

Ares, the side that is paired with the Goddess of love Aphrodite. A pair known in popular language as Mars and Venus. Love and War. Aphrodite/Venus brings to the partnership with Ares feelings of loyalty, service, warmth, love, and companionship that are difficult to find elsewhere in such intensity. Quoting Hillman again, "War is sublime. It brings camaraderie, intensity, great love and great hate, a sense of belonging unmatched."[4] Is it any puzzle then that there was so much awful intensity in the January 6, 2021 attacks on the United States Capital?

Or the shocking invasion of the capital city of Canada, Ottawa, by furious but then orgy-loving truckers, finding camaraderie and relief from the loneliness of the long-distance drives, plunging into saunas, and booze and Dionysian madness. Gripped by Ares, but accompanied by the pleasure-loving Aphrodite, they were escaping the boring, top down rules and restrictions of their governments and the collective consensus to make sacrifices to avoid Covid. Escaping endless traffic jams where they weren't paid, the loss of money due to Covid rules, escaping control by richer more powerful masters. Passion, intensity, anger, violence, but also a feeling of belonging, of fun, of stolen pleasure as the rest of us looked on in outrage, or contempt, or fear. Again, as Hillman says, wars make the headlines. It was impossible to not watch news of the Ottawa invasion; it still is impossible to not watch news about the Jan. 6 insurrection. The point is made, attention is captured.

The Archetype of Illness

And what about the pandemic, our second modern horseman of the apocalypse. We have touched upon the individual experience of Covid-19 in the introduction. Where was the collective memory and where were the historic heroes to inspire us in March 2020? They were not there. Pandemics and plagues may have mobilized populations to undertake pilgrimages in the Middle Ages, but

---

[4] Hillman, 2004, back cover.

the problems with plagues and pandemics is that, unlike in war, there is no glory, no tradition of great poetry, statues and holidays commemorating victories over a plague. Plagues humiliate, kill, cheat, and trick the best of us. There is no camaraderie, no sense of community. They separate more than bring together, isolating, confining, they keep us from having the thing we need most to survive: the presence of our fellow humans. In all plagues, the poor die in greater numbers, the rich can often escape to cleaner, less affected places. In all plagues, the only heroes are the caregivers who stay behind to help the afflicted. Then they may die too soon to be given a medal or maybe it's just that nobody wants to remember the times of pandemics. I would propose that this is even more true of our most recent previous global pandemic, the Flu of 1918 than most. It killed about 50 million people worldwide, and infected about 500 million more, about 1/3 of the world population at that time. It lasted from about March 1918 to March 1920.

It was called the Spanish Flu but had nothing to do with Spain. It was called the Spanish flu simply because newspapers in Spain wrote about it, informed the world about it. Spain was neutral in WWI. It had no reason not to publish news about the terrible flu that was killing so many people. But the countries at war, the US, Britain, France and Germany had many good reasons not to publish about the flu and to censor any publishing about it. It was not allowed. Why? Because the countries at war did not want their citizens to panic in the last days of the war (Nov. 1918) which corresponded to the first year of the flu. All attention was required to focus on the war effort, the victory for one side and the defeat for the other. Censorship and denial prevailed. In fact, it is thought that the so-called Spanish flu began in a Kansas army camp, its soldiers then sent to Europe in spring of 1918, thence spreading the deadly virus all over the world.

In the US, about 675,000 people died. And as of today, some cities fared better than others.

According to a study by the National Geographic, some cities discovered social distancing and quarantine early on and fared best. For example, New York City put quarantines into place early on and that resulted in 432 deaths per 100,000 over 24 weeks. This gave New York the best numbers on the Eastern Seaboard. Philadelphia on the other hand, did not put such measures in place and had 748 deaths per 100,000, resulting in between 14 and 15 thousand deaths in all. The city of St. Louis came in the middle. In the early epidemic they closed down and had only 358 deaths per 100,000 but they released measures after some weeks and the numbers went up.[5]

The cities with low death rates did not have better newspapers and information about the flu. In general, due to government suppression of news in wartime, citizens were not very informed. However, these cities benefited from the presence of a few individuals, particularly astute medical doctors who were aware of the danger and kept up with medical news to persuade local authorities to act. It worked. But who remembers the name of those heroic doctors or even that they existed? We remember the heroes of wars, rarely heroes of a great and catastrophic illness.

Meanwhile few cities closed, few people knew, many died. It was the most devastating pandemic since the great Black Plague that is thought to have killed about one third of the total population in Europe between 1346-52.[6]

But there a was a reason we don't remember the 1918 Flu Pandemic. It was ignorance. Did you, many decades later, learn about the terrible effects of the Spanish flu in school? I didn't, yet my parents were toddlers then in 1918-1920. But neither ever mentioned it, one from Arizona, one from Connecticut.

---

[5] The National Geographic: History and Culture, "How Some cites Cities 'flattened the curve' during the 1918 Flu pandemic" by Nina Strochlic and Riley Champine, March 27, 2020.
[6] McNeill 1998.

I learned about the Black Plague in school but not about the Spanish flu. In March 2020, we had no collective memory to help us cope by remembering our ancestors and how they managed. We lived in the inflated illusion that we were a modern society, with medicines and other tools in the medical arsenal which surely protected against such horrors as new viruses. Our parks are still full of statues glorifying heroes of World War I or II, but how many statues are there to honor the heroes of the 1918 Flu who warned about it, tended the sick, and often died for their efforts? Let's talk about the archetype of illness and health to help us understand more about our reaction as a collective.

The Gods of Healing

The archetype of sickness and healing in the ancient classic world is incarnated in the image of the god Asclepios. He is a god born of a human princess and an Olympian god. He is a god, it is said, who was able to feel empathy, a capacity inherited from his human mother and very different from his cousin Ares the war god, a pureblood god. No empathy there.

You see the gods of Olympus can feel emotions for their own selves, they can feel vanity, lust, anger, and desire, emotions having to do with keeping their power. But they do not have emotions that foster connection in relationship: emotions like empathy, pity, affection, concern, caring. Those feelings belong only to humans. And to humans interested in relationship, as every healer must be. We could even conclude from this that any person who is concerned only with power and who refuses to have empathy or care for others takes him or herself to be a kind of god. All powerful, perhaps, but stunted in their humanity by their lack of emotional connection. Examples of these individuals are not lacking today, whether in positions of greater or lesser political, social, personal or professional power. They may enjoy feeling like gods, but it's a high price to pay for losing one's humanity.

Returning to Asclepios, the Empathetic. Among the priests of his temple in Greece was one who was called Hippocrates, and to this day young doctors take the Hippocratic oath as they set out on their path to healing others. Part of that oath is *Do No Harm*, a reflection of the importance of caring in the process of healing.

But, as wise and balanced as they were, the rituals and teachings of Asclepios were always only in service of helping individuals, not crowds. Until very recently, the practice of medicine has been helpless to deal with the illnesses of thousands, with plagues and epidemics. It's only been since about 200 years ago that modern medicine has been able to deal with the problem of public health and illness of the masses. Vaccination for smallpox had begun in Europe in the 1770s, but it only became widespread and accepted by the 1850s. Other vaccinations would follow as did the introduction of germ theory. Then in the 19th and 20th centuries, more and more discoveries were made about the importance of public sanitation, water and sewers and vaccines for cholera, yellow fever, tuberculosis, as science came into its own about infectious diseases.[7] As a result, as members of a modern society with all these amazing medical tools, we now have no memory of that terrible sickness that killed more people than World War I, soldiers and civilians combined. And yet, as William McNeil the author of *Plagues and Peoples* (1997) writes:

> In spite of the extraordinary record of the past few centuries, the role of infectious disease cannot be left out of future consideration. Infectious disease which antedated the emergence of humankind will last as long as humanity itself and will remain as it has been hitherto, one of the fundamental parameters and determinants of human history.[8]

---

[7] McNeil, William, 1998, p. 256.

[8] McNeil, 1998.

Despite the huge importance of this, we do not have a collective memory, conscious or unconscious to help us through. We know, at least if we read history, that there have been remarkable people who made remarkable discoveries as McNeil mentions, but we don't know, or don't cultivate or celebrate the memory of these heroes and heroines. Is this lack of a name or a specific hero why we are not helped in our struggle to deal with a pandemic that killed millions but seemed to emerge out of nowhere and bring no bygone legendary heroes to guide us through?

Not that some prominent people did not try to take on the role of leader/hero. In the States, there was Dr. Fauci, the nation's medical spokesman who tirelessly tried to explain, guide, and help people through the confusion and contradictions of pandemic information. Then there was President Trump who encouraged people to inject themselves with bleach in order to clean out the virus. Each man had his admirers and followers but in a time of pandemic anxiety and partisan politics, each also had virulent enemies. Each was the object of scorn and attack on social media as if they were actually on equal footing in their medical competence.

In such circumstances no one leader could emerge a hero admired by all. Even in countries with less political division about how to deal with the pandemic, the virus itself ended up tricking, evading and sneaking through whatever barriers were put up against it. The real heroes were the individuals who helped those most in need at the possible expense of their own health and even lives. The doctors, nurses, orderlies, volunteers, family members and neighbors who just stayed. They were heroic and they are forgotten.

To sum up the factors that prevented some kind of positive collective consensus and energy to effectively combat the pandemic in the pre-vaccine period and even after:

- The censoring and erasing of historic memory so that the terrible Flu of 1918 left few helpful lessons for those who followed.

- The progress of modern medicine that led to the hubris of imagining that we as a 2020 society could never succumb to such a thing as a common virus and therefore it took us unaware.
- The extraordinary power of the Covid-19 virus to replicate itself, spread so fast and so invisibly, something most of us had never witnessed up close.[9] It was neither in our memory nor our imaginations.
- The political and social divisions, in greater or lesser form, in most countries or regions that prevented a global consensus and efforts to combat it.
- And last but not least, the very strong desire of most people to forget, put it all behind, and not store memories for future generations.

Archetype of Nature

And what about the nature archetype? What about Climate Change? It is here, it is dire. It is definitely the Third Horseman of the modern Apocalypse. And it comes riding in at a pace unexpected and unimagined ever before. The floods, fires, droughts, heatwaves and storms never before seen in such intensity and volume. A couple examples out of thousands:

The heat wave in British Columbia in summer of 2021, British Columbia a normally cool Canadian province in every sense of the word. But from June to August 2021 the temperatures reached the 100s, people were dying of heat stroke as they lay in the normally green and cool grass of Vancouver parks. According to the British Columbia Coroner's report stated by Canadian Broadcasting, at least 595 people died of the heat in just those few

---

[9] Exception made of course for the brave and tireless individuals who work for organizations like Doctors Without Borders who have certainly seen their share of deadly rapid viruses that kill without warning or preparation.

months.[10] An earlier example, in Europe in the summer of 2003, there were 30,000 deaths from the heat—14,000 in France alone. I know. I was there visiting friends and remember wondering as I lay in my friend's lovely guest bedroom upstairs without a fan, if eyeballs could boil.

Granted these two examples are minor chords in a much louder symphony of daily disasters all over the world. I cite them because it is often the particular individual ones that touch us personally and help bring more consciousness to the situation. You can also read the daily list of horrors chronicled in the news every day. Worst drought in the West for 1200 years. 20,000 people dying a year from chemicals used in producing cotton. 33% of arable soil lost all over the world to erosion, overuse and pollution. Lost. For good. Catastrophes unending as nature explodes and implodes and we become victims of our own heedless actions.

It is often said that Gaia, Mother Nature, is furious at us for treating her so badly for so long. That she is getting back at us by creating an ongoing climate disaster. But I don't think she is angry. I think she has become psychotic. She has been driven mad by all the predation, abuse, rape, and pillaging over the centuries, especially since the Industrial Revolution. She has simply lost her normal ability to self-regulate. To find her own innate balance of hot and cold, dry and wet, calm and stormy. The natural balance that both blessed and terrified humankind for many millennia. But now we have won. We have conquered her. We have invaded and robbed and polluted her most intimate parts, the forests, waters and rich loamy soils, and she cannot recover without our help. All she can do is to keep going on a rampage.

So where do we look in the past for help in the present and future? Where is the collective memory of such a dire situation? Who and where are the heroes that will lead us out of the consequences of these crimes? In collective memory there is not much. Few of

---

[10] CBC news November 1, 2021.

us remember the Great Extinction of the Dinosaurs or the Ice Ages that began 2.6 million years ago and lasted until about 11,700 years ago. Few of us even know about the more recent ice age in Europe said to have lasted between about 1350 and 1850.

Fortunately, we don't have to remember those former times in order to act, and providentially there have been many heroic individuals warning us and acting for change in the past 70 years. Rachel Carlson, author of *Silent Spring*, published in 1962, on the environmental damage caused by pesticides. David Suzuki, now 87, Canadian champion for the environment who has fought all his professional life to bring consciousness of the need to change our ways by creating TV shows, documentaries, and a foundation. Another positive example, a representative of 28 years old who held the first climate change hearings in Congress in 1976 and went on after his political career to make the movie *An Inconvenient Truth* about global warming to awaken the world to what he, Al Gore, called the "greatest crisis in human history." And then there are all the groups that have emerged. Greenpeace, Nature Conservancy, World Wildlife Fund, The Sierra Club, PETA, and the hundreds of others devoted to protecting the flora and fauna of our fragile Earth. Universities now offer degrees not only in environmental sciences, but environmental psychology and environmental history, offerings few of us would have imagined until recently. There are all these efforts, the thousands of people involved and caring who work to tell us how badly off the patient Earth is and what we need to do to heal her and ensure our own survival.

Despite the environment pioneers and groups, thousands of committed individuals, and daily horrible headlines, we don't manage as a species to mobilize enough to heal our home here on Earth. Why? There is inertia, the feeling that we can't do anything. And for some, there is hopelessness because they really cannot do anything. And then there are the many forces against change. Those leaders and people in power who fight against laws and protections of the environment. Greed and short-term interests prevail without empathy or concern for the long-term consequences. These individuals would feel affinities with their Roman counterparts who pillaged the environment and proudly stated in the words of Cicero, one of their orators, "We are the absolute masters of all that the earth provides with our hands. We endeavor to remake it as it were, to make another [kind] of nature."[11] Reading this, we can conclude that a certain inflated human ego, drunk on power and mastery, has not changed much in 2000 years. And we have to say, that Cicero was right. As we shall see a little further on, the Romans did succeed in making another nature out of the one they found. They made desert out of forest, barren hills out of tree filled mountains. We shall look at what the Romans did and the Greeks, too, because there are lessons to learn there, lessons that we never learn in school, and have no collective memory for us.

So yes, there are forces that resist protection of the environment, there is inertia, there is helplessness but I think the problem is even deeper. That is, to repeat again, we don't remember. We lack a global collective unconscious that would emerge from below and spur us on to action. We may have the facts, we know and have seen or lived the terrible effects. But we don't know it in our bones. We know it in our heads. In our social media feeds, our favourite newscasts, and perhaps our own very bad experience. But we don't know it in our bones. We don't remember how the Romans desiccated their environment and left a desert. Meanwhile, the very real heroes of the environmental movement, those named here and many more, are remembered only by a few and celebrated by even fewer.

A recent article published by the journalism department of Oxford University tells us a bit more about this strange lack of interest.[12] It gives a clearer picture of exactly who in the world

---

[11] Hughes Donald J.,1982, p. 74 Cicero on the Nature of the Gods, II 39, 45, 55.
[12] La Presse Canadienne, July 9, 2020, "les Canadiens s'informent peu sur les changments climatiques."

actually cares or doesn't about climate change, according to geographical area and country. The study concludes that people questioned in Latin America, Southern Europe and Asian Pacific care the most about having information about climate change. For example, in Greece, Portugal, Chile and the Philippines, more than half the populations say they are interested and concerned by climate change. In Canada about 39% say they are interested. This puts Canada 31ˢᵗ out of 46 countries. The country with the lowest percentage of people concerned or interested is the United States with just 30%.

Interestingly, those countries whose populations show the most interest in the issue of climate change are not just the ones most affected. They are also ones in which there is the least disagreement among opposing political parties about the need to act on global warming. Knowing this, we learn that in the States, 55% of people to the left politically are interested in information about climate change but only 14% of people on the right are. In all studies, however, youth in all countries are more concerned than older people. More educated people than less educated ones.[13] Is it any wonder given the above statistics and the lack of memory and heroes that there remains a huge distance between what needs to be done and what is being done?

But as mentioned before, this climate crisis is not the first time round for humans. It may be the worst because the earth is running out of resources to take, and we have more modern means to cause damage. But throughout history, some civilizations have misused and abused and destroyed their own environments. We actually have proof of this tendency and records about it from documents written during the years of Greco Roman civilizations, between about 700 BC to 400 AD, documents that supplement the

---

[13] La Presse Canadienne, July 9, 2020, "les Canadiens s'informent peu sur les changments climatiques."

already ample archeological records of environmental destruction during these years.

To set the tone, I'd like to start with these words and expressions: wars, pandemics, rampant inflation, supply scarcities, outrageous impossible prices of fuel. Sound familiar? Sound like our world today? Well, it was also the situation in the Roman Empire around the year 400 because of what they had done to their environment over the course of about seven centuries.

In research for this paper I came across *Deforestation and Erosion and Forest Management in Ancient Greece and Rome*. It is by a Professor Donald Hughes in collaboration with professor J.V. Thirgood in the Journal of Forest History, April 1982. They were pioneer scholars in the field of environmental history. Reading this article created a huge loss of innocence for me and it may for you. I had always imagined nature in ancient Greece and Rome as a constantly balmy, green, fertile place full of forest glades, limpid waters, shady sacred groves inhabited by nymphs and sprites. A place where Artemis, goddess of forest and the hunt, roamed with her retinue of nymphs and hounds, hunting yes, but never over hunting, always caring for her home, the forest.

All of the factual information that follows about the environmental loss of forest land during the Greco Roman Empire between 700 BC and 400 AD is taken from the above-mentioned article.[14] I include some comments regarding certain psychological attitudes especially ones that resemble our own as we face the consequences of our actions on the environment. But most of the historical information is taken straight from the documents studied and written about by Hughes and Thirgood in their article. I think these concrete historical details convey in a way nothing else could exactly how our ancestors made the same mistakes that we are repeating today, even though we have no collective memory at all of this. The section that precedes the one on forests and concerns

---

[14] Hughes, Thurgood, 1982.

the slaughter of most of the wild animals in the Mediterranean basin to feed the appetites of the Roman public for games at the Colosseum are taken from specialized websites cited in the Bibliography.

Nature in classical times, for many of us, is a place of poetry, magical presences, deities, known and unknown, alive with soul. As we wander the marble ruins of this temple or that, we marvel at the beauty that still remains in the splendid fallen or broken pillars but we never stop to wonder why the pillars are always to be found on barren slopes, grassy or stony, rarely surrounded with trees. It is only very recently that historians have begun to take interest in the actual natural environment of the times and to look into the reality of how the Greek and Romans actually used the natural world around them. It isn't always pretty or poetical. The article illustrates the connection between our own modern destruction of the environment and theirs, the Greeks and the Romans. According to Hughes and Thirgood, it is thought by modern scholars of ecology that all of the Mediterranean basin, before the Greco Roman civilization, from around 750BC to 400 AD. was covered in forests, but so was Northern Africa, full of trees, full of animals.[15] And then they weren't. Nothing was covered with trees; the animals were gone.

Before going into more detail about how and why the forest turned into desert or treeless fields, a quick word about those animals. North Africa was full of wild animals, northern Italy too. The Romans had developed a great love of the sport of watching animals fight, either each other or human fighters. This had been a national passion for centuries, but it was only when the first colosseum was built that the real fights and real slaughters began in the life of the Empire. For the opening of the first major colosseum in Rome in 80 AD, the one you can visit and see pictures of today, around 9000 wild animals were caught, thrown into the floor of the

---

[15] Hughes, Donald J., 1982, p. 60.

huge colosseum and killed over a period of 120 days. For another festival in 200 AD, 11,800 animals were slaughtered over 123 days. Some were trained to fight, some tried to escape or fight, all were killed once in front of the blood thirsty eager audiences.

What animals? From North Africa, elephants, giraffes, leopards, lions, hippos, and crocodiles. From the north of Italy, boars, and bears. By the end of the Roman Empire elephants were gone from northern African, so were lions from Greece, hippos from the Northern Nile, lynxes from Eurasia. From afar, the massive and appalling numbers make it seem like it was a terrible gory videogame in which the animals always lost. But it was not a game and they definitely lost.[16] The elephant poachers who kill for tusks today have nothing on our Roman ancestors who killed for war games. What leads us as a human species to be so destructive? Part of the answer is certainly in the words we saw of Cicero when he declared that the Romans were masters of all that nature provided, reflecting an attitude of domination and power only. No relationship, no sense of Nature as Other to be respected and cared for. Clinically that is called narcissism, globally, it results in desecration of the environment and climate change.

And what about the forests, the homes of all those animals, did they fare any better?

We might think of the expression the "groves of academia" and see in our minds eye, the great classic philosophers, wandering and strolling and debating under the shade of majestic leafy trees. But in fact, there are now more trees on the campus of Harvard University in Cambridge, Massachusetts, than there were in Athens in the time of Plato. By his time, around 400 BC, there were no forests to be found in the area surrounding Athens. Plato himself complained, speaking of the mountains around Athens, "What now remains compared with what was then is like the skeleton of a sick

---

[16] Websites cited in bibliography.

man, all the fat and soft earth having wasted away only the bare framework of the land left."[17] What happened?

Well it would be interesting to take a little tour of that long-ago world to see exactly what Plato meant and what the ancients were doing with their forests and especially with wood. Why wood was so important may come as a surprise to many of us for when we think of Rome and Athens, we evoke white marble, not wood. But marble came later, and was especially used for major public buildings when supplies of wood began to wane. Wood was everything for the ancients. In fact, one word for wood in Latin was "materia," the beginning and foundation of all civilization. What were the most common uses of wood? Wood as fuel, wood for building, wood for making war, wood even as food for goats who left to graze in the forests would eat the saplings down to the root, leaving nothing in the earth to grow back.

Taking the uses of wood in more detail: 90% of all wood chopped was used for fuel. It was the fossil fuel, the precious petrol, of the times, and they used it as heedlessly and massively as we have used oil for the past 200 years. At any given time, thousands of men were employed to cut wood, transport it and turn it into charcoal which burned more evenly and with less smoke. As fuel, wood heated houses, cooked food, fed the kilns for pottery, bricks and tiles, stoked the stoves for transforming ore into metal. It burned cracks in the mines to discover that ore. It is said that one metallurgical center could require more than one million acres of forest. One million. In some places, trees cut down or dug up were replaced with new saplings, just as they are today. But not always, just like today. In some places in Greece and Italy where there were major metallurgy mines, the trees have never grown back.

Then there was wood used for building. The Materia, the foundation for all. Wood built houses, public buildings and when it was replaced with stone or brick, wood was still needed

---

[17] Hughes, 1982, p. 67, Plato Critias, 117, 67.

for scaffolding, and to stoke the ovens to heat those bricks. It was used for hinges, for roofs, for household furniture and objects, musical instruments and ship building. There were no plastics, no fiberglass, no synthetic materials. Finally, and fatally, wood was a basic building material for war. Chariots, fortifications and battering rams, ships, and metal weapons forged in fires created by wood.

And then inevitably there was competition for this precious material and thence more wars to procure it and great swaths for forests destroyed in the battles to have it.

As you can see, forests did not have a chance, Plato once said that the ideal city would have its own forests to be self-sufficient, but such was not the case for most cities including his own beloved Athens.

Besides the rampant destruction of forest land to procure wood, there was also the movement to simply destroy forests in order to clear the land for agriculture, for grazing, for building more houses. As populations grew, more land was needed, more forests retreated.[18] Learning all this, you might ask, was nothing sacred to these greedy people who took and took from nature and did not give back? Well, yes, there were the sacred groves. We all know about those, you know, the ones where certain gods are known to live and where it is forbidden to damage or cut any trees. After all they were places of worship, these were carefully demarcated and consecrated by the governments that controlled them. In principle, such sacred places were protected by strict rules. There could be no felling of trees, no tilling of soil, not even removal of dead branches. Breaking the rules could result in fines, even in prison sentences and definitely included ritual curses at you to propitiate the defiled gods. Here there really was soul. Individual trees were said to be

---

[18] This clearing of forest land for farm land is exactly what has happened in Pakistan. At the time of the ongoing flooding there, only 5.7% of the land still has forest cover, while 25% is the recommended percent for sustainability. Climate change is constantly mentioned as the cause of the flooding but there is not enough emphasis put on the catastrophic results of deforestation.

inhabited by nymphs and dryads who, it was believed, died if the tree was cut down. That's pretty important. Something truly sacred.

However, here, too, you may experience a slight loss of innocence because, as in all religions, some of the faithful had more privileges than others. Rich Romans did not seek to buy indulgences from the Church as they might have done in certain later Catholic times. But they did have certain special opportunities. They could for example rent the grove out for a wedding, a party, a celebration. They could also lease the land of a sacred grove, cut the tress, and pay taxes to the local government. In the later years of the Roman Empire, sacred government land was frequently sold to private individuals, even companies, who could exploit it to the fullest while filling the emperor's coffers with gold. I won't belabor comparisons to our modern economies and environmental protected places. You can find such comparisons yourself.

Now the question is, were the Romans completely unaware of the consequences of the deforestation and erosion that came with their lust for timber? It seems they did know to some extent and often planted new tree plantations to replace some cut down forests. But both the lack of greater scientific knowledge and the lack of humility made it impossible to avoid disastrous end of civilization consequences. Remember those words of Cicero: We are masters of nature and all the earth produces. The ego of mankind.

Cutting down the trees, destroying the forests, created erosion all over the Mediterranean basin, created a need to dredge the harbors for ships and without forests, marshlands appeared, increased, malaria and typhoid appeared, floods increased, salination increased, war increased to procure supplies of timber and other forest products. Taxation that formerly went partly to protect forests was more and more spent to maintain armies. Eventually, the system collapsed, wars, inflation, disease, supply shortages in every area, made the Empire ripe for decline and invasion from the North. The Romans were unable to understand the deeper causes of their own destruction. They knew how to use nature but they did not know how to protect her. It is thought that by the 2nd century BC already the rate of soil erosion around Rome had increased from 2-3 centimetres per 1000 years to 20-40 centimetres per 1000 years.[19] And what would it be today?

Conclusion

So how to conclude this tour of wars, pandemics, and climate change? Is the question answered as to why wars mobilize more than each of the others? I think it is. Wars are carriers of past collective emotional memories, as well as memories of heroes. These memories bring on unforgettable scenes of all the consequences of war. Images of blood and destruction, experiences of loss, but these negative memories are coupled with ones of great acts of altruism and heroism. The best and the worst. The brutal and the loving. Mars and Venus. A Death-giving and Life-giving pair. And we witness it all, on our screens, or alas, in our lives. War makes the headlines, Hillman is right.

War is also, at least on the surface, black and white, good and evil. The Manichean division makes it easier for our brains to adhere, get involved. It is so clear. War invites all those involved to participate in some way. It creates solidarity and belonging, calling on our very best and very worst impulses, together.

Pandemics and climate change, on the other hand, don't do that. The dangers they bring are not incarnated in a bad human face we can loathe and fight. The danger is either invisible, i.e., viruses, or one that seems outside of personal individual human range and control, i.e., climate change.

More specifically, to act and fight it, a pandemic requires two very different levels of human organization. On one end, the very specialized experts in hospitals, the specialized world of public health, the specialized laboratories of research and vaccine creation. On the other end, the rest of us. We need not, we cannot

---

[19] Hughes, 1998, pp. 60-74.

bring much to the table. We are not called on to make efforts, to give our best to serve and sacrifice actively, to show our knowledge and courage. On the contrary, we are asked not to participate, to stay away, to just not make trouble and obey the authorities. We are in short, infantilized in order to survive.

How to create proud collective memory and lasting heroes in such circumstances? Between the people dying, the people fleeing, the people isolating, and the social divisions created, pandemics divide and fragment society. People don't want to remember; they don't even want to be heroes. Witness some members of medical staffs expressing extreme discomfort in the early part of the pandemic when they were lauded with the ringing of pots and pans for their professional courage and competence. They did not feel heroic. They just felt exhausted and burnt out. And like everyone, they just wanted it to end.

And so it goes with climate change. There is a similar social division as with the pandemic. It too has called forth experts, incredible minds and hearts and resources. Thousands of individuals who have chosen to defend Mother Nature from the predations of our species. But again, most of us do not, cannot, actually throw ourselves into any kind of glorious heroism. We can do little things, we can follow the advice of the experts, make gestures to save the planet by recycling, turning off the lights, buying electric cars. But these are consumer choices. They count, yes, but they do not lead to a feeling of participating directly in a Great Event as Citizens. When the floods and fires arrive, we ordinary people can only flee, or maybe stay and hope to be saved, just like in the pandemic.

Ultimately, it is a problem of archetypes. Unlike in wars, there is no victory to claim either in a pandemic or the area of climate change. There is progress, there are new vaccines and remedies to help fight off the effects of Covid. But the virus is still with us. As William McNeil cited previously so presciently said, "Infectious disease which antedated the emergence of humankind will last as long as humanity itself and will remain as it has been hitherto, one of the fundamental parameters and determinants of human history."[20]

For climate change there is also progress on many fronts and much, much more awareness and activism especially in younger generations. But it is unlikely that there will come a time in our lifetime when victory will be declared. Nor, hopefully, total defeat. The archetype of winning/losing, victory/defeat, heroes/cowards, just doesn't neatly apply to pandemics and climate as it does to war.

So short of collective memory and lasting heroes, what can help us in the apocalyptic presence of ongoing pandemics and climate change? I would suggest the following, they are neither absolute nor exclusive: expertise, heroes, and above all, leadership.

We have expertise in the areas of virus and climate change that we did not have before. We have knowledge about how it happens and why and ways to diminish their effects. We also have heroes, people in laboratories putting all their considerable brain power into finding better ways to defeat Covid-19 and we have people all over the world giving their energy and even their lives to fight climate change and help nature recover. How to recognize and praise these people, turning from perennial military adoration, to raise up their life-saving efforts in new kinds of heroics?

And finally, what I think is most necessary and most lacking is true leadership.

We know that wars are won by the courage of humans who fight for each other and for leaders they believe in. Wars are lost when leaders are no longer heroes to their people. They may continue to prevail by might but they have lost the most important battle, the one for hearts and minds. As cliché as it sounds, it remains the core of human strength and social coherence. So where are the politicians courageous enough to insist on making climate change a priority in spite of overwhelming resistance from monied interests? Where are the natural leaders who will emerge in the coming years

---

[20] McNeil, 1998, pp. 262-295.

to resist the temptation of war and lead through the moral values that our civilization will depend on as it attempts to avoid global suicide by pandemic, climate change, or by the same old, same old, just war again?

References

Addington, R. and Ames, D. (trans.), *New Larousse. Encyclopedia of Mythology Librairie Larousse,* Paris, France 1968.

Blais, Stephen, July 9, 2020. "Les Canadiennes s'informent peu sur les changements climatiques," *La Presse Canadienne,* From document published by Reuters Institute (2020) of a study done by the Oxford University School of Journalism, Oxford England.

Hillman, James, (2004). *A Terrible Love of War,* New York: Penguin Group.

Hughes, Donald J., (in collaboration with J.V. Thirgood), (1982). "Forest Management in Ancient Greece and Rome," *Journal of Forest History,* pp. 60-75, Chicago, IL: The University of Chicago Press.

McNeil, William H., (1998). *Plagues and People,* New York: Random House-Anchor Books.

Strochlic, N. & Champine, R. (2020). How some cities 'flattened the curve' during the 1918 flu pandemic. National Geographic: History & culture. (March 27, 2020) https://www.nationalgeographic.com/history/2020/03/how-cities-flattened-curve-1918-spanish-flu-pandemic-coronavirus/

Websites on animal extinction during the Roman Empire:
DarkRome.com, January 14, 2022
Longreads.com, Mass Extinction, January 4, 2016.
ThroughEternity.com, Ancient Rome, September 20, 2019

Reconsidering Individuation in the 21st Century: When Archetypal Patterns Shift

Joe Cambray, Ph.D., IAAP

As we will explore here, the notion of individuation emerged during C.G. Jung's *Red Book* (2009) period and evolved throughout the remainder of his life, becoming one of his signature concepts. Although a psychoanalyst in his early career, Jung was also among the first of the adult developmentalists, along with Stanley Hall.[1] Individuation, understood as becoming as fully as possible who one is meant to be, in the context of genetic inheritance and environmental, cultural, and natural forces is a rather broad, complex and elastic idea that can be beneficially reassessed periodically.

Jung's method for approaching individuation experientially, and clinically, is centered on integration of contents of the unconscious, expanding consciousness towards a realization of the Self, occurring in a circumambulatory exploration. According to Jung, the Self "designates the whole range of psychic phenomena in

---

[1] Hall was a founder of the American Psychological Association, and president of Clark University. In the latter capacity he brought Freud and Jung there to speak in 1909 at Clark's historic 20th anniversary conference. While initially a child developmentalist Hall went on to write books on adolescence and the later stages of life. His influence on Jung has been noted though not fully explored.

man [humans];" from the perspective of consciousness it is often represented by a *superordinate personality*, which includes a union of opposites that encompasses both the conscious and unconscious aspect of the psyche (Jung, 1971, para. 790-791). Because his psychology posits a collective as well as personal dimension to the unconscious, the Self, the ordering principle of the psyche, is envisioned as transpersonal (for convenience, I will use the capital S form to represent this, however, Jung did not use this convention). It is of an archetypal nature, as are the primary hubs of the collective unconscious, colloquially referred to as the archetypes. The archetypes pattern human behavior with affect and image, i.e., they are psychosomatic, and marked by a sense of the numinous when encountered by consciousness, giving them a mythopoetic feeling. While integration of the contents of this multilayered unconscious is a type of goal, it is one that can never be fully realized. Hence individuation ultimately is about the individual process rather than being focused on specific contents of that process.

How the archetypal Self is envisioned or expressed is bound to the cultural forms in which it appears. Explicit figurations and images, occurring within a cultural context, never fully capture the totality of the Self but are the ways in which we come to know it. Therefore, how it has manifested in history has varied according to the way the mythopoetic imagination has expressed itself at any particular time and place, often expressed in terms of a god/goddess image. For a thorough, recent study see Corbett (2021).

Although Jung wrote extensively about individuation in his various publications and letters, the subject has remained a vibrant area of scholarship. Academia.edu, at the time of this writing (September 2022), lists more than 1900 books and more than 1100 articles in a search for "Jung and Individuation." Given the volume of material published, a review of the literature in a short chapter is not realistic. Nevertheless, in addition to Jung's classic texts (such as: *Collected Works, Volume 7*, part two of "The Relations Between the Ego and the Unconscious," 1966; and *Collected*

Works, Volume 9, Part I in section VI "Conscious, Unconscious, and Individuation," and "A Study in the Process of Individuation," 1969), the Philemon Foundation has produced a recent volume of seminars Jung gave at Bailey Island (1958/1969) and *Collected Works, Volume 12: Psychology and Alchemy* (1968). The Bailey Island seminars afford further details and insights on how Jung used the concept of individuation in practice as well as in theory (Gieser, 2019).

As mentioned, throughout the years since Jung's death many Jungian and post-Jungian authors have published books and articles exploring various aspects of the topic. A few examples will have to suffice: Marie-Louise von Franz's book exploring individuation as found in fairy tales, a subject on which she had great knowledge (1990); Jolanda Jacobi's classic text, with her clear exposition of Jung's theory (1967); several popular volumes by Murray Stein including a recent reissuing of his main text on the topic (2018). There have also been scholars outside the analytic community, such as Sean Kelly who have linked Jung's ideas on individuation with philosophers such as Hegel (1993).

In this chapter, Jung's development of the concept of individuation will be placed in the context of his personal "confrontation with the unconscious" as documented in his *Red Book* and *Black Books*, where he captured his experiences from this period of inner exploration. This will allow a closer examination of some problems with the idea of individuation as well as some open questions. Jung continued to refine his thinking until the end of his life, and here I will seek to follow the trajectory of his thoughts as they are percolated through some current understandings developed through the application of complexity studies. The suggestion is that a traditional individual "hero myth," so ably described by Joseph Campbell (1968) is no longer as compelling for moderns as it was in Jung's day. Instead, our individuation seems to necessarily be linked to an ecologically based, delocalized and distributed view of the unconscious which has been emerging over the past 30 years.

This embraces an insight Jung had that his time was poised at a:

> kairos—the right moment—for a 'metamorphosis of the gods,' of the fundamental principles and symbol....[and] Coming generations will have to take account of this momentous transformation if humanity is not to destroy itself through the might of its own technology and science. (1970, par. 585)

We are a part of those generations who are now confronting the consequences of our capacity to profoundly alter nature and in that process have set off global warming, pandemics, and a host of related crises. How then is this impacting our understanding and vision of individuation?

The Emergence of Individuation in Jung's Experience

As discussed in other chapters, in the aftermath of severing relations with Sigmund Freud in October 1913, C.G. Jung faced a powerful, personal crisis that led him to question whether his sanity was at risk. Several episodes of waking visions of Europe filling up to the Alps with blood or debris, left him shaken. Rather than avoiding or covering over the issues activated, he chose to explore them and, in the process, develop the technique of active imagination, treating the psyche as real and worthy of research. After several months of intensive work on the upwelling imagery and attendant emotions, his inner world began to settle. The encounters, however, convinced him he had to change his life. In response he resigned his posts and prestigious position, instead focusing on his private practice and allowing himself time for a self-analytic confrontation with the unconscious. In this he was greatly aided by his wife Emma Rauschenbach Jung, who provided a stable home environment, psychological containment, and partnership, along with significant finances to allow him to follow his calling.

As he was recovering, his dreams indicated healing capacities of a collective nature were evolving (dreams of terrible frost descending on Europe but producing grapes with healing juices), as if containing the intense psychic sweetness of a late harvest of soul. Then, a couple of months later World War I broke out and he was faced with questions of prophecy as well as madness. Neither was acceptable and so he toiled for another 15 years or so, seeking a way through this dilemma. Along the way he had numerous experiences that helped form his personality and thinking, molding him into the figure we now commonly think of as Jung, the wise old psychiatrist of Zürich, who bridged science and mysticism, producing a theory of archetypes and plumbing the depths of the collective unconscious.

Jung's psychological development as presented in the RB reveals a gradual confidence and ability to engage with the internal figures and situations of his interior life. Dreams and active imaginations provide the basic substance of his explorations. During WWI he served as the medical director of an internment camp for allied officers.[2] During this time he made a practice of constructing mandalas on a daily basis. A series of these became paintings displaying in abstract form a set of psychological changes indicating the metabolizing of emotional disturbances into enrichments of the personality, but also implying transformational innovations at collective levels, the birth of a new god-image out of trauma and suffering.

After the war ended, Jung began to emerge from his "fallow" period and started to produce a volume of new material. Then, in 1919 as what was then known as the "Spanish Flu" swept the world, Jung contracted a case, which produced a series of fever dreams. He painted a series of images from these dreams but did not include them in the *Red Book*. However, they have been reproduced in *The Art of C.G. Jung* along with his discussion with

---

[2] To retain neutrality in WWI the Swiss had to agree not to repatriate combatants from either side. Their solution was to set up internment camps for the soldiers who made it to Swiss territory and to treat them civilly for the remainder of the conflict. The internment camps were well run and had up-to-date medical care. Jung served in this capacity at Chateau D'Oex.

his biographer Aniela Jaffe of the dreams and vision he had while ill (Hoerni, et. al. 2019, p. 137). The quadrated sphere found in these images was also incorporated into the figure on page 125 of the RB (Jung, 2009, 125). I have demonstrated how this same image has a striking similarity to the image of a juvenal sea squirt found in the marine biological paintings of Ernst Haeckel (2014). My contention then was that Jung was not simply borrowing from science for his images, but was in fact psychologizing the overt contents of science, in particular biology, with a mythopoetic flavor.

Opening the Psychoid Imagination

Now that we know these images of the quadrated sphere are related to fever dreams, I would like to extend the understanding of Jung's visioning in a non-ordinary state of consciousness. I suggest that he was partaking of the "psychoid imagination"[3] and that his artistic intuition was capturing an essential aspect of his illness (Cambray, 2016; 2020). The virus responsible for that pandemic was originally an influenza A virus subtype H1N1 (A/H1N1); a different family of virus from the cause of Covid-19, but with very similar modes of transmission, and sharing roughly the same shape: both are spheroidal with spike proteins punctuating the surface. Note the details of virology including the morphology of viruses were not known during this time.[4] Rather the fever related dreams/ visions appear to have captured this aspect of the infecting agent without the possibility of conscious recognition. Nevertheless, Jung's renderings of spheres from the imagery in his illness are

---

[3] This was a term I coined to give conceptualization to the ability to intuitively perceive aspects of the world generally outside the realm of the psyche. In 1946 Jung created a new term, the *psychoid unconscious* to refer to aspects of the world that were not considered part of the psyche but under some conditions behaved as if influenced by it; he imagined it was wholly inaccessible to consciousness—a notion which I am gently challenging here using Jung's own art work to suggest this, *v.i.*.

[4] The first virus to be imaged was the tobacco mosaic virus in the 1930s (Rossman, 2013).

consistent with other demonstrations of artistic intuition grasping forms not yet available to the cultures in which the artists lived and worked.

Jung's incorporation of some of the fever state images eventually did make it into the RB. On page 131, a luminous, complex sphere glowing whitish blue among the branches of a tree creates a mandala-like form emanating particles and rays— reminiscent of his simpler "Spheric Vision III" of 1919 (Hoerni, 2019, p. 133), which portrays one of his flu dreams. The vector of illness is envisioned through psychosomatic channels and elevated into a form of the *lumen naturae* (the alchemists' light in nature) aglow in the Philosophical Tree. The disease agent has been elevated to a source of wisdom, reversing the disenchantment of the "gods have become diseases" (Jung, 1967, para. 54); so the diseases have become gods.

Recognition of the re-enchantment of the world through psychic reality is an aspect of the RB not yet fully developed. In this regard, it may be important to note that the author of the notion of the "disenchantment of the world" through modern science, renowned sociologist Max Weber, also contracted "Spanish Flu" and died of it in 1920. Weber's declaration of disenchantment was first delivered in a lecture in 1917, subsequently published in 1918 in German; the first English translation was in 1946 (Weber, 1946). Jung was likely aware of this notion and his own experience with the pandemic may have increased sympathy with the author and his fate. That his fever dream made it into the RB, seems at least a nod in the direction of reversing disenchantment, which Weber would have certainly found valuable.

Several scholars have shown links in the thought of Weber and Jung. In particular Roderick Main has written on how the work of the philosopher, Charles Taylor, makes a valuable bridge between the two, and makes Jung more relevant for contemporary sociology (Main, 2013). Gavin Walker has also made links, especially with Weber's categories of religious experiences of "ascetic" and "mystic" states as having close parallels to Jung's ideas. He also finds relevancy for Jung's thought in modern sociology (Walker, 2012).

The Self and the Process of Individuation

Referring to this period Jung remarked: "During those years, between 1918 and 1920, I began to understand that the goal of psychic development is the self. There is no linear evolution; there is only a circumambulation of the self" (1961).

This circumambulation continued throughout his life, but reached a culmination in the RB with his "Liverpool" dream of 1927:

....The various quarters of the city were arranged radially around the square. In the center was a round pool, and in the middle of it a small island. While everything round about was obscured by rain, fog, smoke, and dimly lit darkness, the little island blazed with sunlight. On it stood a single tree, a magnolia, in a shower of reddish blossoms. It was as though the tree stood in the sunlight and were at the same time the source of light. My companions commented on the abominable weather, and obviously did not see the tree. They spoke of another Swiss who was living in Liverpool, and expressed surprise that he should have settled here. I was carried away by the beauty of the flowering tree and the sunlit island, and thought, "I know very well why he has settled here." Then I awoke. (Jung, 1961, pp. 197-198)

In his analysis and commentary, Jung notes:

The dream brought with it a sense of finality. I saw that here the goal had been revealed. One could not go beyond the center. The center is the goal and everything is directed towards that center. Through this dream I understood that the self is the principle and archetype of orientation and meaning. Therein lies its healing function….Out of it emerged a first inkling of my personal myth. (Jung, 1961, pp. 197-198)

From the introduction to the recently published *Black Books* (2020), Jung's original journal entries which he used to construct the RB, we learn that he felt:

This dream described the apex of the whole unconscious process of development….My life would have actually lost its meaning without such a vision. But the meaning was expressed here. (Jung, 2020, V. 1, pp. 98-99)

Black Books editor Sonu Shamdasani noted: "The realization was that the self was the goal of the process of individuation" (Jung, 2020, p. 99). Jung also went on to give the dream pictorial representation as "The Window on Eternity," found on page 159 of the RB. The question then arises, with the realization of the concept of the Self, why did Jung continue for several more years working on his inner material, giving it form first in his journals which were ultimately published as the *Black Books*, then in the *Red Book*?

Synchronicity: An Innovative Jungian Concept

As I have shown elsewhere (2014), Jung's all-encompassing commitment to inner work continued until he discovered the notion of synchronicity.[5] This finally released him to "return to the human side and to the world" (2009, p. 219). For this chapter I hold that Jung was not fully satisfied with a personal revelation of the transpersonal Self, as important as that was. Rather, he needed

---

[5] As I show in the 2014 paper, it was the synchronistic receipt of the manuscript of *The Secret of the Golden Flower* from R. Wilhelm which contained an image of the Vajramanda, just as Jung was working on a mandala of a walled city, with some striking parallels that provided the path back to the world. There were other elements in this story that are recounted in the paper, but this meaningful coincidence gave Jung the opportunity to pursue historical parallels to his own experiences and broke through his isolation.

a new cosmogonic principle and indeed his work with Wolfgang Pauli from 1932 until Pauli's death in 1958, was essential.[6] In exploring Jung's description of synchronicity, Pauli refers to it as an "act of creation in time" and may have been Jung's source for his implicit reference to "big bang" cosmology (our scientific story/creation myth):

...since experience has shown that under certain conditions space and time can be reduced to almost zero, causality disappears along with them because causality is bound up with the existence of space and time and physical changes, and consists essentially in the succession of cause and effect. For this reason synchronistic phenomena cannot in principle be associated with any conceptions of causality (Jung, 1969, para. 855).

The point of disappearance of space and time is the theorized preceding singularity of Big Bang cosmology. Hence this is a cosmological conception about the fundamental nature of the universe. Individuation then is not only about seeking wholeness for the individual person, but also reflects a unitary imagining of all of reality, including a re-enchantment of the world. I believe this is what intuitively Jung was seeking in continuing his work in the *Black Books* and *Red Book* until 1932. He then returned to university teaching, no longer in psychiatry but now in general psychology.

This also was the time of his pivot towards alchemy. Transformations of personality, helping others move towards states of "golden" consciousness, paralleling and overlapping the transformations of substances in alchemy became his great work. The alchemical secret of the golden flower with its synchronistic

---

[6] For the unfolding of their thoughts on the synchronicity hypothesis see their correspondence in *Atom and Archetype* (Meier 2001); an excellent study of their collaboration by Suzanne Gieser (2005); and the work of Harald Atmanspacher and colleagues on The Pauli-Jung Conjecture (2014) as well as his many other publications on the topic.

revelation set the path for the tremendous, bold task of individuation of self and environment. As he ends in his last great alchemical text:

> Alchemy, therefore, has performed for me the great and invaluable service of providing material in which my experience could find sufficient room, and has thereby made it possible for me to describe the individuation process at least in its essential aspects. (1970, para. 792)

In the spirit of Jung's search, I would like to now consider how new fields of knowledge have opened up understandings of the world since Jung's death in 1961. In particular, I would like to turn to complexity studies and ecological applications.

New Paradigms

In the sixty years since Jung died, there have been remarkable developments in understanding the complex nature of the world. For our purposes I will focus on some findings from complexity studies, in particular, complex adaptive systems. These are systems of interacting agents, which can be almost anything from subatomic particles to clusters of galaxies, including biological systems and even collective human behaviors, from traffic jams to stock markets. The interactions being considered occur within a competitive environment and the interconnectedness of the agents allows them to spontaneously self-organize, without top-down hierarchies, to produce emergent properties. These are holistic features not discoverable within individual agents but only as a manifestation of the whole. The liquidity of water at room temperature is a simple example: on an individual molecular basis water might be anticipated to be gaseous at room temperature, but due to the hydrogen bonding between molecules, liquidity results as an emergent property. In the analytic field, the appearance of a third subject is likewise an emergent property of the clinical encounter. The third often enters the process as a co-construction, not fully belonging to either partner. This is not reducible to either of their internal worlds but comes out of their interactions with one another within their shared environment.

As a first foray into this area I looked at synchronistic phenomena in terms of emergence in complex adaptive systems (Cambray, 2002). Others looked at complexes, archetypes and the Self along similar lines—for a brief sampling of a few inaugural works, see Hogenson, 2004, 2005; Martin-Vallas, 2006, 2008; and Knox, 2003. The literature in this field has flourished and grown over the past two decades.

For present purposes, network models, especially scale-free networks are valuable. These have self-similar morphologies at a minimum of three levels of scale, e.g., tree-branch-twig being such a set; river deltas, airline route maps, the structure of the internet are all common examples of such systems. Network maps are informational structures composed of nodes, which are small collection points, while hubs are nodes with many links (connections to other nodes). These types of maps have widespread applicability and utility. For example, the brain can be represented as an extremely complex 3-D network of different kinds of neuronal fibers interconnecting in and between various substructures. Visualizing connections helps to indicate patterns of interaction and flow (e.g., of energy or information). Often hidden relationships can be discovered through tracing connective interactions, which would be too complex to identify without the mapping.

Ecological systems have been usefully explored through network analysis and mapping. These include food networks as found in nature (who eats who), which identify hub predators. When such hub animals are removed from the ecosystem there is often a trophic cascade, which can be catastrophic for a local environment. Fortunately some are reversible as when the US forest service reintroduced wolves into Yellowstone Park after they had been hunted to extinction locally, and after several years the environment rebounded, see: (https://www.yellowstonepark.com/things-to-do/wildlife/wolf-reintroduction-changes-ecosystem/).

Although Jung did not have access to sophisticated ecosystems maps, he was interested in the phenomena. His orientation came from an interest in rhizomes. These are plants that have "horizontal underground plant stem[s] capable of producing the shoot and root systems of a new plant" (from https://www. britannica.com/science/tuber). Common examples include bamboo, ginger, lotus, aspen, and turmeric. Individual shoots look as if they are separate plants above ground but are all part of a single entity once the root system is examined. Hence these plants serve as models of highly interconnected networks, invisible upon first inspection but revealed by looking more deeply below the surface, a valuable metaphor for the psyche itself. Jung also traced the notion of connected networks back to the ancient Greeks, for whom the rhizomes referred to the four elements, especially following Empedocles. These were powers included in the alchemical vision of the world, and so Jung also understood them symbolically. Jung used a rhizomatic analogy to describe life and the psyche:

> Life has always seemed to me like a plant that lives on its rhizome. Its true life is invisible, hidden in the rhizome. The part that appears above ground lasts only a single summer. Then it withers away— an ephemeral apparition. When we think of the unending growth and decay of life and civilizations, we cannot escape the impression of absolute nullity. Yet I have never lost a sense of something that lives and endures underneath the eternal flux. What we see is the blossom, which passes. The rhizome remains. (Jung, 1961, p. 4)

In recent years the study of rhizomal systems has expanded our vision of connectivity in nature. Suzanne Simard is a top researcher in the field of forest ecology whose work has helped to reveal forest structures consisting of multispecies networks. Simard's research on Douglas fir trees opens into a convergence of the symbolic and ecological, especially with the notion of the "mother tree" (Frazier, 2015; Simard, 2021). In an early project she sought to understand how fir seedlings survive at the forest floor with only 4 to 5% of the light from the sun reaching them. Following intuition, she designed an experiment demonstrating that parent trees feed and care for their seedling offspring through interconnected root systems. Anthropomorphizing this reveals what we would identify as maternal caretaking behavior. This is consistent with mythopoetic beliefs about certain kinds of trees in various traditional cultures (often placentas are placed in the roots of a "twin" tree imagined to share the fate of the individual, and in some cultures the dead are buried in hollows of trees, returning the body to a maternal womb in nature).

Extending her research, Simard has turned to even more complex systems, mycorrhizal networks. These are comprised of fungal (mykes) species that share roots (rhizia) with various species of trees within a single forest. The networks created are comprised of multiple species forming an interconnected web that can achieve great size. One was discovered in the western US which constitutes the largest known organism on earth, see: http://www.scientificamerican.com/article/strange-but-true-largest-organism-is-fungus/. It is reported to occupy 2,384 acres (about 10 square kilometers); its longevity is also impressive, estimated to be between 2,400 and 8,650 years old.

These networks have remarkable interactive capabilities. In the systems Simard has studied, Douglas firs photosynthesize and supply sugars to the fungi which symbiotically infiltrate the tree roots by dramatically increasing the plant's water and mineral absorptive powers via their vast network of filaments (Frazier, 2015). Furthermore, fungal networks transport nutrients for storage and distribution, e.g., dying trees download their nutrients into these mycorrhizal networks, which then move these nutrients to other members of the network. The network also differentially distributes phytohormones used, for example, in warning signals and defensive alterations in biochemistry, e.g., against herbivores such as insects (beetles, caterpillars, etc.).

As I've discussed previously, mycorrhizal networks serve as a conduit and communication pathway between trees of several species, allowing cooperative coordination previously undetected between the partners of the network (Cambray, 2018). From an ecological perspective, these multi-organism systems have a sophisticated communication and distribution network with a kind of adaptive intelligence. Given fungi and trees have such a rich communal interconnected life, what then of ourselves with brains composed of incredibly rich neural nets engaging with one another and our worlds? Does not our core consciousness emerge from such deep roots? And, might there be noetic qualities inherent in these roots that we perceive via intuition and imagination, often significantly in advance of cognitive process as discussed above?

About a decade ago images from NASA telescopes gave views of the universe at its largest scale. Within days compelling visual comparisons finding similarities with thin sections of mammalian brains were made. More recently there has been quantitative comparisons between these structures which have led observers to note:

> ...the natural physical processes lead to similar structures even when differences in scale can be greater than 27 orders of magnitude.
>
> The human brain contains approximately 69 billion neurons, whereas the observable universe consists of a web of at least 100 billion galaxies. In both galactic and neural networks, just 30% of their masses are composed of 'working' masses, such as galaxies and neurons. The rest of the 70% of matter plays an apparently passive role: water in the brain and dark energy in the observable cosmos. (https://www.zmescience.com/science/human-brain-cosmos-05832/).

The fractal similarities between such radically different systems is amazing and the physicists commented on this versus the components of their networks: "These two complex networks show more similarities than those shared between the cosmic web and a galaxy or a neuronal network and the inside of a neuronal body" (Tibi Puiu 2020). What is shared is the emergent property of each network as a whole. This would indicate a profound archetypal patterning spanning the physical, biological, and perhaps psychological universes. While claiming the universe is a giant mind is not yet warranted it does hint at the profound similarity between nature and the psyche, perhaps with consciousness as a fundamental background quality to the universe. This would also point towards the *unus mundus*, the alchemical idea of a unitary background to all phenomena, also referred to as the *pleroma*, or the one world.

The link to the *unus mundus* becomes a key aspect of what we understand to be Jung's final view of individuation, as articulated in *Mysterium Conunctionis* (1970). It can be seen as the deepest fundament to reality, it exists prior to the separations of opposites such as mind and matter. In a discussion of the "stages of the conjunction," Jung refers to sixteenth century alchemist Gerhard Dorn, linking his views on the "chemical marriage" with the individuation process:

> The second stage of conjunction, the re-uniting of the unio mentalis with the body, is particularly important, as only from here can the complete conjunction be attained—union with the unus mundus. The reuniting of the spiritual position with the body obviously means that the insights gained should be made real....The second stage of conjunction therefore consists in making a reality of the man who has acquired some knowledge of his paradoxical wholeness. (1970, p. 476)

A bit further on Jung then considers the meaning of this with regards to the environment:

> If Dorn, then, saw the consummation of the mysterium conjunctionis in the union of the alchemically produced caelum with the unus mundus, he expressly meant not a fusion of the individual with his environment, or even his adaptation to it, but a unio mystica with the potential world....That even the psychic world, which is so extraordinarily different from the physical world, does not have its roots outside the one cosmos is evident from the undeniable fact that causal connections exist between the psyche and the body which point to their underlying unitary nature. (Jung, 1970, pp. 537-538)

Here Jung is moving towards a conception of union with the cosmos, a profound connectedness of the psyche with the whole of nature, reminiscent of the Indra's Net of the Buddha's the Avataṃsaka Sūtra sermon. In such a vision, a person is inextricably a part of the universe. According to von Franz this is "the ultimate stage of the process of individuation, a becoming one with the collective unconscious" and this culminates at the "point where out and inner reality (heaven and earth) become one with the goal of individuation" (von Franz, 1979, p. 115). What then are the implications for the archetypal pattern at the core of individuation?

A Twenty-First Century Vision of Individuation

As noted above, one of the most important advances in knowledge since Jung's death has been the development of complexity theory. This has opened up an eco-spiritual view of the psyche, as non-local, distributed, wholly intertwined with nature and spirit, in a rich, complex, holistic universe. How then is the notion of individuation impacted by this more extended view of reality?

While individualism, which is egocentric, was seen by Jung as far less important than individuation, which is about realizing and developing a relationship with the transpersonal Self, traces remain. For example, the use of the hero archetype as the blueprint for individuation within the family, leaves a person pursuing psychological development from an intrapsychic base, identifying with heroic acts of famed individuals, as in geniuses. This tends to bring in a perfectionism, often with lofty goals, but frequently at the expense of the environment, human and natural. This can take the form of seeking spirit while denigrating the physical and all that is symbolically linked to it.

Instead, I suggest we begin by acknowledging our fundamental embeddedness in the world but allow for an ecological expansion, especially of our psyches. The synchronicity hypothesis is a valuable conception that can move us in this direction as the boundaries between subjective and objective realities are necessarily viewed as more porous in the face of acausal, meaningful coincidences. To expand our vision of the psyche, I believe it is helpful to recognize that synchronicities are not confined to individuals, but can occur within groups and cultures—including between cultures—and now we may be seeing global synchronicities.

In a previous book, I devoted a chapter to introducing the notion of cultural synchronicities with a variety of examples (2009). In the face of cultural traumas there are records of many people having premonitory dreams with shared elements, e.g., black birds falling out of the sky just prior to the 9/11 attack on the Twin Towers of the World Trade Center. Similarly, in a non-traumatic setting, the use of social-dreaming at conferences, frequently is marked by issues being raised in the symbolism of participants' dreams that emerge in reality during the course of the event. While the dream material can seem intimate and private to the dreamer, when placed in the larger context in which the phenomena occur, it often reveals what could be understood as a shared symbolic field.

The participants each have their own idiosyncratic view but when assembled and collated, an ecological vision of the psyche emerges.

If one important aspect of synchronicities is communications of what is, or has been rendered, inexpressible, then reading these events for their potential insights into cultural traumas could offer some psychosocial relief. A grim example of this happened during WWII with regard to the tomb of Timur. In June of 1941 a Soviet archeological expedition commissioned by Joseph Stalin was sent to Samarkand, Uzbekistan to open the tomb of Timur/Tamerlane. This was followed by a set of curious coincidences:

> Two days after the opening of the Timur's tomb, on the night of June 22, Nazi Germany without declaring the war invaded the Soviet Union..... The turning point in the war came with a victory in the Battle of Stalingrad. A month earlier Stalin ordered to return the remains of Timur and his dynasty to Samarkand and to bury them with full honors.
>
> (https://www.advantour.com/uzbekistan/legends/ tamerlane-curse.htm).

If even a figure like Stalin, so convinced of the correctness of his action, could alter course in the face of synchronistic evidence, might we revision our model of the psyche?

Moving back from synchronicity to individuation, since we have extended the one to interacting groups, might the other then be extended to cohesive collectives? As cultural complexes are metabolized, however slowly, is cultural individuation fostered? The United States' struggle with its racist history and proclivities has been intensifying since the murder of George Floyd. Would not a pathway towards repair and resolution help society move beyond the polarizations rending the social fabric, which can be so easily exploited by the tyrannical? Without this we face cultural fragmentation and disintegration.

Similarly, grasping the severity of the impending ecological crises associated with global warming requires a more holistic vision of the world and ourselves. The Covid-19 pandemic may be an early harbinger of what is to come. Shifting patterns of nature on the planet due to climate stress is not only dislocating species, but soon to unleash great waves of climate migrations in humans with enormous repercussions for all. Working through one's personal traumatic history is of course valuable but can no longer be separated from environmental considerations. We desperately need a new vision of our psyches through which the complex interrelationships between everyone and the planet can be acknowledged and lived in an integrated fashion.

A concern in retaining the individuation metaphor as psychological goal, even inclusive of collective levels, is how to conceive of the Self in the more expansive versions of the psyche. Revising the Self as intrinsically part of, and non-separable from the world, could be a valuable step. One dilemma of the Self, even in the Jungian corpus, which at an archetypal level makes it equatable to the god image, is the tendency to collapse into strict monotheism. As Weber pointed out this monotheism is the path to disenchantment and ultimately as monotheistic religion is superseded by science the world falls into a disenchanted reductive materialism (https://plato. stanford.edu/entries/weber/ accessed 9/28/2022). The proposal here is to step back and reconsider strict monotheism as a reduction of the emergent form (the one and only god) into a single entity without its roots in the agents from which it emerged. Yet reclaiming the emergent process is not a flight back into a polytheistic cosmos, as tempting as that might be at first glance.

An emergent version of the Self remains in process and is vulnerable to loss if the process is not adequately attended. The complexity model clearly links the emergent form back to its underlying agents in a loop of mutual interaction. Conceived as such, this Self cannot be reified into a single entity with a detached separate existence, but must renew itself at the edge of order and chaos, where it was born. The essence of this chapter is to suggest this reconsideration is a natural, normal, and necessary aspect of individuation, an ongoing reflective process on the nature of the self in the context of a changing world. A task that I believe Jung himself envisioned:

> Every advance in culture is, psychologically, an extension of consciousness, a coming to consciousness that can take place only through discrimination. Therefore, an advance always begins with individuation, that is to say with the individual, conscious of his isolation, cutting a new path through hitherto untrodden territory. To do this he must first return to the fundamental facts of his own being, irrespective of all authority and tradition, and allow himself to become conscious of his distinctiveness. If he succeeds in giving collective validity to his widened consciousness, he creates a tension of opposites that provides the stimulation which culture needs for its further progress. (1969, para. 111)

We might frame this as the need for innovation as a part of the individuation process. How then might this manifest today?

A Personal Example

In 2019 I introduced the concept of the *adjacent possible* into the Jungian literature (Cambray, 2019). This is another idea coming out of complexity theory, especially in the work of Stuart Kauffman (1996; 2000), further developed by a group in Rome (Gravino, et. al 2016). It models innovation pathways in nature (e.g., evolution) and in culture (e.g., in films). The model can be readily applied to psychology, as seen in dreams in which the dreamer discovers a new room in a dwelling (often a new or previously unnoticed space within the realm of the familiar). Entering into the new psychic space, inhabiting and exploring it, leads to a development of new capacities or awareness. A series of such innovative moves, if integrated into the personality can provide a pathway for individuation.

Several moments in my own life point to this kind of trajectory. In one, while living in Japan as a visiting faculty in a chemistry department, my first career, I joined a Soto Zen meditation group. The practice of sitting zazen was quite psychoactive and produced a series of dreams in which I found new rooms in the condo I was staying in on the campus. The rooms were a combination of contemporary western and more traditional Japanese rooms. While the Zen sensei acknowledged the dreams, they said they would pass and to let go of them. I agreed they would pass but wanted to explore them and so began reading Jung on dreams to more deeply enter the material. This inaugurated a path which eventually lead me from chemistry to becoming an analyst.

For a number of years, I sought to build bridges between my vocational aspirations. The most effective link came in my clinical work with traumatized clients. Elsewhere I have reported the case of the "Black Forest" in which a person suffering from sustained, early childhood abuse, dreamt of my being in the Black Forest and lost to her, while I was on vacation (2002). During that trip I learned to scuba-dive, and my first ocean water dive was to a site called "the Black Forest," a reference to the black corral found at 30 to 60 feet below the surface. In seeking to understand the meaning of this coincidence, I was drawn into an extended reflection on Jung's notion of synchronicity. This occurred around the time that complexity theory was becoming popularized through the writing of a number of authors associated with the Santa Fe Institute. The timing of this was most fortuitous for me as it allowed me to begin building the bridge between my interests in a sustained manner.

While writing and thinking about complexity as applied to synchronistic phenomena, a wide array of new arenas presented themselves (an extended series of *adjacent possibles*). This included renewed interested in ecology, which had advanced greatly in the years from my original science career. Soon rhizomes came into view, and I found shoots of this sort in many places: biology, neurology, astrophysics, as well as in diverse authors Jung, Empedocles, Deleuze, and many contemporary thinkers. The work of Suzanne Simard has been particularly inspiring, see for example her autobiography (2021). She details the fascinating complexity of the rhizomal networks operating below ground in forests. Richard Powers fictionalized this work in his bestselling novel, *The Overstory* (2018).

Thus 20 years after I first wrote about the Black Forest dream of my client, synchronistically connected to my initial dive in the depth of the sea, I find myself continuing to work inside the image of what lies beneath the ground in forests. The psychological and the physical worlds seem ever more porous and interpenetrating to me. As I age I find myself feeling drawn to the final statement of *Memories, Dreams and Reflections* where Jung, in old age, reflected on Lao Tzu and our relationship to nature:

> …there is so much that fills me: plants, animals, clouds, day and night, and the eternal in man. The more uncertain I have felt about myself, the more there has grown up in me a feeling of kinship with all things. In fact it seems to me as if that alienation which so long separated me from the world has become transferred into my own inner world, and has revealed to me an unexpected unfamiliarity with myself. (1961, p. 359)

Conclusions

Since all psychological writing carries an autobiographical element, explicitly using aspects of my own story is part of a strategy of contemporizing concepts that have been profoundly meaningful as well as challenging to me. As a person living through the various developments as the world moves from the twentieth into the twenty-first century, I am attempting to chronicle how the notion of individuation has been shifting in my experience.

I have used my story rather than that of clients not only to ensure confidentiality but also because I have more history and data to explore. I can see how my various interests have become interwoven to create a unique tapestry. In doing so, it has become evident how interconnected we all are; that nothing happens in isolation, though the connections may remain hidden like the rhizomal networks in forest. While these may be discoverable, we need both the tools to detect them and the openness of mind to explore the unknown and uncertain. For the depth psychological traditions, I believe this requires us to continue to evaluate where unconscious processes lie. As we examine the unconscious aspect of ourselves and others, the boundaries are ever shifting but the mystery persists.

References

Atmanspacher, H. and C. Fuchs, eds. (2014). *The Jung Pauli Conjecture: And its Impact Today,* Exeter, UK.: Imprint Academic.

Cambray, Joseph, (2002). "Synchronicity and emergence." *American Imago 59* (4), pp. 409-434.

_____. (2009). *Synchronicity: Nature & Psyche in an Inter-connected Universe* (Fay Lecture Series). College Station, TX: Texas A & M University Press.

_____. (2014). *The Red Book: Entrances and Exits in The Red Book: Reflections on C.G. Jung's Liber Novus,* T. Kirsch and G. Hogenson, eds. New York & London: Routledge.

_____. (2016). Intuizione artistica e immaginazione psicoide: un ponte tra realta simboliche e ecologiche, in Enkelados, 4, 117-133.

_____. (2018). "Complexity, ecology, symbolism, and synchronicity," in *Research in Analytical Psychology - Volume 1: Applications from Scientific, Historical, and (Cross)-Cultural Research,* J. Cambray and L. Sawin, eds. New York & London: Routledge.

_____. (2019). "Enlightenment and individuation: syncretism, synchronicity and beyond." In *Journal of Analytical Psychology,* 64, 1, 53–72.

_____. (2020). 21st Century unconscious: altered states, oracles and intelligences, in *Depth Psychology and Climate Change: The Green Book,* ed. Dale Mathers, New York & London: Routledge.

Campbell, J., (1968). *The Hero with a Thousand Faces,* (2nd ed.). Princeton, NJ: Princeton University Press.

Corbett, L., (2021). *The God-Image: From Antiquity to Jung.* Asheville, NC: Chiron Publications.

Gieser, Suzanne, ed. (2019). *Dream Symbols of the Individuation Process: Notes of C.G. Jung's Seminars on Wolfgang Paulil's Dreams.* Philemon Series. Princeton and Oxford: Princeton University Press.

_____. (2005). *The Innermost Kernel.* Berlin, Heidelberg, New York: Springer.

Gravino, P., Monechi, B., Servedio, V.D.P., Tria, F., Loreto, V. (2016). 'Crossing the horizon: exploring the adjacent possible in a cultural system.' *Proceedings of the Seventh International Conference on Computational Creativity,* June 2016.

Hoerni, Ulrich, Fischer Thomas, Kaufmann, Bettina, eds. (2019). *The Art of C.G. Jung* (P. D. Young and C. J. Murray, Trans.) New York, London: W.W. Norton & Company.

Hogenson, G., (2004). Archetypes: emergence and the psyche's deep structure, in Analytical Psychology: Contemporary Perspectives in Jungian Psychology, (J. Cambray and L. Carter, eds.) East Sussex and New York: Brunner-Routledge.

Hogenson, G.B., (2005). The Self, the symbolic and synchronicity: Virtual realities and the emergence of the psyche. *Journal of Analytical Psychology,* 50(3), 271–284.

Jacobi, J., (1967). *The Way of Individuation.* (R.F.C. Hull, Trans.) Hull. New York: Harcourt, Brace & World, Inc.

Jung, C.G., (1961). *Memories, Dreams, Reflections.* New York: Vintage Books.

_____. (1963). *Mysterium coniunctionis, CW Vol 14,* (R. F. C. Hull, Trans.) (H. Read et al., Eds.). Princeton, NJ: Princeton University Press. (Original work published 1955-56)

_____. (1966), *CW, Vol. 7, Two Essays on analytical psychology.* Princeton, NJ: Princeton University Press.

_____. (1967). *CW, Vol. 13, Alchemical studies.* Princeton, NJ: Princeton University Press.

_____. (1968). *CW, Vol. 12, Psychology and alchemy.* Princeton, NJ: Princeton University Press. (Original work published 1953)

_____. (1969). Archetypes of the collective unconscious (R. F. C. Hull, Trans.). In H. Read et al. (Eds.), *CW Vol. 9.1, Archetypes and the collective unconscious* (2nd ed., 3-41). Princeton: Princeton University Press. (Original work published 1954) https://doi.org/10.1515/9781400850969.3

_____. (1969). Psychology and Religion. In H. Read et al. (Eds.), *CW Vol. 11, Psychology and religion* (2nd ed., 3-105). Princeton, NJ: Princeton University Press. (Original work published 1940)

_____. (1969). Synchronicity: An acausal connecting principle (R. F. C. Hull, Trans.). In H. Read et al. (Eds.) *CW Vol. 8, Structure and dynamics of the psyche* (2nd ed., pp. 417-519). Princeton. NJ: Princeton University Press. (Original work published 1952)

_____. (1969). On psychic energy (R. F. C. Hull, Trans.). In H. Read et al. (Eds.), *CW Vol. 8, Structure and dynamics of the psyche* (2nd ed., 3-66). Princeton, NJ: Princeton University Press. (Original work published 1928)

_____. (1970). *CW, Vol. 10, Civilization in transition* (2nd ed., 3-28). Princeton, NJ: Princeton University Press. (Original work published 1918)

_____. (1971). *CW Vol.6, Psychological types.* Princeton, NJ: Princeton University Press. (Original work published 1921)

_____. (2009). *The Red Book,* (S. Shamdasani, Ed.). New York and London: W.W. Norton & Company.

_____. (2020). *The Black Books,* (S. Shamdasani, Ed.; M. Liebscher, J. Peck, & S. Shamdasani, Trans.). New York and London: W.W. Norton & Company.

Kauffman, S.A., (1996). *Investigations: The nature of autonomous agents and the worlds they mutually create.* Santa Fe Institute.

_____. (2000). *Investigations.* Oxford, New York: Oxford University Press.

Kelly, S., (1993). *Individuation and the Absolute: Hegel, Jung, and the Path Toward Wholeness.* Mahwah, NJ: Paulist Press.

Knox, J., (2003). *Archetype, Attachment, Analysis.* Hove and New York: Brunner-Routledge.

Main, Roderick, (2013). In a secular age: Weber, Taylor, Jung. *Psychoanalysis, Culture and Society, 18,* 277–294. https://doi.org/10.1057/pcs.2013.10.

Martin-Vallas, F., & Kutek, A., (2006). The transferential chimera: A clinical approach. *The Journal of Analytical Psychology, 51(5),* 627–641. https://doi-org.pgi.idm.oclc.org/10.1111/j.1468-5922.2006.00624.x.

Martin-Vallas, F., (2008). The Transferential Chimera II: Some Theoretical Considerations. *The Journal of analytical Psychology, 53(1),* 37–59.

Meier, C.A., (ed., with the assistance of C. P. Enz and M. Fierz; translated from the German by David Roscoe; with an introductory essay by Beverley Zabriskie) (2001). *Atom and Archetype: The Pauli/Jung Letters,* 1932-1958. Princeton, NJ: Princeton University Press.

Powers, R., (2018). *The Overstory: A Novel,* New York, London: W.W. Norton & Co.

Rossmann M.G., (2013). Structure of viruses: a short history. *Quarterly Reviews of Biophysics, 46(2):* 133-80. doi: 10.1017/S0033583513000012. PMID: 23889891.

Simard, S., (2021). *Finding the Mother Tree: Discovering the Wisdom of the Forest.* Alfred A. Knopf: New York.

Stein, M. (2018). *The Principle of Individuation: Toward the Development of Human Consciousness.* Asheville, NC: Chiron Publications. (Original work published 2006) von Franz, M. -L., (1979). *Alchemical Active Imagination.* Irving, TX: Spring Publications, Inc.

_____. (1990). *Individuation and Fairy Tales, revised edition.* Boston & London: Shambhala.

Walker G., (2012). Sociological theory and Jungian psychology. *History of Human Sciences, 25(1):* 52-74. doi: 10.1177/ 0952695111427360. PMID: 27656724.

Weber, M., (1946). *Science as Vocation,* (H. H. Gerth & C. Wright-Mills, Eds. & Trans.). New York: Free Press.

Moving Forward

Joe Cambray, Ph.D., IAAP

This book has provided a Jungian-based perspective on where we are now in terms of uncertainty on many levels. We have explored seminal Jungian concepts including the role of the unconscious, projection, synchronicity, the nature of shadow and working with images. We have proposed ways to approach current concerns and offered paths to move forward in terms of personal growth and managing uncertainty.

Importantly, the book poses this question: *Does this time of increasing uncertainty over many areas of life offer opportunities for personal growth and for enhancing our participation in community as we all grapple to find ways to interact with the multiple challenges facing our world?* The answer is a firm yes, a clear message that change starts with the individual and knowing yourself is an essential first step.

Our authors have proposed new approaches to thinking about the social concerns we are all facing and understanding how our world has changed and will continue to change. New approaches to understanding our relationship to the collective (conscious and unconscious), to nature and to science are offered. In this final chapter, we review where we are through Jungian concepts and offer observations for the future.

Coping with Uncertainty

As noted in previous chapters, coping with uncertainty is not a new problem, it is very deep in our evolutionary history, a part of life itself. Nevertheless, the intensity of events over the past several years has increased the degree of uncertainty in many people's lives (examples cited herein include climate change and climate refugees, more pandemics, recrudescence of wars and violence against civilian populations, and strife stemming from racial and ethnic tensions). We have made the case that the Jungian approach can be particularly helpful in tolerating unknowing, offering potentials for transformative growth of the personality.

Core concepts in Jungian psychology involve increasing our capacity for using systemic forms of uncertainty. Individuation, the Jungian process of self-realization and expansion of the personality through integration of unconscious contents, is a never completed work, but evolves with the challenges of life and thrives on our ability to engage reflectively with the unconscious, a fundamental source of unknowing. This process can train us to extend this way of knowing to events in our world, often outside of our personal control. One element in individuation is inherently surprising, synchronicity. This concept points to events that bring us into contact with meaningful unknowns that manifest at particular moments in our lives. The personal realization of these moments is often fraught with unanticipated significance. The ability to reflect on such events and plumb their meanings necessarily engages us with uncertainties and unknowing. Intuition is a most useful faculty in encountering the unknown as it points us toward where we might fruitfully explore. Jungian psychology with its respect for the psyche begins with the recognition that much of the psyche and the sense of Self are unconscious and can never be completely known, though the boundaries can be expanded.

The Jungian perspective is one of a number of ways to approach our uncertain times. The focus on the interconnectedness of conscious and unconscious seems to us a natural process in understanding and living with uncertainty. As noted above, it is based on the premise that change of any kind starts with the individual.

Like any approach, the Jungian perspective has limits. Personal work of this nature may not appeal to everyone. It has limitations in terms of time and working with unfamiliar concepts and processes. It is a very person-based approach. There are other avenues of thought that can also be pertinent here. As will be described below, scientists working in the areas of neuropsychology and quantum physics are beginning to offer other ways to understand the mind, its properties and how they work. The study of emergent properties can also offer a different perspective on the problem of uncertainty.

In reading this book, the Jungian way of relating to the unknown has hopefully emerged for you. This approach cannot banish unknowing, but helps us in our psychological, emotional, and spiritual response to the natural human tendency to feel some anxiety or tension when confronted with various unknowns. If we are fortunate, we learn to befriend the unknown for what it can reveal in its own way. Thus, as you have made your way through this book, we hope you have found it useful in reconsidering the way in which you experience uncertainty. From a depth psychological perspective, we need to befriend uncertainty, perhaps as it is figured in our dreams, rather than try to eliminate or avoid it. How might we take our reflections and move forward in life while embracing the unknown?

Nature and Process for Personal Work

According to Jung, the value of the soul affirmed by the presence of archetypal images allows a person to realize the nature of projections and become conscious "that the conflict is in himself, that the discord and tribulation are his riches, which should not be squandered by attacking others" (Jung, 1955, para. 511). This statement by Jung underscores the value of doing shadow work.

Still relevant for soul work today, turning us inward to face the hidden hostilities that lie within, often unknown to us before we fully engage in this work.

While extremely important, we do have to acknowledge limits, as in dealing with psychopathic personalities, especially in leadership roles and the damage they can do. Often our best course under such conditions is to be cultural critics, raising our voices in protest and not leaving it to others.

Archetype of the Apocalypse

We are currently in cultural and even global processes that lead to change. Several authors in this book have reminded us that apocalyptic periods are not new. They are a repeating phenomenon in our history. One way of understanding where we are now is as another apocalyptic moment in time. The millennial fantasy of the apocalypse highlights the role of suffering in healing and growth; this is not in itself a bad thing; it is a natural part of the process. The notion of an apocalypse also includes a critical element of growth at the end. The apocalypse, historically, is a method that leads to change, to something new. Its endpoint is a new beginning not total annihilation. It is needed to support the emergence of growth and development when old ways of being have collapsed. Suffering during this process is natural and can be a productive part. Jungian approaches can help understand the process of that suffering and offer ways to work within the process to encourage growth and understand personal responses during that time.

Edward Edinger wrote a full-length book on the topic of the apocalypse from an archetypal perspective. He examines the psychology of the Christian *Book of Revelations* by the Gospel writer St. John (1999). The rich potentials in the apocalyptic imagination are explored in this, as well as a case study on the dangers of possession by this archetype, which have a long, sad history.

Our current situation with the pandemic, violence, and danger of destruction of the planet make us all feel we are on the edge of an apocalypse. As noted above, underlying these threats and dangers can be fertile ground for growth and change. This doesn't dismiss the stark realities but the long view can give us a bit of hope, perhaps enough to allow our imaginations to open to ways of experiencing and engaging with the apocalypse archetype in a non-destructive manner.

Collective Change and Opportunities

Part Two of this book focuses specifically on the current national and communal issues facing us. As noted in the introduction of Part Two, at the community level, we are in a time of strife and dread. We are being challenged by upheaval, isolation, anger, exhaustion, and grief. These are issues that are not going to be resolved immediately. It is an archetypal time of social change and development. The authors in this section offer insight about three specific challenging topics: racial justice, political polarization, and mechanisms that mediate responses to communal issues. Other writers talk about collective issues in terms of climate change, the pandemic and war.

New Perspectives on Interconnectedness

We desperately need a new vision of our psyches through which the complex interrelationships between everyone and the planet can be acknowledged and lived in an integrated fashion. A new synthesis of the mythopoetic imagination with complexity science offers possibilities, some of which are mentioned in this book. The origins of this can be traced back to the German romantics who would marry subjective experiences to objective observation in attempting to create a new, broader form of knowing, which went by the name "natur-philosophie," the philosophy of nature. This was revived and reconsidered by depth psychologists, especially Jung, who in his last iteration of the concept of the archetype expanded it into the psychoid realm, so that the archetypes of the collective unconscious are seen as a formative aspect of both psyche and nature. The archetypes provided the basis for the mythopoetic imagination, which Jung also envisioned as being integrally a part of the psychological background to scientific formulations, guiding the choice of metaphors and ways of describing reality. We can look at interconnectedness from multiple vertices, including recent advances in biological and sociological considerations. These can be seen as a reflection of the shifting archetypal dominants of our age. That which has been marginalized by society in the past now returns as harbingers of what needs to be integrated into our societies. First articulated by Sigmund Freud, the return of the repressed often comes as a severe challenge. Nevertheless, Jung taught us the transformative value in engaging, honoring and coming to grips with these challenges. In our contemporary world this might transcend Jung's own position to include non-binary thinking, such as is emerging in the presentation of gender fluidity. Similarly, reconceiving racial matters as a part of re-valuing diversity, equity, and inclusion into a new form of democracy which can become more complex and enriched by such an embrace. In effect we are seeking to link personal responsibility to collective needs at both conscious and unconscious levels of reality.

Some Thoughts for the Journey

When considering facing uncertainty, modern societies have turned not to religions but the sciences. At its core the scientific method is about testing predictions. Hypotheses are constructed based on what is known, to test possible new directions or refine models of how the current understandings of things might evolve. Naturally, this process is marked by great uncertainties and the ability to use feedback from experiments to improve hypotheses is fundamental to the method. In this sense, science has been our best attempt at contemporary versions of oracular prediction for more than 150 years.

Science in the Future: A Holistic Vision

For potential directions we could also turn to futurology as a field employing an expanded view of the predictive qualities of science to imagine futures. This is based on extrapolation of current trends applied in a deliberate, focused manner. A Jungian contribution to such an expansion would be by way of a holistic vision of knowledge, including conscious and unconscious forms of knowing. To complement this, might we think about collective intuition? Is there a collective pre-conscious aspect to the psyche, not belonging to any one individual but which we may tap into using our intuition. There is often a convergence of research onto innovative discoveries appearing close together in time (this is where concerns about priority become heated). Unfortunately, the attention on personal acclamation has tended to overshadow the more collective dimensions activated in those particular moments in culture. A depth sociology of discovery could help us see and appreciate the more collective, collaborative contributions to innovation. In many ways this was a project Jung was discovering in his *Red Book*, and it behooves us to make it contemporary and relevant to our times, while noting the parallels from the past. However, this is not the only way forward but just some musing for consideration.

En-visioning/Re-visioning

Throughout this collection we have implicitly been using forms of *re-visioning* and *re-flection* as key ideas in grappling with and tolerating uncertainty. Years ago, James Hillman linked the "re" prefix with the nature of psychological thought itself. He saw this mode as a return to things/events that have already occurred, in order to understand them in terms of psychology.

Extending this logic we might also turn to the prefix "en" as in "en-chantment" or "en-liven" "en-able," etc. for additional insights. Dictionary definitions of "en" include: a prefix occurring originally in loanwords from French and productive in English on this model, forming verbs with the general sense "to cause (a person or thing) to be in" the place, condition, or state named by the stem; more specifically, "to confine in or place on" (enshrine; enthrone; entomb); "to cause to be in" (enslave; entrust; enrich; encourage; endear); "to restrict" in the manner named by the stem, typically with the additional sense "on all sides, completely" (enwind; encircle; enclose; entwine). This prefix is also attached to verbs in order to make them transitive, or to give them a transitive marker if they are already transitive (enkindle; enliven; enshield; enface). https://www.dictionary.com/browse/en accessed 2/18/2023.

For the future, we may want to consider the combination of "re" with "en" to draw attention to the growing body of studies on *re-enchantment* (post dis-enchantment) as a way of using imagination to *re-en-soul* the world. This can be read as the deepest goal of Jung's individuation model (Main, 2022). At the end of *Mysterium Coniunctionis* Jung drew on the writings of the alchemist Gerhard Dorn, with his three stages of alchemical union, the *unio mentalis*, the *caelum*, and finally the *unio mystica*, resulting in whole individual (body, soul, spirit), joining with the *unus mundus*, the archetypal base of reality (1970, paras. 759-775). Marie-Louise Von Franz referred to this last stage as "a becoming one with the collective unconscious...to reach that point where outer and inner reality (heaven and earth) become one" (1979, p. 115).

An important step in this direction can be found in the recently published book by Roderick Main: *Breaking the Spell of Disenchantment: Mystery, Meaning, and Metaphysics in the Work of C.G. Jung* (2022). Main looks at the triad of enchantment, disenchantment, reenchantment from the perspective of Jung's theory of individuation and explores the archetypal patterns being expressed. All three stages have their place and meaning in the context of individuation, being of the whole person.

Altered/Non-ordinary States of Consciousness

A broader area of research which has been revived that might assist in engaging uncertainty is the exploration of altered/ non-ordinary states of consciousness. The noetic value of some states has been known and used throughout history, though religions which insist upon strict orthodoxy generally have marginalized or demonized exploration of these states, as well as those who seek to employ them. Nevertheless, the history of divination and the oracular traditions in the ancient world could teach us much about how to engage with uncertainty. The goal would not be to literally reinstate those activities, but to learn from them, to re-engage them through the lens of re-enchantment.

Coupled with the renewed interest and research in psychedelics, including their use as entheogens, we now have a greater range of approaches to investigate the fullness of the psyche and its engagement with the world; e.g., see several recent conferences at Pacifica Graduate Institute, *Psychedelia: The History and Science of Mystical Experience* (October 2-3, 2021) https://retreat.pacifica.edu/psychedelia/; *Accessing the Ineffable: Depth Psychology, Religious Experience, and the Further Reaches of Consciousness*, (June 19, 2021) https://retreat.pacifica.edu/accessing-the-ineffable/ and *Altered States: Dreams, Vision, Renewal* (June 21-23, 2019). This is also leading to renewed exploration and application of altered states in psychotherapy and analysis, an area of growing interest to many in the Jungian community. Efficacy has been shown in the treatment of certain refractory depressions, fears of dying, and addictions (Pollen, 2018, pp. 331-396).

How to best integrate the use of these substances with psychotherapy is currently under intensive investigation. The value of Jungian contributions will be an important part of these studies. Thus we are finding new tools and methods even as we face into times of profound uncertainty.

References

Edinger, E.F., (1999). *Archetype of the Apocalypse*. Chicago and LaSalle: Open Court.

Jung, C.G., (1970). *CW, Vol. 14, Mysterium Coniunctionis: An Inquiry into the Separation and Synthesis of Psychic Opposites in Alchemy* (2nd ed.; H. Read et al., Eds.). Princeton, NJ: Princeton University Press.

Main, R., (2022). *Breaking the Spell of Disenchantment: Mystery, Meaning, and Metaphysics in the Work of C.G. Jung.* Asheville, NC: Chiron Publications.

Pollen, M., (2018). *How to Change Your Mind*. New York: Penguin Press.

Von Franz, M. -L., (1979). *Alchemical Active Imagination*. Irving, Texas: Spring Publications, Inc.

Author Biographies

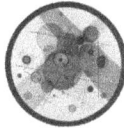

Jan Bauer, MA, was born and raised in the USA, lived in various European countries for 20 years, and has sort of resolved her tension of opposites by settling in Quebec, Canada for the last 40 years. She has been involved in training with the Inter-Regional Society of Jungian Analysts as Director of Admissions and then of Training. And in Quebec, she gives seminars and presentations for professionals and the public in French and English, as well as maintaining an active bi-lingual private practice. Particular areas of interest are individuation, the shadow, the democracy of the psyche.

Joe Cambray, Ph.D. is past President/CEO of Pacifica Graduate Institute; he is Past-President of the International Association for Analytical Psychology; has served as the U.S. Editor for *The Journal of Analytical Psychology* and is on various editorial boards. He was a faculty member at Harvard Medical School in the Department of Psychiatry at Massachusetts General Hospital, Center for Psychoanalytic Studies; and former President of the C.G. Jung Institute of Boston. Dr. Cambray is also a Jungian analyst now living in the Santa Barbara area of California. His numerous publications include the book based on his Fay Lectures: *Synchronicity: Nature and Psyche in an Interconnected Universe*, a newly edited volume, with Leslie Sawin, *Research in Analytical Psychology: Applications from Scientific, Historical, and (Cross)-*

Cultural Research and a volume edited with Linda Carter, *Analytical Psychology: Contemporary Perspectives in Jungian Psychology.* He has published numerous papers in a range of international journals.

Sean Fitzpatrick is the executive director of The Jung Center, where he has worked and taught since 1997. Sean holds master's degrees in religious studies from Rice University and in clinical psychology from the University of Houston — Clear Lake. He received his PhD in psychology, with a specialization in Jungian studies from Saybrook University. His book *The Ethical Imagination: Exploring Fantasy and Desire in Analytical Psychology* was published by Routledge in August 2019. He is a psychotherapist in private practice and teaches internationally.

Donald Kalsched, PhD, is a Jungian Analyst and Clinical Psychologist who practices in Brunswick, Maine. He is a member of the C.G. Jung Institute of New England, a senior faculty member and supervisor with the Inter-Regional Society of Jungian Analysts, and lectures nationally and internationally on the subject of trauma and its treatment. He is the author of numerous publications including *The Inner World of Trauma*, 1996 and *Trauma and the Soul*, 2013.

Jeffrey Kiehl, PhD, is a Diplomate Jungian Analyst and senior training analyst for the C.G. Jung Institute of Colorado and the Inter-Regional Society of Jungian Analysts. He is the author of *Facing Climate Change: An Integrated Path to the Future*, which provides a Jungian perspective on climate change. He has also published articles on *US Cultural Complexes and Climate Change*, and *The Green Man and Climate Change*. Jeffrey's current interests include alchemy, the relationship between psyche & matter, and amplification of film through a Jungian lens. Jeffrey has presented on these topics at national and international conferences. He lives in Santa Cruz, CA.

Margaret Klenck, MDiv, LP, is a Jungian analyst in private practice in New York. She graduated from Union Theological Seminary with a Masters of Divinity. She is past president of the Jungian Psychoanalytic Association in New York, where she teaches and supervises trainees and she was the JPA's representative to the Executive Council of the IAAP for 6 years. Margaret has lectured and taught nationally and internationally.

Leslie Sawin, M.S. develops programs and edits work focusing on community-based efforts to bring Jungian ideas to the general public. She has a master's degree from the Harvard School of Public Health. Her previous editorial works include *Jung and Aging: Possibilities and Potentials for the Second Half of Life,* with Lionel Corbett and Michael Carbine and *Research in Analytical Psychology: Applications from Scientific, Historical, and Cross-Cultural Research* with Joseph Cambray.

Thomas Singer, MD, is a psychiatrist and Jungian psychoanalyst who trained at Yale Medical School, Dartmouth Medical School, and the C.G. Jung Institute of San Francisco. He is the author of many books and articles that include editing a series of books on cultural complexes that have focused on Australia, Latin America, Europe, the United States, and Far East Asian countries, in addition to another series of books featuring Ancient Greece, Modern Psyche. He serves on the board of ARAS (Archive for Research into Archetypal Symbolism) and has served as co-editor of *ARAS Connections* for many years.

Morgan Stebbins, MDiv, LMSW, DMin, LP, is a supervising analyst, faculty member, and former President and Director of Training at the Jungian Psychoanalytic Association in New York, where he also maintains a private practice. Holding a doctorate in Religious Studies and Hermeneutics, he began his Zen training at the San Francisco Zen Center where he was also a monastic resident. He has written on symbol formation, dreams, the role of mindfulness in analysis, the meaning of compulsion, and the archetypal psychology of Buddhist sutras and precepts. His main concerns are to help people develop a contemplative psychological life and to promote a symbolic awareness of the world.

Murray Stein, Ph.D. is a training analyst at the International School for Analytical Psychology in Zurich, Switzerland. He is the author of many articles and books. He lectures internationally on topics related to Analytical Psychology and its applications in the contemporary world.

Ann Ulanov is an internationally known and practicing Jungian analyst in New York City; Professor Emerita of Psychology and Religion at Union Theological Seminary; and lecturer in the U.S. and abroad. She is the author of many books including *Cinderella and her Sisters: The Envied and the Envying, Transforming Sexuality: The Archetypal World of Anima and Animus*; with Barry Ulanov, and *The Psychoid, Soul and Psyche: Piercing Space/Time Barriers*; *Back to Basics*; and *Madness and Creativity*.

www.ingramcontent.com/pod-product-compliance
Lightning Source LLC
Chambersburg PA
CBHW020335270326
41926CB00007B/187